MULTICULTURALISM WITHIN A BILINGUAL FRAMEWORK

Language, Race, and Belonging in Canada

This book explores the roots of multiculturalism and bilingualism in Canada to show that these two important Canadian policies are inextricably linked and operate together as a contemporary national narrative, famously formulated by Pierre Trudeau as 'multiculturalism within a bilingual framework.'

Both official bilingualism and multiculturalism emerged out of the Royal Commission on Bilingualism and Biculturalism of the 1960s, which was established to address the emerging contestations to Anglo-Celtic hegemony from not only francophone but also Indigenous and other racial and ethnic communities in Canada. Eve Haque undertakes a comprehensive analysis of archival material, including transcripts of royal commission hearings, memos, and reports, to reveal the conflicts underlying the emergence of multiculturalism policy. This book explains how, in this era, the push from historically marginalized communities for recognition and national belonging led to a decisive shift of the national narrative onto the terrain of language and culture in order to maintain white settler hegemony while disavowing racial and ethnic exclusions.

EVE HAQUE is an associate professor in the Department of Languages, Literatures, and Linguistics and the Department of Equity Studies at York University.

EVE HAQUE

Multiculturalism within a Bilingual Framework

Language, Race, and Belonging in Canada

UNIVERSITY OF TORONTO PRESS
Toronto Buffalo London

© University of Toronto Press 2012
Toronto Buffalo London
www.utppublishing.com
Printed in Canada

ISBN 978-1-4426-4078-8 (cloth)
ISBN 978-1-4426-1016-3 (paper)

Printed on acid-free, 100% post-consumer recycled paper with
vegetable-based inks.

Canadian Cataloguing in Publication Data

Library and Archives Canada Cataloguing in Publication

Haque, Eve
Multiculturalism within a bilingual framework : language, race, and
belonging in Canada / Eve Haque.

Includes bibliographical references and index.
ISBN 978-1-4426-4078-8 (bound).   ISBN 978-1-4426-1016-3 (pbk.)

1. Multiculturalism – Canada.   2. Bilingualism – Canada.   3. Language
policy – Canada.   4. Language and culture – Canada.   5. Canada – Race
relations.   I. Title.

FC105.M8H37 2012   306.44'60971   C2011-907814-7

University of Toronto Press acknowledges the financial assistance to its
publishing program of the Canada Council for the Arts and the Ontario
Arts Council.

 Canada Council   Conseil des Arts
for the Arts   du Canada

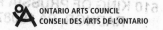 ONTARIO ARTS COUNCIL
CONSEIL DES ARTS DE L'ONTARIO

University of Toronto Press acknowledges the financial support of the
Government of Canada through the Canada Book Fund for its publishing
activities.

This book has been published with the help of a grant from the Canadian
Federation for the Humanities and Social Sciences, through the Aid to
Scholarly Publications Program, using funds provided by the Social
Sciences and Humanities Research Council of Canada.

Contents

Acknowledgments

This project could not have been realized without the help and support of a number of people. These people, to whom I owe heartfelt thanks, include Sherene Razack, Jim Cummins, Normand Labrie, Roger Simon, and Ruth Wodak. Other people I need to thank include Ellen Cray, Sandra Acker, Shahrzad Mojab, Kari Dehli, George Dei, Amir Hassanpour, Ruth Roach Pierson, Rinaldo Walcott, Allison Felker, Sheryl Nestel, Amar Wahab, Carrianne Leung, Lorena Gajardo, Jane Ku, Helen Moore, and many others both at OISE/UT and in Osaka, Japan. Thanks must also go to Sylvie Lamoureux, Darryl Leroux, Kerrie Kennedy, and Claire Horsnell, as well as the manuscript reviewers.

Last but not least, I thank my family for their ongoing patience and support.

MULTICULTURALISM WITHIN A BILINGUAL FRAMEWORK

Language, Race, and Belonging in Canada

Introduction:
'I'm Talking Language'

On 30 October 1995, the night of the sovereignty referendum in Quebec, Premier Jacques Parizeau became infamous for his comment that 'money and ethnic votes' had defeated the sovereignist cause. The vote was an incredibly close victory for the 'No' side (a margin of 53,000 votes), which may have fuelled the frustration that drove Parizeau to make his remarks. His speech, and in particular his comment regarding the role of ethnic voters, triggered major national media coverage, analysis, and discussion. Within the next twenty-four hours Parizeau had tendered his resignation, and over the next few months he virtually disappeared from public and political life.

What is interesting about this incident is not so much Parizeau's speech, which sustained a surfeit of media analysis, commentary, and public discussion on all sides of the debate, but rather his own explanation of his controversial remarks, made years later in an hour-long documentary about his life. This documentary, entitled *Public Enemy Number One* (2003), directed and narrated by journalist Francine Pelletier, traces Parizeau's early life and the build-up to his successful political career. The climax comes near the end of this documentary, when Parizeau explains what he meant by his 'money and ethnic votes' comment:

> It's true that we were beaten . . . but by what? By money and ethnic votes. I know that I'm supposed to be a fascist . . . I'm supposed to be a racist but I never put anyone in jail. I never prevented anyone from saying what they wanted to . . . and it's true that I can't be compared to that great democrat Pierre Elliott Trudeau who put 500 people in jail . . . It's not 'hating'? I've tried to describe reality as I saw it . . . It's true we know now that that love-in cost more than twice what the Yes campaign and No campaign were

authorized to spend for the full campaign . . . so I said it . . . money . . . yes indeed . . . The ethnic vote – the words might not have been very well chosen – but the fact is that that is what happened . . . the non-francophone vote . . . and I'm not talking here . . . I'm talking language . . . I'm not talking . . . ethnic origin or whatever . . . that's why my words were not necessarily well chosen but . . . it was a language issue – the non-francophones more than usually as was the case voted No and some polls were zero – I had never seen that . . . (Cartier and Henriquez, 2003)

Although Parizeau holds firm to his position and backs it with analysis, he also tries to unpack exactly what he meant by 'the ethnic vote.' In this portion of the documentary, Parizeau, who had been quite articulate until then, starts to struggle. He begins by admitting that his words 'might not have been very well chosen.' In his attempt to delineate exactly who was covered by the term 'ethnic,' he notes that what he had in mind was not 'ethnic origin or whatever' but rather language: 'it was a language issue.' Significantly, he is not specifying the Quebec anglophone minority either, for then he could simply name it as such; instead, he is trying to find a way to identify the 'No' voters among the 'non-francophone' and, by extension, non-anglophone groups. If this is not a group of voters/non-voters that can be acceptably delineated through 'ethnic origin' – for, after all, this is what ignited the country-wide storm of reaction against Parizeau's speech – then Parizeau's own effort to find the acceptable words and offer the appropriate explanation ('that's why my words were not necessarily well chosen') reveals that language was a good substitute: 'I'm talking language.'

Parizeau's explanation provides an entry point into the central questions of this book. More than a semantic slip, Parizeau's shift onto the terrain of language to clarify and support his comments was illustrative of the convenient alibi for racial ordering that can be provided by a multicultural nation established on the foundation of a putatively open linguistic duality – articulated in national policy as 'multiculturalism within a bilingual framework.' Yet I am not interested in vilifying Parizeau, nor the political position from which he speaks; rather, I wish to use his comments as a basis from which to explore questions about language, race, and nation-building. The animating question of my analysis is this: how, in Canada, did language come to be the site for articulating exclusions which can no longer be stated in terms of race and ethnicity? Flowing from this is my specific goal of tracing how a national formulation of 'multiculturalism within a bilingual framework' emerged to install a racial order of difference and belonging through language in the ongoing project of white settler nation-building.

At the centre of the book is the work of the Royal Commission on Bilingualism and Biculturalism (1963–70), commonly known as the B and B Commission. Established by the Liberal government of Lester B. Pearson as a response to growing nationalist sentiment among French Canadians in Quebec, the mandate of the commission, as laid out in its terms of reference, was primarily to

> inquire into and report upon the existing state of bilingualism and bicul-turalism in Canada and to recommend what steps should be taken to de-velop the Canadian Confederation on the basis of an equal partnership between the two founding races, taking into account the contribution made by the other ethnic groups to the cultural enrichment of Canada and the measures that should be taken to safeguard that contribution. (Canada, *Book I*, 1967, Appendix I)

The terms of reference go on to specify that this would include deter-mining the extent of bilingualism in the federal bureaucracy, the role of the public and private sectors in promoting English-French harmony, and the opportunities open to both English and French Canadians for becoming bilingual. Central to the commission's view of Canada, es-pecially in its early phase, was the notion that the country rested on an equal partnership between the English and French 'founding races'[1] and that the reality of this partnership needed to be fully recognized in national institutions and society at large. In time, as this vision was challenged by non-English and non-French Canadians during the commission, it evolved into what became known as multiculturalism within a bilingual framework.

Those are the basic facts of the B and B Commission; the full story is more complex and multilayered. As the 1960s began, a confluence of events resulted in challenges to the existing Anglo-Celtic dominant na-tional narrative of belonging, and the B and B Commission became the 'apparatus' through which the federal government addressed these is-sues. It is my contention that, at this particular historical juncture, the need to rearticulate the formulation for nation-building and national belonging meant a decisive shift onto the terrain of language and cul-ture for organizing and maintaining white-settler hegemony while also disavowing racial and ethnic exclusions.

Archival records and commission reports reveal the conflicts that underlay the emergence of this ostensibly seamless linguistic and cultural policy of 'multiculturalism within a bilingual framework,' a policy enshrined in the commission's own report as well as, subsequently, the Official Languages Act (1969) and the Multiculturalism Policy (1971). The emergence of these two defining legislative texts on foundations laid by the B and B Commission required the elision of substantive contestation from both Indigenous communities and 'other ethnic groups' (which is how non-French and non-English immigrant groups were defined throughout the inquiry). Against the background of the commission's terms of reference, which spoke of only 'two founding races,' it is possible to trace how Indigenous groups' claims were eventually set aside and other ethnic groups' demands were muted, all culminating in the commission's final report. The shift from overt racial distinctions between founding and other ethnic groups onto the terrain of language and culture meant that racial exclusions could be disavowed even as they were smuggled back in through the contradictory operation of language and culture. This strategy emerged just as obvious, biologically based racial exclusions became increasingly politically and socially disreputable; therefore, particular cultural forms – especially language – became essential ascriptions for the constitution and exclusion of various groups along racialized lines. Consequently, language was identified as a fundamental element of culture by the commission and mobilized as an essential component of culture for the 'founding races,' even as it was deemed to be a private and peripheral element of culture for 'other ethnic groups.' Furthermore, by fixing narrow definitions of 'multicultural' and 'integration' in federal legislation, claims for substantive and collective forms of recognition from the state for other ethnic groups could be limited. In this way, with the concurrent changes to immigration legislation that were also taking place in the 1960s, language and culture were mobilized through the national formulation of multiculturalism within a bilingual framework in order to incorporate people into the contemporary, racialized hierarchy of belonging and citizenship rights.

Though my main goal is to explore the roots of multiculturalism within a bilingual framework and the implications of this concept for the Canadian social structure, I attempt to answer a set of subsidiary questions as well. First, what was the confluence of events and factors that required the rearticulation of the white-settler national mythology in terms that disavowed Anglo-Celtic dominance and racial exclusion?

Second, what arguments did non-English and non-French communities present to the B and B Commission to support their claims of belonging within the nation? Third, how did the commission respond to such views and, in the end, interpret them in such a way as to maintain white-settler hegemony? Finally, how precisely does this disavowal of racial exclusion operate through language and culture to naturalize the notion of a putatively open multicultural nation, while at the same time organizing the racial order of a new white-settler bilingual and bicultural nation?

First, a few words concerning this book's scope and structure. The B and B Commission published a *Preliminary Report* in 1965 and a final report in six books between the years 1967 and 1970. (With the death of André Laurendeau – co-chairman of the commission – on 1 June 1968, the planned seventh volume on constitutional reform never appeared [Smart, 1991, 9].) My analysis focuses on the *Preliminary Report* and Books I (*The Official Languages*) and IV (*The Cultural Contribution of the Other Ethnic Groups*); the remainder of the Books – II: *Education*; III: *The Work World*; V: *The Federal Capital*; and VI: *Voluntary Associations* – fall outside the scope of this discussion. The study proceeds as follows. In chapter 1, I position my study within the larger theoretical literature on language, race, and nationalism, and outline the analytical approach adopted for this archival research project. Chapter 2 examines the relevant historical context in which the commission was conceived and operated, as the 1960s was a watershed decade for the reworking of Canadian settler nationalism on many fronts. In particular, I examine the concurrent and significant changes that were taking place within immigration policy, where a historic shift from race-based policies to a point system was taking place – a shift which would have momentous implications for the demographic future of Canada and, consequently, the implementation of the commission's recommendations. As well, controversial changes were being proposed with respect to the federal policy on Indigenous peoples; changes which would see historical relations between the State and Indigenous people completely transformed through the proposed elimination of the Indian Act. Finally, revolutionary changes were taking place in relation to French-language politics, particularly in Quebec, which gave particular urgency to the work of the Royal Commission.

Chapter 3 analyses the commission's preliminary hearings and subsequent *Preliminary Report*, drawing on Foucault's genealogical method to trace the emergence of a specifically singular notion of 'crisis,' meant to both animate and circumscribe the precise limits of the Royal Commission's mandate. Specifically, this chapter traces how the range of concerns presented by Indigenous groups and 'other ethnic groups' during the preliminary hearings was distilled into an overall national 'crisis' between the French and English groups in the preliminary report of 1965. In chapter 4, submissions to the commission from various groups challenging the hegemonic formulation of the terms of reference as mainly a crisis between the French and English are analysed. Drawing on Nikolas Rose and Peter Miller's (1992) notion of 'expertise,' this chapter also examines the commissioner's subsequent use of research reports and related documents to confirm their authority in contesting or reinforcing findings from the public hearings in the production of the final report. Chapter 5 examines *Book I* of the final report, which gave rise to Canada's first Official Languages Act in 1969. First, this chapter explores the contradictory mechanism by which language and culture are defined in the opening 'blue pages' of this volume in order to re-inscribe the disavowed racial and ethnic hierarchies of the terms of reference. Next, Adam Ashforth's (1990) idea of 'reckoning schemes of legitimization' is used to trace the process whereby some facts were legitimized against others to justify the primacy of a white-settler bilingual and bicultural Canadian nation. Chapter 6 examines *Book IV* and its conception of and recommendations regarding 'other ethnic groups,' which ultimately led to the federal government's announcement of the Multiculturalism Policy in 1971. In this chapter, the contradictory mobilization of language and culture is used to redefine 'other ethnic groups' as 'cultural groups' even as recognition of their group rights is foreclosed. Specifically, non-official language rights are individualized and relegated to the private sphere as a form of cultural 'integration' and entrenched as such in the Multiculturalism policy – in direct contrast to the group rights accorded to official language communities. A concluding chapter reflects on the various current manifestations of multiculturalism within a bilingual framework, most significantly as it is embedded in the Canadian Charter of Rights and Freedoms. Finally, as a way to think outside the limiting, racialized hierarchy of belonging put into place through the white-settler national formulation of multiculturalism within a bilingual framework, Jacques Derrida's notion of hospitality is considered. Specifically, the *aporia* between conditional and unconditional hospitality is examined as a potential driving force for the improvement of national 'laws of hospitality' (Derrida, 2000) in an effort to rethink the theoretical limits of nation and community in the present.

1 Language, Nation, and Race: Framing the Inquiry

The durability of the white-settler bilingual/bicultural formulation in the present, and its contemporary mode of ordering racialized immigrant Others, is worth examining in order to suggest ways to rethink the theoretical limits of language planning and policy in nationalist projects. The context for this project lies in the relations between language, race, and nation-building; therefore, it is important to frame this analysis within these larger issues of race, language, and nation – and to outline the analytical approach to the data before narrowing the focus to the Royal Commission on Bilingualism and Biculturalism.

Language and Nation

Conventional scholarship on nationalism organizes theories of nation and nationalism into four schools of thought. Although the following examples are not exhaustive, it is clear that – although its operation in each school of thought varies widely – language is a significant and constitutive aspect of nation formation. The first school of thought is what Anthony D. Smith (1998) refers to as the primordialists: those who argue that nations are part of a natural order, ancient and ubiquitous, with modern nations evolving from an original and enduring group. Second (and often seen as a subset of the first) are the perennialists, who, although they agree that nations have a primordial nature, deny their predestination and rather see them as temporally continuous or recurrent in history. Third are the modernists, who treat the nation as a recent, socio-political fact derived from the processes of modernization. Finally, and usually lumped together in one category as the postmodernists, are those who unpack the discursive construction of the nation, emphasize the fragmentation of contemporary national identities, and unravel the gendered and racialized discourses of nation-building (Smith, 1998). Despite the impression of clearly delineated categories, it is important to note that there is in fact considerable overlap among them as well as disagreement about who belongs in which classification. Further confusion arises from the fact that there is little consensus on the definitions of terms such as nation, nationalism, and state.

In the primordialist school of thought, language is a central point around which the nation is organized.[1] In his prize-winning and influential essay (1770) 'Über den Ursprung der Sprache' (The Origin of Language), Johann Gottfried Herder wrote: 'Language is the medium through which man becomes conscious of his inner self, and at the same time it is the key to the understanding of his outer relationships. It unites him with, but it also differentiates him from, others' (as cited in Barnard, 1965, 57). He believed that the sustaining and integrating power of language would lead to a higher rate of social cohesion and the emergence of a *Volk*, or 'people.' Most important, Herder felt that, if language was capable of arousing a sense of identity in a community, it would also simultaneously give rise to the community's consciousness of difference from those speaking another language. This formulation of language and *Volk* meant a close association between language and politics that led to a change in the meaning of 'nation.' A nation was no longer a group of political citizens united under a political sovereign; rather, it was now a separate *natural* entity whose claim to political recognition rested on the possession of a common language (Barnard, 1965, 56–9). Similar to Herder, Wilhelm von Humboldt[2] made it clear that language was the 'spiritual exhalation' of the nation, and that nothing was more important for national culture and continuity than the ancestral tongue (ibid., 25). Another thinker, Johann Gottlieb Fichte (1762–1835), was one of the most famous disseminators of Herder's views, and built on them to develop his own theory of national superiority based on the supposed linguistic purity of the German language (ibid.).

This ethnolinguistic formulation of the concept of 'nation' set the stage for what in the present day is more popularly known as the 'blood and belonging' form of nation. In this category, groups who perceive themselves as possessing a common culture and language come together to make a political state, with 'blood' and language as the main criteria for belonging (Wright, 2000, 41). Germany and Japan are the classic examples of this formulation – that is, states where the main organizing principle is the belief in a common cultural and linguistic heritage. It is also clear that, according to this view, one does not 'join' a nation; rather, one is born into it.

It is through language, too, that Joshua Fishman[3] seeks to answer why nationalism so often generates a political community occupied with a common cultural heritage. He identifies three main attributes of language in the message of nationalism. The first is language as a link with the glorious past, where mother tongue becomes history itself (Fishman, 1972, 45). The second is language as a link with authenticity, which is the now-familiar primordial and Herderian formula (ibid., 47). The final is a contrastive self-identification via language, which is described best by Fichte's formulation of language 'purity' as reflective of ethnic superiority (ibid., 52). For Fishman, both the primordial and modernist links between language and nationalism are clear: 'Nationalism intends that language use and language planning both should encourage and facilitate behaviours of broader unity, deeper authenticity, and various modern implementations of sociocultural and political-organizational integration' (ibid., 66). This is precisely the form of language-planning exercise that the B and B Commission became engaged in as they took on the task of reformulating Canadian nationalism.

In the modernist account of nation formation, nations arise out of specific social, economic, and political circumstances. Their emergence as the primary social community in the modern era is related to the advent of modernization, the concomitant rise of the state, and the ideology of nationalism (May, 2001, 63). In this school of thought, language plays a crucial, unifying role in the rise of the modern nation, but this standard language is not so much a primordial, essential precursor to nation formation as something that emerges through the processes of modernity. Language as a unifying force in the formation of the nation can most famously be traced back to the French Revolution and the emergence of a 'national' standard of French (Wright, 2000; Higonnet, 1980; Grillo, 1989).

The French Revolutionary model of linguistic uniformity has given rise to the present-day conceptual framework of French integration, where assimilation is compelled through a hegemonic monoculturalism and monolingualism. The philosophy that underlies membership in this type of nation can be summed up as, 'You are here, therefore you are "X" or must become "X"' (Wright, 2000, 41). Ernest Gellner builds on this model. For him, the material changes associated with industrialization at the end of the eighteenth century are the main causes of the rise of the modern nation. He highlights the shift from localized, feudal agrarian societies to the modern industrialized society, with its literate, mobile, and occupationally specialized division of labour (Gellner, 1983). This shift, where the substitutability of the worker – that is, the ability of the worker to move between increasingly complex and differentiated roles – became increasingly important to industrialized work, is the space wherein Gellner locates the emergence of the modern nation-state and the need for cultural and linguistic standardization. The prior development of a strong state culture, from which a homogeneous nation could be shaped in response to the requirements of industrialization, is the central element in Gellner's definition of nationalism as 'primarily a political principle, which holds that the political and the national unit should be congruent' (Gellner, 1983, 4). Gellner argues that a nationalism flourishes because 'well-defined, educationally sanctioned and unified culture[s]' offer a path to modernity, a basis of political legitimacy, and a means of shared cultural and linguistic identity (ibid., 55; May, 2001); this becomes the rationale for the B and B Commission's overt shift from an ethnic to linguistic basis for nation-building.

Like Gellner, Benedict Anderson is generally seen as a modernist, but he is often differentiated as a late modernist as well. In his frequently cited book *Imagined Communities*, Anderson elaborates that the nation is imagined 'because the members of even the smallest nation will never know most of their fellow-members, meet them, or even hear of them, yet in the minds of each lives the image of their communion' and in this way, the nation is conceived of as a deep, horizontal comradeship (Anderson, 1983, 15). Locating himself squarely amongst the modernists, Anderson points to the Enlightenment – when rationalist secularism arose and religious belief ebbed – as the point when the nation emerged. In his theory of modern nation-building, the emergence of a standardized national language is traced back to the gradual demotion of the sacral languages, such as Latin (ibid., 24).

Anderson identifies printing – particularly newspapers – as the technology that made it possible for growing numbers of people to think about themselves, and relate themselves to others, in profoundly new ways (ibid., 40). Print capitalism's restless search for markets forced the production of texts in the vernaculars of the masses, which then went on to create unified fields of exchange and communications below Latin and above the spoken vernaculars (ibid., 47). This meant that speakers of widely different varieties of English, French, and so on, who might not even be able to speak to one another, became capable of understanding each other through print. Print capitalism also gave a new fixity to language, since the printed book was able to keep permanent form; and it created new languages of power, since certain dialects that were closer to the print language became the dominant standard (Anderson, 1983, 48). Anderson also emphasizes the affective role of language in nation formation. First, he stresses the primordialism of languages – even those known to be modern – as appearing to loom up imperceptibly out of a horizonless past (ibid., 132). Second, he draws on the image of *unisonance*, which occurs when people wholly unknown to each other form a 'special kind of contemporaneous community,' most effectively in the form of poetry and songs. Examples include national anthems sung on national holidays, in which, 'no matter how banal the words and mediocre the tunes, there is ... an experience of simultaneity' (ibid.). In this way, Anderson's conclusion that 'from the start the nation was conceived in language, not in blood' (ibid., 33) finds a parallel in the B and B Commission's eventual shift from an overtly ethnic basis for national unity to a linguistic one. Thus, for Anderson, the role of language is central in suturing the past, present, and future of the nation together, and points to the importance of culture in creating the affective community of the nation. This lays the groundwork for postmodern conceptions of nation-building.

In postmodern accounts of nation formation, there is a wide array of approaches. However, to a large extent, Homi Bhabha's interpretation – as outlined in his essay 'DissemiNation: Time, Narrative and the Margins of the Modern Nation' – is typical. In this essay, Bhabha examines the ambivalence that 'haunts' the idea of nation, because it is the cultural representation of this ambivalence in modern society, he suggests, that can be the site of possible resistance to the certainty of the nation's 'origins' (Bhabha, 1990a, 1).

Bhabha identifies the ambivalence of the nation as a narrative strategy which produces a 'continual slippage into analogous, even metonymic, categories, like "the people," minorities, or "cultural difference," that continually overlap in the act of writing the nation' (ibid., 292). These metonymic categories do not arise simply out of historical events; rather, they are a 'complex rhetorical strategy of social reference where the claim to be representative provokes a crisis within the process of signification and discursive address' (ibid., 297). The metonymic 'people' are historical objects of a nationalist 'pedagogy' and also subjects of a living, repeating, 'performative' principle of daily life. It is out of this tension between the pedagogic and the performative that a space marked internally by cultural difference and the heterogeneous histories of contending peoples arises (ibid., 299). Therefore, between the pedagogic and performative, the cohesive limits of the Western nation shift to a 'contentious internal liminality,' where 'difference' turns from the boundary outside to within, making cultural difference a problem no longer of 'other' people but a question of otherness within the nation (ibid., 300–1).

Bhabha traces the role of language in nation-building by examining how migrants who 'speak the foreignness of language split the patriotic voice of unisonance' (1990a, 315). This recalls Anderson's notion of the imagined unisonant nation, one that is split by the silenced dissonance of the 'alien.' The very visibility of this splitting is written across the alien body and becomes a languageless presence that evokes an archaic anxiety and aggressiveness within the unisonant nation-space (ibid., 316). In short, the presence of the Other within the metropole does not evoke a harmonious patchwork of cultures; instead, it challenges the totality of national culture by bringing in the Other's history of elsewhere and articulating a narrative of cultural difference that disrupts the national history. This can be seen in the Canadian case where, although there is the assertion of a mosaic of multiple cultures, there is still a totality of national culture as white settler bi-culture.

Bhabha's postmodern model of nation-building introduces notions of ambivalence, resistance, and liminality to destabilize the certainty of national history. This model disrupts a finite conception of the nation and its 'origins,' and also ruptures its boundaries by highlighting the turn of difference from outside the nation to within. Within the contentious liminal space between performative and pedagogical, there is the possibility for supplementary strategies of resistance which eschew simple confrontation with and negation of master discourses. In this model, language reveals the relation of the Other to the nation as the Other's words are rendered opaque and the unisonance of the nation is split by their silence. This model exemplifies postmodern nation-building in that it allows for a complex accounting of the relationship between language, nation-building, and the Other.

During the course of the royal commission, this question of the 'cultural difference' of the Others within the nation became salient as contending and heterogeneous histories of hitherto 'silenced' ethnic groups and Indigenous peoples were made visible by representative groups throughout the preliminary and public hearings in order to contest the commission's notion of 'two founding races.' As a result, the commission had to contend with a crisis in their claim to be representative of the people, pushing them to rearticulate a hierarchy of racialized national belonging on the basis of language and culture. The next section will examine how language lends itself to the project of racial differentiation.

Language and Race

Language provides a convenient basis for racial differentiation because, even as the universal nature of language is claimed, the deterministic and immutable origins of separate languages provide the basis for dividing and hierarchicalizing groups of people along cultural and racialized lines. Geoffrey Galt Harpham's (2002) insights about language provide a starting point for understanding how racial differentiation can move into the realm of language in the first place. Tracing the emerging dominance of language as the locus of explanation for contemporary philosophical and linguistic scholars, Harpham shows that language has become a fetish because it 'has served as a proxy for other issues that resist resolution on its own terms'; that is, there has been a 'recourse to language as a way of thinking other thoughts and answering other questions' (Harpham, 2002, 65). He specifies that language allows us to disavow our agency, while at the same time it gives us assurance that we possess some universal 'species-endowment that is more meaningful than mere anatomy' (ibid.). In this way, language has become a fetish or an 'empty signifier' for our displaced fears and anxieties, protecting us from full self-recognition (ibid., 66). As well, the fact that language is possessed by every member of our species provides the basis for a 'universal ethical imperative' which allows language to function as a possible site of 'of moral law' (ibid., 193). It can thereby serve as the basis for an optimistic 'hope' for the realization of a dream for a 'new universal community' (ibid., 48).

This universalizing imperative that lies at the core of language ties into David Goldberg's identification of the liberal paradox at the heart of modernity. Goldberg (1993) states that modernity's insistence upon its universal identity – that is, the idealization of the liberal principles of equality and the moral irrelevance of race – in fact emerges out of, and is embedded in, a deeply racialized framework of differentiation. In the case of Canada, then, the country's reconfiguration as a modern nation-state can be seen as an exercise in which racialized differentiation is disavowed through the projection of a dream for a 'new universal community' onto the fetish of language. This theme is critical to the project of this book – namely, the process whereby racial exclusion continues to operate on the terrain of language and culture in a social model based on multiculturalism within a bilingual framework.

The modern connection between language and race can be traced from the establishment of philology, which Foucault describes as the 'science' of objectivizing the speaking subject (Foucault, 1982, 208). Ernst Renan, a noted nineteenth-century philologist-historian as well as influential Orientalist, wrote voluminously on the topic of language and race. His work on the differences between the Semitic and Aryan languages explicitly connects language and race through the scientific discourses of philology. One of the leading influences on his scholarship was Herder, discussed earlier, whose work on the primordial links between reason and language informed Renan's studies on language and race (Ashcroft, 2001).

Renan's views on the 'linguistic races' are framed in the racialist thinking embedded in the scientific discourses which flourished with the rise of modernity. Drawing on the common racialist views of his time, his work is concerned only with the 'white races,' since he considers these to be the races that have contributed to the development of world civilization. Having set out this premise, however, Renan proceeds to move away from the racialist thinking current in his era. He begins with the assertion that there are no pure races in Europe, since all European nations are the product of intermixing. Instead of the physical determinism of race, Renan proposes that language is the basis upon which the white races – the Aryan and the Semitic – can be distinguished, so much so that these peoples are in fact 'linguistic races.' Renan not only asserts a relation between language and race, but he also attests to their 'solidarity' (cited in Todorov, 1993, 32). Thus, as Tzvetan Todorov observes, Renan's theories mark the shift from using such terms to describe languages to using them to describe people (ibid., 144). Perhaps Said explains this best when he draws on Renan's writings to outline how the distinction of languages from each other meant that language users – their minds, cultures, potentials, and even their bodies – could also be deemed as ontologically and empirically different in similar ways:

> The point to be emphasized is that this truth about the distinctive differences between races, civilizations, and languages was (or pretended to be) radical and ineradicable. It went to the bottom of things, it asserted that

there was no escape from origins and the types these origins enabled; it set the real boundaries between human beings, on which races, nations, and civilizations were constructed; it forced vision away from common, as well as plural, human realities like joy, suffering, political organization, forcing attention instead in the downward and backward direction of immutable origins. (Said, 1979, 233)

In this way, the racialist doctrine of modernity remained, since a linguistically based determinism was 'no less inflexible for being cultural rather than physical' (Todorov, 1993, 145). This was a central strategy in the work of the royal commission, which organized the groups of people who are delineated in the terms of reference as linguistic categories, but then smuggled racial differentiation back in through a hierarchicalization of the very same categories.

The establishment of the link between language and race in the crucible of modernity meant that, in contemporary nation-building projects – as that of the B and B Commission – language could become the basis of the Other's exclusion. Language could be modernity's empty signifier of promise for a universal community, disavowing racial exclusion even as it simultaneously divides this putative universality through the deterministic and immutable origins of separate languages. Foucault's notion of dividing practices, whereby 'the subject is either divided inside himself or divided from others' (Foucault, 1982, 208), is the process whereby divisions of the population through language come to provide an acceptable cultural basis for nation-building, as in the case of Canada.

As they operate linguistically, such practices divide the population into separate groups through the purported immutability of languages, reprising the exclusions of racial taxonomies. An example of language operating in this way was the tendency of Europeans, in their early years of contact with Indigenous peoples in settler colonies, to dismiss Indigenous languages as mere dialects. As Alfred Arteaga explains, the linguistic 'proof' of the inferiority of the Indigenous languages lay in the fact that they had no words for 'Jesus, for money, for opera, ergo, the Indian is uncivilized, savage, and quite likely, subhuman' (Arteaga, 1996, 22). Upon a landscape that is therefore *lingua nullus* (Eggington, 1994), the imposition of a European mother tongue can occur. Further, language provides an important site of struggle for control over social and cultural resources, but it is also connected to struggles of political power in all its guises: 'Language ... has served a key means by which social inequalities and different forms of cultural oppression have been hegemonized' (Rassool, 1998, 90). Even the project of creating a national language is inherently violent, as it is literally and symbolically forged from the marginalization of the vernaculars and dialects of the modern state (Willinsky, 1998, 199). This loss of the 'right to signify' (Bhabha, cited in ibid., 197) amounts to the loss of the right to exist. Specifically, divisions in language are about the distinctive differences between races and civilizations, and they set boundaries between human beings; thus, they become the justification for colonization and genocide (Said, 1979). The marginalization of all 'non-official languages' in Canada arises from what Tony Crowley describes as the challenge to the nation from within by 'dissident forces' and 'subnational interests' (Crowley, 1996, 182), who are also the heavily policed and internally colonized 'others' (Rassool, 1998, 91). The challenge to national unity that these groups are purported to present can be addressed through the deployment of language, which pits unity against division. This has been a dominant theme in the discourse of Canadian nation-building.

Membership in the Canadian nation is achieved through designation into one of four groups: English, French, Aboriginal, and 'Multicultural.' Although linguistic dividing practices operate to collapse race and ethnicity into language in the case of English, French, and Aboriginal (a homogenizing term that itself points to the suppression of distinct Indigenous languages) groups, this is not the case for the group designated Multicultural. However, being positioned as Multicultural in opposition to English or French implies a *de facto* linguistic status, and a homogeneous one at that, particularly in a contemporary, liberal moral climate that steers clear of the word 'race.' In fact, a doubling occurs with the omission of language from the designation Multicultural – one that allows this group to be defined only through culture while it still emerges as a category in opposition to other linguistic groups. The maintenance of these divisions, as we will see, was a central concern of the B and B Commission, which sidelined the contesting subnational interests of 'other ethnic' and Indigenous groups in the larger project of establishing a new bicultural form of Canadian white-settler nationalism.

Canada as a White-Settler Society

Given the recent history of European settlement in Canada – especially in relation to Indigenous groups – the English and French claims for 'founding race' status could not be built on assertions of the Herderian principles of primordialism. Rather, founding race status for the English and French groups could only be claimed on the basis of a racialized settler nationalism which has its own specific geographic, political, social, cultural, and historical antecedents. Therefore, understanding how Canada came to be established as a white-settler society requires attention to the specificities particular to the category of those nation-states that are described as breakaway settler colonies (McClintock, 1992), creole states (Anderson, 1983), ex-British settler societies (Anderson, 2000), and white-settler societies (Devereux, 1999; Anderson, 2000; Bannerji, 1996; Razack, 1999). The precise understanding of what comprises a settler society is to some degree contested by scholars, yet there are some fundamental points on which they agree.

Ronald Weitzer (1990), focusing mainly on Northern Ireland and Zimbabwe, defines settler states as those 'founded by migrant groups who assume a super-ordinate position vis-à-vis native inhabitants and build self-sustaining states that are de jure or de facto independent from the mother country and organized around the settlers' political domination over the Indigenous population' (24). Daiva Stasiulus and Nira Yuval-Davis (1995) add that this process of establishing settler societies was accompanied by varying levels of physical and cultural genocide; alienation of Indigenous land; disruption of Indigenous societies, economies, and governance; and movements of Indigenous resistance (7).

Although Weitzer's interest lies in the settler states of Northern Ireland and Zimbabwe, his identification of the three main conditions for stable settler rule is relevant for other settler societies such as Canada and Australia. Weitzer identifies the first imperative of stable settler rule as achieving autonomy from the metropole in the exercise of political authority and coercive power. He states: 'The greater the degree of autonomy, the greater the settlers' room for manoeuvre in moulding economic, social, and political structures' (Weitzer, 1990, 26). His second condition is the consolidation of control over the Indigenous population, in order to prevent and/or contain natives' political mobilization and unrest (ibid., 27). His final and most important condition is the maintenance of settlers' caste solidarity and the states' cohesion: 'Although the great divide is that between settlers and the Indigenous population, settler unity is never a foregone conclusion' as 'internal conflicts within the state and dominant community – along class, ethnic, political, or cultural lines – can be dangerous' (ibid., 28).

In their discussion of the theoretical construction and use of the term 'white settler colony,' Frances Abele and Daiva Stasiulus (1989) reveal the historically gendered and racialized usage of this term by scholars. They discuss how the concept of 'white settler society' is a historical construct, which reveals as much about the hegemonic myths of colonial settlers as it does about historical patterns of white settler societies' development and state formation (Abele and Stasiulus, 1989). In fact, the gendered and racialized nature of these hegemonic myths has been absorbed into the political and legal-judicial institutions, 'myths of origin,' and national metaphors of these countries (Stasiulus and Yuval-Davis, 1995, 8) but are also contested in the competing claims of Indigenous peoples, and other groups of subordinated settlers and migrants.

At the end of the nineteenth century, the development of the two largest white-settler colonies, Canada and Australia, out of the expansionist tide of the second British Empire, gave rise to the original, unique position of the settlers in these territories: caught between their location as colonial in relation to the metropole, and as colonizers themselves in relation to the Indigenous populations. As well, in those places where settlers from the metropole were dominant in number (be it through sheer immigration numbers, annihilation of Indigenous populations, or a mixture of both), very particular discourses around white women's bodies collapsed this European settler presence into the 'virgin' territories of the white-settler states (Devereux, 1999). This represented a historical overlooking of the labour of migrant bodies of colour (Anderson, 2000; Bannerji, 1996), as well as an erasure of Indigenous bodies, both literally and physically – all of which combined to create a socio-historically specific space.

It is necessary to understand the unique formation of these white-settler territories in order to begin to understand the centrality of language to the construction of the white-settler nation-space. Michael L. Herriman and Barbara Burnaby (1996) examine the historical and contemporary linguistic landscapes of Canada, the United States, New Zealand, and Australia in their book *Language Policies in English-Dominant Countries*. The book outlines the dominance, in these states, of English as a colonial language which served to suppress other migrant languages and eradicate Indigenous languages. However, in recent years claims for the recognition for these and other languages have grown with increasing waves of immigration and Indigenous rights movements (Herriman and Burnaby, 1996). Although the appellation 'English-dominant countries' provides a good entry point into understanding the singularities and similarities of the formations of these specific nations, there are particularities to each context and the characterizations of each as white-settler societies. While the totality of the nation as a white-settler society is made unstable when it is described as English-dominant, it is this very instability which would drive the B and B Commission in Canada to seek the solution it did in a reformulation of the nation as multicultural within a bilingual framework.

Therefore, based on Weitzer's model, it is possible to conclude that Canada established itself on the basis of all three pillars of settler rule. That is, it achieved autonomy from the mother country (Britain) through a long period of mostly non-violent resistance (the rebellions of 1837–8[4] being the most notable exception); control of the 'Native population' through a systemic process of genocide, displacement, land theft, and containment; and, from the early years of Confederation, upheld settler caste solidarity and social cohesion through the institution of an Anglo-Celtic hegemony. However, the act of establishing Anglo-Celtic hegemony did not go unchallenged. Concern for national unity led the federal government to create the B and B Commission at a specific historical juncture, when the legitimacy of established modes of articulating social cohesion – that is, through a framework of Anglo-Celtic dominance – was being questioned. It was in this project of finding a new basis for articulating social cohesion that the commission would finally have to contend with reconciling the challenges to Anglo-Celtic dominance from the Others within the nation.

Race and Nation-Building

It is through the Other that the nation forms its boundaries. Julia Kristeva argues that a social being is constituted through the expulsion of the 'abject': that which society deems to be impure. Furthermore, these expelled elements can never be fully obliterated and will haunt the edges of the subject's identity with the threat of disruption and dissolution, since the abject is 'something rejected from which one does not part' (cited in McClintock, 1995, 71). Although Kristeva's notion of the abject is broad, her model illuminates how the Other demarcates the boundaries of culture and nation. The link between the psychoanalytic elements of subject formation and the concrete material history of nation formation is vital to understanding how it is that the 'non-belonging' of the Other helps to define the borders of the nation – at the same time as the Other exists within the nation and remains necessary, in a very material way, to its construction.

In all models of nation-building, language performs an important and constitutive role. Nation-building also requires an accounting of the place of the Other in the quest for national unity, even as the inhabitants of the category of the Other shift through history. In the case of Canada, therefore, it is only to be expected that the nation-building project has been pursued in the context of language and immigration policy. This point will be explored in greater detail in the next chapter. Suffice it to say that in the 1960s the Canadian nation-state rethought how its boundaries would be demarcated. Moving from white-settler, Anglo-Celtic dominance to a bicultural hegemony meant the reorganization of the category of Other, even as this category was also being rearticulated on linguistic and cultural terms. Substantively, this involved the passage of the Official Languages Act – to mediate a putatively equal relationship between the French and the English – and the introduction of the policy of multiculturalism, which would outline the place of the other ethnic groups in the nation. At the same time, Canada's immigration policy was being overhauled (as will be discussed in the next chapter), which would result in the 'cultural groups' of multiculturalism policy increasingly became a racialized category, signalling yet another transformation in the category of the Other.

The management of the Other in Canada occurs through the regulative practices of key documents such as the Immigration Act and the Multiculturalism Act. These policies locate the racialized immigrant on the boundaries of the nation and as constitutive elements of these borders; thus, tensions arise from the desire for immigrant labour, the celebration of pluralism, and anxieties about the Other. Multiculturalism policy – which became the Multiculturalism Act in 1988 – performs the domestic task of management and containment of the Other within the nation. This regulation of the modality of inclusion can also be understood as an internal policing of the nation-state. Therefore, the nation-state's dominion is not a fixed entity; rather, its internal construction comprises a series of ranked borderlines which demand constant observation and enforcement (Yegenoglu, 1998, 136). Furthermore, Ghassan Hage locates multiculturalism along a continuum of 'domestic' white management techniques designed to enforce and maintain unity, asserting that multicultural policy was a means for regulating the mode of inclusion of the racialized other and ensuring the nation's social cohesion (Hage, 2000, 237). Positioning relations of minorities to core cultures as domestic matters – through such orthodoxies as multiculturalism – turns the gaze inward and severs the link to transnational considerations of how Canadian imperialism and globalization processes of late capitalism bring migrants from the South to 'our door' (Razack, 1999, 174). Therefore, multiculturalism is a state policy that, while serving to impose a dominant basis for social cohesion, also positions immigrant labour into specific patterns. In Canada, multiculturalism also performs the crucial role of maintaining Weitzer's third pillar of white-settler rule: it ensures caste solidarity among settlers, who – in contemporary Canadian society, organized through a policy of multiculturalism within a bilingual framework – can be understood to be white citizens.[5]

Although state policies such as multiculturalism serve to enact 'control' over the Other and ensure societal cohesion, they also function to distance Canada from its mother country, Britain, and position it in the international community with a distinct identity of its own. The gaining of this autonomy from the metropole is Weitzer's first pillar of white-settler rule. In Canada's case, this is accomplished by presenting it as a uniquely colourful 'mosaic' where multiculturalism means equality for all immigrants in a harmonious multicultural melange (Anderson, 2000, 386) or as a multicultural exhibition of an idealized, tolerant national self through the exhibition of otherness (Hage, 2000, 153). The need for a distinct international Canadian identity stems, as Himani Bannerji explains, from the fact that 'the very discourse of nationhood in the context of "Canada," given its evolution as a capitalist state derived from a white-settler colony with aspirations to liberal democracy, needs an ideology that can mediate fissures and ruptures' (Bannerji, 1996, 9). Therefore the usually 'undesirable others,' who consist of non-white peoples with their traditional ethnic or 'underdeveloped' cultures, are 'discursively inserted in the middle of a dialogue of hegemonic rivalry' (ibid., 9). This projection, both domestically and internationally, of Canada as a multicultural, bilingual, tolerant, and diverse nation not only severs the link to the mother country but also grounds the formation of a distinct Canadian identity in opposition to other nation-states. In particular, it distinguishes Canada from the American 'melting pot' to the south, and allows Canada to portray itself in contrast as a cultural 'mosaic' and a 'kinder, gentler' nation.

In the Canadian context, then, the Other has always been an essential element of nation-building even as the category of the Other has shifted historically. Although the Other is always a racialized construction in a white-settler nation, in the aftermath of the B and B Commission and the concurrent changes to immigration policy, the increasingly racialized 'immigrant' has come to occupy this particular category in the contemporary multicultural nation. Although required for economic reasons, this racialized immigrant Other is out of place within the national boundaries of the Canadian white-settler nation, and its modality of inclusion must be regulated through the policy of multiculturalism. Severing the immigrant body from its labour by designating them 'cultural groups' and policing this internalized yet out-of-place Other, multiculturalism also promotes state cohesion while it projects, both domestically and internationally, a uniquely tolerant multicultural identity that sets Canada apart from both Britain and the United States. Thus, the emergence of multiculturalism within a *bilingual* framework out of the work of the B and B Commission signalled a particular shift in the category of Other, the reworking of the white-settler category, and the rearticulation of the national formulation. Even as the Other remained a racialized category – increasingly visible, given the changes to the immigration policy – the marginal positioning of the Other was maintained through the operation of immigration and multicultural policies.

Conceptualizations of language, race, and nation provide a broad framework for the specific questions of this book. As a constitutive feature of nation-building, language provides the perfect proxy for national anxieties about the management of the racialized Other within the boundaries of the unified nation-state. In the aftermath of the B and B Commission's project of Canadian white-settler nation-building, this produced the Official Languages Act and the Multiculturalism Policy. Precisely how these two regulative texts come together to be articulated as a new national narrative of 'multiculturalism within a bilingual framework' requires a particular reading of selected data.

Analytical Approach and Data

Although the literature on language, race, and nation-building frames the analysis of the B and B Commission, the particular approach of this analysis to the data also needs to be outlined. The data is mainly textual in nature, drawn in most part from the archival records of the royal commission. As well, there are two important elements which structure the analysis of the commission: Foucault's genealogical method and the work of scholars who have theorized the emergence of government commissions in the legitimization of state regulation.

The focus of this data analysis is on the role and place of the other ethnic groups and Indigenous groups in the work of the B and B Commission. It can be argued that the other ethnic and Indigenous groups who participated in the inquiry hearings were inserting themselves into the dominant discourses of the commission's terms of reference in order to resist and renegotiate the master narratives of bilingualism and biculturalism. As Chris Andersen and Claude Denis summarize, public inquiries do not just gather facts; rather, they authorize certain forms of social discourse, which ultimately become truths because of the supposed neutrality of the inquiries themselves (Andersen and Dennis, 2003, 381). However, a study such as this one, which is 'patiently documentary' in its examination of various briefs, submissions, hearings, conference proceedings, research reports, policy statements, and memoranda, reveals the 'said and not-said' of the inquiry and the resistance – supplementary and otherwise – of other ethnic and Indigenous groups to the master discourses of the inquiry's terms of reference.

Given that the project's aim is to track the national narratives of nation-building into the present, the bulk of the data used consists of federal government documents connected with the B and B Commission, with an emphasis on internal commission documents and reports, submitted briefs and materials from the public (particularly the other ethnic groups), transcripts of commission hearings, and the commission's final report. A large portion of these data, of course, is archival material located in the Library and Archives Canada – national memory institutionalized into one drab government building at the foot of the bridge that joins Ottawa, the nation's capital, to Gatineau, the federal government's physical entry point into Quebec. The decision to locate the national archives here was a calculated and placatory geographical gesture, one that arose out of the B and B Commission's recommendation for a bilingual national capital region. Stored at this particular site, these documents reflect the overt and covert struggles of selection, which organized everything deemed relevant to this royal commission under a single accession number. This collection of primary sources was part of the process that led to the establishment of a national memory and the enunciation of Canada's bilingual and bicultural heritage. However, for the researcher, there are opportunities inherent in the singularity and concern with detail which is part of 'archival reason' (Featherstone, 2000, 170). This approach shifts the focus down into the details – the mundane elements of everyday life. Although these documents are

meant to be a collection of materials which are the archival underpinning of a unitary enunciation of the nation, a 'patiently documentary'
study of them – in all their minutiae and detail – can reveal the counter-
stories, the discontinuities, deviations, and disjunctures lodged there.
Consequently, it is possible to do a study of multiculturalism within
a bilingual framework, which reveals myriad challenges to the master
discourses of bilingualism and biculturalism pursued by other ethnic
and Indigenous groups during the course of the inquiry.

Data selection was guided by the extent to which given documents
were germane to the positioning of other ethnic and Indigenous groups
during the commission. As well, related data, which further illumi-
nated the questions being explored, was drawn upon across various
genres. These included parliamentary debates, newspaper articles
from the ethnic and mainstream press, conference reports and proceedings, a published diary, a published speech, and a documentary film.
These textual materials were examined not as discrete artifacts unto
themselves, but as elements linked to the real-world concerns which
originally animated the overall project. Dorothy Smith explains texts
as coordinators of ruling relations; 'text-mediated relations are the
forms in which power is generated and held in contemporary societies' (Smith, 1999, 80). If our knowledge of society is largely mediated
through the ruling relations of texts designed to create an objectified
and hegemonic understanding of the world, then the researcher's interpretative practices are also embedded in a relational process (Ng, 1995,
36). This means that reading practices – such as Foucault's genealogical
method – that eschew the foundationalist claims of objective 'reading'
and interpretation can be used to unravel the hegemonic national formulation that government documents profess.

Foucault begins by describing genealogy as 'gray, meticulous, and
patiently documentary' (Foucault, 1977, 139). The genealogical method
evolves out of Foucault's mistrust of the search for origins and essence,
since 'what is found at the historical beginning of things is not the in-
violable identity of their origin; it is the dissention of other things,' and
'it is disparity' (ibid., 142). Genealogy does not see history as a continuous development of an ideal schema; rather, it is oriented to revealing discontinuities in the supposedly continuous development of
history, and by implication, discontinuities in the present social formations (Tamboukou, 1999, 203). This is the 'history of the present' (Dean,
1994) that genealogy undertakes; instead of criticizing the past in terms
of the present, it criticizes the present by reflecting upon the ways the

discursive and institutional practices of the past still affect the constitution of the present (ibid., 205). To begin to unpack the linear narration of the officially bilingual Canadian nation, a method of historical inquiry that is oriented towards discontinuities is necessary.

Three aspects of the genealogical methodology that are relevant to my inquiry are *eventalization, descent,* and *emergence.* Foucault sees genealogy as eventalization, or a method that can attribute different dimensions to the ways traditional historians have dealt with the notion of events (Tamboukou, 1999, 207). He elaborates that eventalization must begin with interrogation, 'making visible a singularity at places where there is a temptation to invoke a historical constant' (Foucault, 1977, 77), as this forces a rethinking in terms of 'a multiplication of a pluralization of causes' (ibid., 76) – and a rethinking of various power relations that, at a certain historical moment, decisively influenced the way things were socially and historically established (Tamboukou, 1999, 207).

For Foucault, descent is used to disrupt the notion of uninterrupted continuity, and emergence serves to dispel the notion of a final term in historical development. Descent is not the reconstruction or tracing of past events on the present; rather, the search for descent 'disturbs what was previously considered immobile; it fragments what was thought unified; it shows the heterogeneity of what was imagined consistent with itself' (Foucault, 1977, 145). In this way, it demonstrates that the truth does not lie at the root of what we know and what we are, but that the things that continue to exist and have value for us may arise from accidents, reversals, errors, and faulty calculations among other deviations (ibid., 144).

Emergence, or the moment of arising, always occurs in the interstices that designate a place of confrontation; however, this place is where, instead of a closed field of struggle among equals, there is pure distance between the adversaries and an 'endlessly repeated play of dominations' (Foucault, 1977, 148). Foucault elaborates: 'The domination of certain men over others leads to the differentiation of values, class domination generates the idea of liberty, and the forceful appropriation of things necessary to survival'; it is here where the moment of emergence arises (ibid.). Therefore, these elements can produce a genealogical reading of the various collected data which can disrupt the historical continuity of the national narrative that emerged out of the B and B Commission.

Foucault introduces the *dispositif,* or 'apparatus,' as a conceptual tool that can be used to cut across the usual analytic frameworks of class, institutions, and cultures in order to reveal new and different elements, association, and relations (Rabinow and Rose, 2003, xv). Foucault's notion of the apparatus provides insight into the workings of a royal commission as the 'apparatus' is described as a 'contraption whose purpose ... is control and management of certain characteristics of a population,' which brings a 'grouping of heterogeneous elements into a common network' at a particular 'historical conjuncture' (ibid., xvi). The elements of an apparatus includes the 'said and the not-said,' as exemplified in the heterogeneous groupings of institutions, policy decisions, laws, administrative measures, scientific statements, among other things, all joined together in a 'strategic bricolage' to 'define and to regulate targets constituted through a mixed economy of power and knowledge' (ibid.). In short, these strategic assemblages are formed as initial responses to crises and specific historical problems, or perceived challenges to those who govern (ibid.). Thus, a royal commission can also be thought of as an apparatus, in that it is a response to a crisis or a perceived challenge to those who govern at a particular time, and draws a heterogeneous grouping of elements such as research reports, conference proceedings, hearings, briefs, submissions and memoranda, and policy statements into a common network. Foucault's notion of the apparatus is useful for conceptualizing the work of a royal commission; however, the writings of scholars who have theorized the evolution and function of government commissions for the legitimization and accumulation of state regulation also give necessary insight into the development of multiculturalism within a bilingual framework.

Philip Corrigan and Derek Sayer trace the historical emergence of government commissions as important political forms in English state formation (Corrigan and Sayer, 1985, 33). They link the information-gathering and policy-enforcement functions of such commissions with 'ideological consolidation, on a scale unknown previously' and the visibly increasing *definition* of a nation state (ibid., 70). Commissions, however, were not so much about the fine details of policy enforcement or proclamation of statutes as about the cumulative weight of growing state regulation, the overall effect of which was to give the state a 'palpability and presence it had not enjoyed before' (ibid.). In the modern period, the state eventually came to represent a neutral, natural set of institutionalized, routine practices that could successfully claim a legitimate monopoly on national administration (ibid., 123). A key component of this legitimization was the centralization of knowledge, which requires facts – specifically, the legitimization of some facts, and the methods used to collect them, against other facts – in order to justify features and forms of *policy* (ibid., 124). The relation between facts and policy is essential to the functioning of commissions, which contribute to the centralization of knowledge and the increasing density of state regulation, both of which are central to modern nation-state formation.

Ashforth (1990) builds on Corrigan and Sayer in his discussion of commissions of inquiry in the modern era. He describes these commissions as engaging in a process of reckoning schemes of legitimation – that is, they are attempts to systematize and explain the principles underlying policy and the ends of state power, and are characterized by statements expressed in a language observing the rules of 'objective' knowledge or facts (Ashforth, 1990, 6). Ashforth usefully describes the three phases within the institutional processes of commissions of inquiries. The first is the investigative phase, when the commissioners – the official representatives chosen by the state – engage in discussion with representatives of selected social interests within the institutional, jurisdictional, and epistemological parameters of the investigation (ibid., 6–7). Important here is the idea that oral hearings are not just modes of scientific investigation, but performances which serve to authorize a form of social discourse; as he states, 'they are in this sense institutions which draw upon the authority of science to present the state of Truth and the majesty of judgment to represent the truth of State' (ibid., 7). Central to the investigative phase is the singularity of 'the problem,' which must have a rational cause and eventually, with application of relevant facts, a reasonable solution. This attribution of singularity to the objects of inquiry has more to do with what Ashforth calls 'the epistemic predilections of modernity' than any intrinsic unity within the myriad social phenomena under scrutiny (ibid.).

Next comes the persuasive phase, which ensues upon the publication of the inquiry's report(s), symbolizing an invitation to public discussion or dialogue between state and society (Ashforth, 1990, 7). Ashforth argues that it is this symbolic dimension of the public dialogue or discussion that helps to 'constitute the neutrality of the State as an institutional domain separate from Civil Society yet dedicated to the advancement of the "common good,"' with the report(s) becoming the authoritative statement pertaining to political action (ibid.). The final phase is the archival one, when the report(s) become a means of both interpreting events and entering into a dialogue with history (ibid., 8). Ashforth summarizes commissions of inquiry as theatres of power, where the state ventures out from its official spaces to both listen to society and inspect conditions; its objective gaze culminates in the symbolic materialization of this search for truth in the form of a published report (ibid., 9). Although an extension of the state, commissions of inquiry maintain their authority through their construction as independent bodies, made so by the appointment of people who – while representing different interests – will, once appointed, strive to consider the common good (ibid.). Their limits of investigation are also determined through the terms of reference that formally structure and produce the authoritative form of reality the commissioners are seeking to understand (ibid., 8).

Since Confederation, there have been several hundred royal commissions in Canada, though governments of the past two decades have resorted to royal commissions less frequently than was previously the case (O'Neil, 2001, 15). Jane Jenson states that, in Canada, royal commissions are institutions that represent ideas and have often been the 'locales for some of the major shifts in the ways that Canadians debate representations of themselves, their present and their futures' (Jenson, 1994, 39–40). She goes on to specify that such representations are crucial not only to policy making but to politics in the larger sense, because 'they set out the terms of who we are, where we have been and what we might become' (ibid., 40). These issues of 'who we are, where we have been and what we might become' were certainly a central concern for the B and B Commission.

An analysis of the emergence of a new national formulation from the B and B Commission must be located in relation to the broader literature on language, race, and nation-building in order to provide an appropriate context for the examination of the relevant data. However, the B and B Commission also arose out of a particular national, historical context which had crucial implications for how this new national, white-settler formulation would develop. The next chapter will outline the historical context in which the B and B Commission was created and pursued its work – in particular, the confluence of events and factors which led to the perceived need for a rearticulation of the national formulation, as well as the model of multiculturalism within a bilingual framework that followed in its wake.

2 Historical Context

In the quest to understand the constellation of language, race, and nation that organizes Canada in the present, there must be a mapping – along the lines proposed by Foucault – of the 'contingent pathways along which the taken-for-granted possibilities and limits of our present have come into existence' (Rabinow and Rose, 2003, xiii). What this means for our purposes here is this: in order to render visible how multiculturalism within a bilingual framework came to operate as a technology for organizing difference and belonging in the present – and how the fault lines of language and race came to be embedded within this policy – it is necessary to go back to the moment when previously established ways of thinking about and organizing national belonging in Canada came into question. This means revisiting the early 1960s, when critical changes were taking place in Canadian society that would lay the groundwork and conditions for the emergence of a new configuration of national unity and belonging. Although there were various events taking place in this period which signalled these changes, three main areas directly germane to the B and B Commission were the radical changes taking place in immigration policy, the federal government's attempts to abolish the Indian Act, and the rise of Quebec's linguistic nationalism and independence movements.

Immigration

One of the most momentous changes of the 1960s involved a fundamental transformation in immigration policy – one that saw selection criteria based on race or geography abandoned in favour of new criteria emphasizing education and skills. The consequences of this shift for the way in which Canadians perceived their country, and for the royal commission that attempted to frame their evolving views within the parameters of language, were profound.

At the beginning of 1962, Minister of Citizenship and Immigration Ellen Fairclough announced in the House of Commons that immigration would in the future emphasize 'education, training and skills as the main condition of admissibility, regardless of the country of origin of the applicant' (Canada, *House of Commons Debates*, 1962, 9). This announcement represented a pivotal turn away from earlier immigration policies, which were based on racial and geographical exclusions; from 1885 until 1962 Canadian immigration law was explicitly racist in wording and intent, openly discouraging and/or prohibiting non-white, non-European immigration (Taylor, 1991, 2). This history of racial exclusion was built on such policies as the 'single continuous journey' provision, the Chinese Immigration Act and its subsequent revisions, and a variety of 'all-purpose exclusion provisions' outlined in the 1906 Act; when these restrictive measures failed, the government could issue a proclamation to 'prohibit the landing in Canada of any specified class of immigrants' (cited in ibid.).

In the immediate post–Second World War era, the federal government of Mackenzie King made certain changes to the details of Canada's exclusionary immigration policy while reinforcing its overall thrust. In a 1947 speech given in Parliament, King laid out his government's objectives. He began with a short statement of principle: 'The policy of the government is to foster the growth of the population of Canada by the encouragement of immigration. The government will seek by legislation, regulation, and vigorous administration, to ensure the careful selection and permanent settlement of such numbers of immigrants as can advantageously be absorbed in our national economy'; he also warned that 'the people of Canada do not wish, as a result of mass immigration, to make a fundamental alteration in the character of our population' (Canada, *House of Commons Debates*, 1947, 2644). He then explained the new approach to racial exclusion that would henceforth guide Canadian immigration policy: although the King government would repeal the specific discriminatory exclusions regarding Chinese and East Indian immigration, it would do so within a framework that asserted the authority of the Canadian government to maintain exclusionary principles by formulating immigration as a 'privilege' and a question of domestic policy as opposed to a 'fundamental human right' (ibid., 2646). It was this same principle that allowed the government to maintain the prohibition on Japanese immigration. The primary concern here was that the post-war repeal of legislation specific to Asians should not result in an increase in their immigration since, as King stated, 'Large-scale immigration from the orient would change the fundamental composition of the Canadian population' (ibid., 2646); thus, the government's changes to immigration legislation, while repealing the most notorious exclusionary measures, were not meant in any way to alter the type of immigrants who were coming to Canada. In particular, fears that 'Asiatic' immigration would give rise to social and economic problems remained in place, as did the regulations allowing for the continued exclusion of immigrants – non-Chinese and non-East Indian ones, at any rate – on racial grounds. Furthermore, Hawkins points out that the term 'Asiatic' was broadly construed: 'In the minds of the Canadian Liberal government in 1947, Asia meant almost everything in the Eastern Hemisphere outside Europe,' and therefore it was possible that 'by excluding Asian and, by association and extension, Africans also (except white South Africans), Canada was prepared to accept only one kind of immigrant from the Eastern Hemisphere – the European immigrant' (Hawkins, 1988, 94–5).

Five years after this speech, in 1952, a new Immigration Act was passed that reflected the principles that King had outlined. The Japanese had been removed from the list of 'enemy aliens' by then, and the new act placed Germans back on the same basis as other European immigrants. At the same time, however, the act set out limited annual quotas for Indian (150), Pakistani (100), and Ceylonese (50) immigrants – quotas that remained in place until 1962 (ibid.). The exclusions outlined in the Immigration Act of 1952 gave the governor-in-council wide powers to prohibit or limit the admission of persons by reason of

1. Nationality, citizenship, ethnic group, occupation, class, or geographical area or origin;
2. Peculiar customs, habits, modes of life, or methods of holding property;
3. Unsuitability, having regard to the climatic, economic, social, industrial, educational, labour, health, or other conditions of requirements existing temporarily or otherwise, in Canada or in the area of country from or through which such persons come to Canada; or

4. Probable inability to become readily assimilated or to assume the duties and responsibilities of Canadian citizenship within a reasonable time after admission. (Hawkins, 1988, 102)

These provisions meant that King's desire to avoid any alteration to the fundamental character or composition of the Canadian population could be respected.

With a strong demand for labour in the primary industries and in the professional and skilled occupations, immigration rates began to increase in the late 1950s (Hawkins, 1988, 99). As well, by the later part of the decade, a deep conviction about the benefits of immigration was growing among the younger post-war recruits to the public service (ibid., 72). Against the background of declining immigration from Europe, a memorandum emerged from the Department of Citizenship and Immigration in 1960 which called for revisions to existing immigration policy and emphasized that the 'need for immigration and its economic advantages should be clearly explained to the Canadian public' (ibid., 75). This set the groundwork for a series of revisions, culminating in 1961 with the decision to proceed with a complete overhaul and revision of the immigration regulations (ibid., 105).

With the rise in unemployment rates among unskilled workers, pressure from the Department of Labour for more skilled 'manpower,' the decline in European immigration, and the increasing stigma attached to overt racial discrimination, the time was ripe for a new set of immigration regulations which emphasized skills and education. But there were other motives at play as well. Three weeks before Fairclough's announcement, an internal departmental memorandum stated that the prime objective of the proposed revisions was to 'eliminate all discrimination based on colour, race or creed' (Hawkins, 1988, 130). Fears that this would unleash an influx of people from the 'coloured parts of the world' remained strong, however, as the memo went on to note: 'This means that, if we continue to allow Greeks, Poles, Italians, Portuguese and other Europeans to bring in the wide range of relatives presently admissible, we will have to do the same for Japanese, Chinese, Indians, Pakistanis, Africans, persons from the Arab world, the West Indies and so forth' (ibid.). Thus, in the end, despite overturning the most objectionable immigration regulations, a discriminatory clause which retained the racial restriction for family unification was inserted into the new act at a very late stage as an extra precaution against a flood of non-European relatives of people now in Canada (ibid., 131). As Harold

Troper (1993) has argued, this was in order to 'assuage public concern, particularly in British Columbia, about any sudden influx of dependent Chinese or South Asians' (266).

If immigrants from 'the coloured parts of the world' were now to benefit from these changes to immigration legislation, their good fortune was due to many factors, including declining numbers of immigrants from Europe, the demand for more skilled workers, and the need for the Canadian government to show that it had moved away from racist immigration policies. Valerie Knowles writes that the new regulations introduced by Fairclough were 'foreshadowed by the Bill of Rights that John Diefenbaker presented so proudly in 1960'; since that bill rejected discrimination on the basis of race, colour, national origin, and religion, the government could no longer justify exclusionary immigration policies on those grounds (Knowles, 1997, 152). As well, it has been argued that the racist provisions of Canada's immigration policy hampered the country's role in the United Nations and multiracial Commonwealth (Wayland, 1997, 44); therefore, it was clear that if Canada wanted to retain any international credibility it would have to change course. Thus, Troper concludes, the motivation to abandon overtly racist immigration policies was 'less to court non-white immigration than it was to improve Canada's international image and bring immigration legislation in line with domestic human rights policy more generally' (Troper, 1993, 266). The King government's exclusionary policies had ensured that, between 1947 and 1961, only 9.6 per cent of the people admitted to Canada as permanent settlers were from outside Western Europe, the United States, and Australasia (Satzewich, 1989). With the lifting of racial restrictions in 1962, immigration numbers began to increase, most notably with respect to immigration from Asia (Hawkins, 1988).

In late 1965 – with Lester Pearson's Liberals in office – the government announced the appointment of a new minister of immigration, Jean Marchand,[1] and a new name for his department: the Department of Manpower and Immigration (Hawkins, 1988, 151), which would be responsible for immigration and many of the immigration-related matters hitherto handled by the Department of Labour. The following year, on 14 October 1966, a long-awaited White Paper on Immigration was tabled in the House of Commons. Designed to assist in public discussion in and out of Parliament on the principles and policies which the government believed should be embodied in new immigration legislation (Canada, Department of Manpower and Immigration, 1966, 5), the

White Paper was significant in that it articulated in general terms the new framework for immigration now that it had moved away from explicit racial criteria. Most striking was its emphasis on the economic importance of immigration, as opposed to the pre-1962 focus on immigration's role in maintaining the fundamental character of the nation.

In addition, the development of national identity and international stature was particularly important to counter the pull of 'our neighbour to the South.' In short, the emphasis in this White Paper was on the future and not the past. Yet the end of overtly racist immigration regulations did not mean an open-door policy on immigration, as this statement from the Department of Manpower and Immigration makes clear:

> Canada is an under-populated country by most standards of measurement. It must appear almost barren to people of many of the countries of Africa and Asia with their teeming millions, and indeed some of the densely populated countries elsewhere. Many Canadians are attracted to the theory that to fill up our empty spaces as rapidly as possible with any and all immigrants willing to cast their lot with us would serve not only the humanitarian purpose of helping to redress the world's population imbalance but also the national economic goal of providing an enlarged market for domestic production. Some people conclude that we should open our doors wide to a very large flow of immigrants ... The fact, however, is that economic conditions have changed ... Our people are moving off the land, not on to it. We are not a country of virgin lands and forests waiting to be settled by anyone with a strong back and a venturesome spirit. Despite its low population density, Canada has become a highly complex industrialized and urbanized society. And such a society is increasingly demanding of the quality of its workforce. If those entering the workforce, whether native born or immigrants, do not have the ability and training to do the kinds of jobs available, they will be burdens rather than assets. Today, Canada's expanding industrial economy offers most of its employment opportunities to those with education, training, skills. (Canada, Department of Manpower and Immigration, 1966, 8)

Here, an almost Malthusian conception of Canada as a desolate nation of irresistible appeal to the larger populations of Africa and Asia is outlined. At the same time, the statement makes clear that Canada's necessity for immigration had changed: rather than requiring immigrants to settle 'virgin' land, there was now the need for immigrants who would be economic 'assets' because of their education, training, and skills. In this way, although the explicitly racial exclusions of immigration policy had been lifted, a different set of selection criteria – education, training, skills – had been set in their place; the concerns remained the same, but now a new set of selection criteria would control this movement.

Developing alongside the anxieties about this newly broadened range of immigrants from various parts of the world was an increasing concern about national security. In the past, inadmissible classes of immigrants had included 'mentally or physically defective and diseased persons' as well as a variety of people belonging to the 'criminal' classes. By contrast, the White Paper of 1966, drawing on scientific knowledge and medical advances, took a broader approach that articulated these concerns for national security on reasons that still sound familiar: 'Canada is altogether a convenient place of refuge for criminals of all kinds ... It seems essential, therefore, to include in the prohibited classes the person who is known or suspected on reasonable grounds to be associated with criminals or who is a fugitive from justice, even though not actually convicted of any specific crime ... ' (Canada, Department of Manpower and Immigration, 1966, 25). Based upon these and other related apprehensions, the White Paper suggested an extensive set of rules and regulations for immigrant selection, control, deportation, security screening, and appeals, as well as a detailed list of classes of persons deemed ineligible for immigration (ibid., 26).

According to Hawkins, the major objective of the White Paper was to develop 'a reasonable control over the sponsored movement,' given the prevailing worries about opening up the country to a large influx of unskilled sponsored relatives, particularly from the 'coloured parts of the world'; therefore, a large portion of the document was devoted to the development of a complex formulation to achieve this goal (Hawkins, 1988, 160). The White Paper sought to eliminate any overtly discriminatory clause and, to this end, it proposed a complicated formula for sponsorship, with the most significant change being that only immigrants who became Canadian citizens after five years could sponsor relatives. A joint committee of the House of Commons and Senate rejected this proposal, forcing the Department of Manpower and Immigration to rethink admission categories all over again (ibid., 162). Eventually, the government settled on three different categories for admission – independent applicants, sponsored dependants, and nominated relatives – and established a point system for immigrant selection. By October 1967, the new immigration regulations went into effect. According to the minister, these regulations would increase recognition of family relationships and be more closely attuned to Canada's economic needs.

The mainstream media paid close attention to the dramatic changes in immigration policy. The end of race-based immigration policies was announced in headlines declaring 'Welcome to All Races' (Farquharson, 1966), 'Immigration Policy Eased' (Wilson, 1966), and 'Geographical Qualifications Dropped; Selectivity Remains' (ibid.). Although most of the press coverage was positive about the elimination of racially and geographically based restrictions, concerns were voiced about the sponsorship and selection criteria. Many editorials pointed out that these criteria explicitly targeted Italian immigrants. Douglas Fischer and Harry Crowe, in an article in the Toronto *Telegram* entitled 'That White Paper Is Anti-Italian,' stated that 'there's no doubt that the intended victim of the Liberal Government's new immigration policy is the Italian immigrant' (Fischer and Crowe, 1966). Some newspapers also pointed to the colour bias that was entrenched in the 'southern European' selection criteria. As Lubor J. Zink explained in articles entitled 'The True North White and Free?' and 'A Hollow Equality,' the White Paper and the new policies flowing from it were designed to ensure that 'Canada will remain a white man's country while creating the impression that all forms of racial discrimination had been eliminated from our immigration practices' (Zink, 1966a). Zink went on to argue that the barrier lay in the new selection criteria, as the increase in educational requirements would guarantee that the trickle of coloured immigrants to Canada remained negligible, 'for no colored country can compete with Europe in general availability of high school education' (ibid.).[2] Another letter to the editor stated that, in fact, there was no dearth of 'skilled' Asians to apply for immigration; rather, there was a backlog of applications as a result of the limited capacity for screening them in New Dehli (Mannil, 1965). In 1965 there were only three Canadian immigration offices in all of Asia, compared to fifteen in northern Europe, five in southern Europe, and seven in the United Kingdom (Parai, 1974).

Regardless, from 1962 to 1970 there was a steady increase in immigration numbers from Asian, African, and South and Central American countries whereas, after a peak in 1967, European immigration numbers began to decline significantly (Hawkins, 1988, 57). Perhaps most telling was the shift in the top immigration-source countries from 1967 on. In 1967, Britain and Italy were the leading two immigration-source countries, accounting for 62,420 and 30,055 immigrants, respectively; by 1970, their numbers had dropped to 26,497 and 8,533, respectively, while Asian immigration numbers had increased approximately seven-fold, from 3,912 in 1963 to 23,319 in 1969 (ibid.).

What became clear was that, during the course of the B and B Commission, major changes were occurring in Canadian immigration policy. A decrease in European immigration numbers, changes in the domestic economic and labour situation, and increased international pressure all meant a shift away from an overtly racialized immigration policy. Inevitably, changes to immigration policy, especially around selection and sponsorship criteria – and despite the attention to national security issues and inequities in the distribution of Canadian immigration offices abroad – began to result in a change in source countries and the distribution of immigration. This signalled a fundamental shift in who came to inhabit the cultural group category in the B and B Commission's formulation of multiculturalism within a bilingual framework. Jean Burnet[3] traces this shift in relation to multiculturalism:

> The policy of multiculturalism was framed under pressures from and in regard to the aims of Canadians who had come, or whose ancestors had come, from Europe. To the eye they were similar, and, although in the past they had been subjected to discrimination, by the 1960s and the 1970s the concern of their spokesmen was with boundary maintenance, and with language as an important ethnic marker. But since 1967 a considerable portion of the immigrant stream had come from the West Indies, Asia, and Africa. It had been composed of people visibly different from the majority of Canadians. Boundaries between particular South Asian or East Asian groups may be hard to maintain, but boundaries between South or East Asians and Europeans have physical markers. (Burnet, 1978, 109)

Multiculturalism, then, emerged within the context of pressure from other ethnic groups – which, as Burnet suggests, were mainly those groups who had come or whose ancestors had come from Europe. She makes the important point that, by the 1960s and 1970s, language had become the most salient marker of ethnic identity for this group, while during the same period a more visibly marked, or racialized, group of immigrants was beginning to arrive in increasing numbers. Manoly Lupul divides these two groups into the 'white ethnics' and the 'real minorities.' He describes the 'white ethnics' as 'undistinguished in external appearance and therefore socially invisible,' a group whose main concerns were therefore 'language and cultural retention and development,' whereas the 'real minorities' were the 'visible peoples whose facial features prevent assimilation' (Lupul, 1983, 104). The strategy to gain recognition for the other ethnic groups (of the B and B terms of reference) or the 'white ethnics,' as exemplified in certain presentations to the B and B Commission, was to argue for their inclusion into the white-settler category alongside the 'founding' groups. However, this strategy was forever out of reach for the 'real minorities,' since the visibility of their racialization thwarted any such possibility. Thus, cultural groups increasingly came to signify a racialized category while the 'white ethnics,' who were the original 'other' ethnic groups around which multiculturalism was initially framed, slowly assimilated into the white-settler category and became 'socially invisible.'

The White Paper (1969) and Indigenous Groups

In the 1960s, another group that the federal government attempted to force assimilation upon and make 'socially invisible' was the Indigenous communities of Canada. In 1969, Jean Chrétien (then minister of Indian Affairs and Northern Development under Prime Minister Pierre Trudeau) put forward the *Statement of the Government of Canada on Indian Policy*, also known as the White Paper. This White Paper proposed the abolition of the Indian Act and the Indian Affairs Branch as well as the rapid assimilation of Native people into mainstream society. The *Statement* begins by defining what an 'Indian' is: 'To be an Indian is also to be different. It is to speak different languages, draw different pictures, tell different tales and to rely on a set of values developed in a different world' (Canada, *Statement*, 1969, 3); thus, right from the opening statements, the White Paper defines 'Indians' as culturally distinct from other Canadians. The *Statement* clarified that this difference had set Indians apart and was a problem: 'But to be a Canadian Indian today is to be ... apart – apart in law, apart in the provision of government services ... ' (ibid.). The central philosophy of the White Paper hinged on this 'apart'-ness; in particular that the legal distinction between Indians and other Canadians lay at the root of the disadvantages that Indigenous people have suffered, and hence that eliminating this 'discriminatory' legal distinction would lay the groundwork for true equality and justice for Indigenous people. Among other things, the White Paper proposals minimized the importance of treaties and land claims, and, although acknowledging the importance of cultural heritage, the *Statement* made clear that ultimately all these issues would cease to be federal concerns within a short, transitional five-year period. Thus, although acknowledging the importance of Indigenous languages, the White Paper ultimately devolved responsibility for their maintenance: 'The Indian culture can be preserved, perpetuated and developed only by the Indian people themselves' (ibid., 8–9).

The White Paper reflected Trudeau's philosophy of common citizenship, which was premised on an individualized notion of equality as well as his reluctance to redress historical injustices (Cairns, 2000, 52). As will be discussed in chapter 6, this philosophy would also underlie Trudeau's attempts to implement and circumvent the recommendations for biculturalism from the B and B Commission. Most notably, Trudeau also ignored the input from Indigenous leaders during the extensive consultations in the summer of 1968 which had preceded the issuance of the White Paper, as well as the recommendations of the 1966–7 *Hawthorn Report*. The *Hawthorn Report* was commissioned by the Department of Citizenship and Immigration in 1964 in order to review the situation of Indigenous peoples in Canada. The resultant two-volume report, *A Survey of the Contemporary Indians of Canada: Economic, Political, Educational Needs and Policies*, was edited by Harry B. Hawthorn and recommended that Indians should be regarded as 'citizens plus' since, in addition to the normal rights and duties of citizenship, they had added rights as charter members of the Canadian community (Hawthorn, 1966–7). The *Hawthorn Report* also rejected assimilation in any form and argued that the special 'citizens plus' status acknowledged historical relationships and ensuing injustices to Indigenous people (Cairns, 2000, 52). Cairns has argued that the proposals of the White Paper fit 'very comfortably into the basic policy toward Indians of the previous century' (ibid., 51).

As far back as 1857, the United Province of Canada passed an Act to Encourage the Gradual Civilization of the Indian Tribes in this Province, which would be accomplished through the 'gradual removal of all legal distinctions between the Indian and Her Majesty's other Canadian subjects' (Johnston, 1993, 354). Thus, any Indian man could be 'enfranchised' – that is, deemed to no longer be an 'Indian' or able to make any claims based on Indian status – if he met language (English or French) and education requirements, was of 'good moral character,' and had no debts (ibid.). There were limited monetary and property incentives for this enfranchisement, but very few individuals came forward to be enfranchised (ibid.). Shortly after Confederation in 1867, a new consolidated Indian Act of 1876 reprised similar conditions for enfranchisement but in a more transitional, three-stage process to ensure that there was a period of 'good behaviour' before an Indian could be enfranchised. Again, very few individuals came forward for enfranchisement, so in 1884 an amendment was made to allow the government to circumvent the requirement for the band's consent for enfranchisement – displacing community authority over its members and disposition of land (ibid., 361). Between Confederation and 1920, only 201 individuals came forward to be enfranchised, reflecting Indigenous people's historical reluctance to leave their communities, renounce their Indigenous cultural identities, and in most cases give up on communal stewardship of land (ibid.). As a result of the low enfranchisement numbers, in 1920 the government introduced another amendment which granted it the power to enfranchise individuals against their will, giving the rationale that 'our object is to continue until there is not a single Indian in Canada that has not been absorbed into the body politic, and there is no Indian question and no Indian department' (ibid., 363). These compulsory provisions were repealed in 1922, restored in 1933, and not repealed again until 1951, although voluntary enfranchisement was left in place until 1985. Thus, despite the clear historical evidence that Indigenous people had rejected enfranchisement in any form, it is this history of enfranchisement that Trudeau revived in the White Paper of 1969: a history of compulsory assimilation, historical erasure, and cultural eradication.

There was a strong reaction from Indigenous communities to the White Paper. In 1970, a brief entitled *Citizen Plus*, which also came to be known as the Red Paper, was drafted in response by the Indian Association of Alberta under the leadership of Harold Cardinal (Cairns, 2000, 67). Presented directly to cabinet, this brief condemned the White Paper proposals, stating they would lead to the loss of Indigenous lands within a generation and the relegation of future generations to 'urban poverty in ghettos' (ibid., 68). The Red Paper affirmed the importance of the treaties and the guaranteed special status of Indigenous groups, reminding the government that the only way to maintain Indigenous culture was to 'remain as Indians,' which would mean the preservation of status, land, and traditions (ibid., 5). As well, the Red Paper refuted the paternalistic positioning of the White Paper and asserted Indigenous rights for determining their own priorities and future developments. Shortly after these challenges, the White Paper was withdrawn by the government.

The terms of reference for the B and B Commission clearly omitted any reference to Indigenous groups in Canada. This does not mean that the government was not concerned with the place of Indigenous communities in the nation during this period. Rather, the omission reflected the assimilative plans that the government had for these groups which, as McRoberts argues, meant that 'even for native peoples, equality could only mean individual equality'; that is, equal status as individuals (McRoberts, 1997, 121). This plan of Indigenous assimilation proposed by the White Paper fit well into the reformulation of Canada as having only two – English and French – founding nations. With Indigenous groups assimilated into the larger Canadian body politic through the logic of individual rights, claims for collective recognition could be reserved for the two selected founding groups and the logic of a bicultural, white-settler nationalism would be complete. However, again, Indigenous groups were not content to be left out of the monumental national reformulation project that was going on in the B and B Commission, and as the next few chapters will show, these groups came out to be heard and to challenge this bicultural logic at both the preliminary and public hearings of the commission.

Language and Politics in Quebec

Alongside these changes in federal policy towards immigration and Indigenous groups, equally far-reaching changes in the relationship between English- and French-speaking Canadians were taking place. In response to French-Canadian demands for equality in Confederation, particularly in the area of language rights, the assumptions on which the country was based came into question, as did the institutions that bound it together. At the same time, the very terms of the debate on French Canadians' place in Confederation had the effect of pitting the two founding races against other groups. The result was a clash, played out during the hearings of the B and B Commission, between the language rights of French Canadians and the cultural rights of non-English Others, the eventual outcome of which was a new model of multiculturalism within a bilingual framework.

Prior to Confederation in 1867, the laws governing the use of French and English in the territories that would eventually become Canada varied extensively depending on the political situation. With the division of the colony into Upper and Lower Canada in 1791, bilingualism was preserved in Lower Canada but abolished in Upper Canada. Following Lord Durham's report in the aftermath of the Rebellions of 1837–8, the Act of Union was adopted, uniting Upper and Lower

Canada into the Province of Canada and abolishing the use of French entirely. However, French was reintroduced in the legislative process a year later, and while bilingualism was abrogated again in 1848, it did endure in the judicial system. In 1867 language rights were enshrined in the Constitution, with section 133 of the British North America Act guaranteeing the use of English or French in legislation and in courts, a provision applicable both to the federal Parliament and to Quebec. The British North America Act of 1871 confirmed the validity of the Manitoba Act (1870), which had brought Manitoba into Confederation and guaranteed English and French language rights in the province's legislature and courts.

With an increase in immigration and industrialization through the later nineteenth century and the first half of the twentieth, Anglicization of the economy increased, resulting in the marginalization of French in the economy and federal bureaucracy – as well as directing immigrant assimilation mainly into English-speaking communities. Although French-language rights were gradually reduced in many provinces, especially Manitoba, there were minor gains in French-language schooling in Nova Scotia, the Northwest Territories, and Ontario. However, in 1916, English became the sole language of instruction in Manitoba, and in 1934 this also became the case in Saskatchewan. At the federal level, bilingualism made gradual progress in the civil service and in Parliament. In 1960 the Canadian Bill of Rights was instituted, guaranteeing rights to an interpreter in courts, commissions, and boards or other tribunals (Bastarache, 2004).

These gains were not insignificant, but to many French-speaking Canadians they hardly amounted to the full equality they were seeking. Particularly in Quebec, French dissatisfaction with their subordinate economic status to the English, a growing disgruntlement with the heavy presence of the Roman Catholic church in almost all aspects of Quebecers' lives, and an increasing concern for the future of the French language all laid the groundwork for the major shifts in political relations between the French and English – between Quebec and the federal government – that were about to take place during the critical period of the 1960s. Although many of these concerns could be traced back to before Confederation, they began to take on a particular saliency in the post–Second World War period.

By the 1950s, almost all of the major economic institutions and industries of Quebec were controlled by anglophones and English had become the language of work from middle-management on up, skewing management positions in favor of anglophones throughout almost all of the private sector (Levine, 1990, 18). This meant that francophones were relegated mainly to subordinate and peripheral economic activities, with French merchants concentrated in small businesses and oriented, at best, to regional markets (ibid., 19). These occupational disparities translated into significant wage differences, as researchers for the B and B Commission found a 51 per cent wage gap between English speakers and French speakers in 1961 (ibid., 24). This produced one of the best-publicized conclusions of the B and B Commission, which was that Canadians of British origin fared far better in Montreal than anywhere else in the country; in fact, unilingual anglophones had higher incomes than both bilingual and unilingual francophones (ibid., 25). Although increasing awareness and dissatisfaction with these economic disparities helped to fuel the mobilization of Quebec's nationalist movement, it was also fuelled by long-standing changes in sociocultural conditions within Quebec.

Between the 1930s and 1960s, significant urbanization was taking place within Quebec and, by 1961, approximately 40 per cent of the francophone population of Quebec had left rural areas to move to metropolitan Montreal (Levine, 1990, 43). The rising density of the urban francophone population meant a surge in cultural activities – refocusing francophone identity in an urban rather than rural context – and an expansion of a francophone middle class. This new middle class found itself increasingly frustrated by the social and economic conditions of Montreal during the 1950s and felt a growing dissatisfaction with the authority retained by the Roman Catholic Church in the provincial political regime of premier Maurice Duplessis and his Union Nationale party. In particular, there was a rising concern with the Church's stranglehold on social services, including education and health, as well as a growing sense that the provincial government's clerical conservative nationalism was incompatible with modernity. As the federal government increased centralization through expanded national programs related to education, health, transportation, natural resources, and defence, Duplessis brought about his own crisis of political legitimacy by refusing to participate in a number of federal conditional grant programs for the provinces (McRoberts, 1997, 28). One notable example includes his direction to cash-strapped Quebec universities to refuse direct federal grants based on the rationale that education was a provincial concern (Handler, 1988, 86). Duplessis's opposition to the growth of governmental bureaucracy and his policy of giving discretionary as opposed to statutory grants led to the denouncement of his regime and a call for the expansion of the social and economic responsibilities of the Quebec state (ibid., 87). Thus, the emerging francophone middle class pushed for social and political changes against both the anglophone economic establishment as well as the traditional francophone elites. After the death of Duplessis in 1959 and the subsequent death of his successor, Paul Sauvé, Jean Lesage led his Liberal Party to victory over the Union Nationale in 1960, propelling Quebec into an era now commonly known as the 'Quiet Revolution' – a time of accelerated social, political, and economic reforms spanning the early to late 1960s.

The Quiet Revolution ushered in dramatic changes to the political organization of Quebec, with a massive expansion of the role of the provincial government into areas previously controlled by the Church. During the 1960s, provincial expenditures per capita rose over 200 per cent; the provincial bureaucracy more than doubled to 70,000 employees; and the Quebec state, under control of the new francophone middle class, became the most visible presence in provincial life (Levine, 1990, 46). The emergence of political power in the growing francophone middle class also gave them a growing sense of being a cultural majority seeking much more than just equal rights for French alongside English; rather, there was a mounting concern that English was a threat to the future integrity of the French language and culture (ibid., 48). As such, escalating pressure was put on the provincial government to act on linguistic issues.

Historically, there have been relatively few conflicts over the place of English and French in Quebec. Notable examples include the Rebellions of 1837–8, the Tory riots of 1849,[4] and the conscription controversies of 1917 and 1942.[5] However, the period leading up to the 1960s saw linguistic issues emerge as the central locus of conflict; a conflict that would usher in revolutionary changes to both Quebec and Canadian nationalism in the following decades. In 1953, as a response to the massive centralization of the federal government, Duplessis struck the Royal Commission of Inquiry on Constitutional Problems headed by Judge Thomas Tremblay. In 1956, the Tremblay Commission issued its landmark report on the status of French-Canadian culture, 'calling to public attention the possibility that the French-Canadian language and culture faced a dangerous future' and that responsibility for the future of French-Canadian culture lay with the Quebec government (Handler, 1988, 94). This report laid the groundwork for the rise of linguistic nationalism in Quebec for the coming decade.

The Government of Quebec took its first serious step into language politics in 1961 with the establishment of the Office de la Langue Française (OLF) within the Quebec Cultural Affairs Department (Handler, 1988, 169). With a philosophy based in linguistic purism, the main focus of the OLF was status and corpus planning (ibid., 170). Alongside the establishment of the OLF was a growing concern with the issue of immigrant Anglicization – particularly in Montreal, which had seen a significant growth in immigration levels in the post–Second World War period; between 1960 and 1970, over 150,000 non-French and non-English immigrants arrived in Montreal, so that by 1970 they comprised 23 per cent of Montreal's population (Levine, 1990, 55). The linguistic schooling choices for the children of these immigrant families would become a spark that would inflame the language wars in Quebec.

By the 1960s, almost 40,000 of the 43,000 'allophone'[6] children in Montreal were attending English-language schooling (Levine, 1990, 56). Immigrants were choosing to send their children to English schools primarily to ensure their future economic mobility. As well, in contrast to the mainly English Protestant school board, the Catholic school board offered French-language education but would not enroll non-Catholic children; streamed many students away from university; spent less money per student; had less qualified teachers, a dated curriculum, and very poor second-language instruction programs in English; and, in short, was oriented away from integrating immigrants in favour of a focus on maintaining the purity and homogeneity of the francophone community (ibid., 58). These factors all served to steer allophone children into English-language education and inflamed francophone concerns about the French language. Well-publicized, alarmist demographic projections as well as a declining francophone birthrate only fuelled the hysteria that francophones were well on the way to becoming minorities in Montreal. This served to openly politicize the linguistic cleavage in Montreal, setting the stage for one of the most significant events on this issue: the impending crisis that was developing in Montreal's Saint Leonard neighbourhood.

By the 1960s, Italian immigrants in Saint Leonard formed about 30 per cent of the population of what was previously a quite homogeneous French neighbourhood. Therefore, in 1963, the local Catholic school board decided to respond to the area's growing ethnic diversification by opening bilingual elementary schools in which classes would be taught in both French and English (Levine, 1990). By 1967, over 90 per cent of

Saint Leonard's allophone elementary school children were enrolled in these bilingual schools; however, upon graduation, more than 85 per cent went on to the local English-language secondary school. Not only were the children of allophones following this linguistic path in their schooling, but a number of children of francophone parents were, too (ibid., 68). This effect was neither planned nor predicted by the franco-phone-controlled Saint Leonard Catholic school board, and given the direction of linguistic politics of this era, the school board decided to withdraw bilingual schooling and phase in French-language instruc-tion, adding the requirement that all children entering Saint Leonard's elementary schools starting in the fall of 1968 would be required to at-tend French-language schools (ibid.). Allophone parents reacted nega-tively to the imposition of French unilingualism and their loss of choice in the medium of instruction for their children. They threatened to withhold school taxes and keep their children out of school, and some started basement classes for their children. These community tensions served only to galvanize francophone language activists and, by 1968, the Mouvement pour l'intégration scolaire (MIS), with links to radical separatist organizations such as the FLQ and RIN,[7] emerged. At first, their goal was to fight for 'French as the sole language of instruction in the public schools of Saint Leonard,' but this was soon broadened to include the creation of '10, 20, 50 Saint Leonard crises across Quebec' (ibid., 69). After the MIS won control over the local school board a new unilingual mandate was declared. The resultant, dramatic escalation in demonstrations, protests, and political activity on both sides of the matter soon catapulted the issue into national prominence. Meanwhile, an expanded version of the MIS, the Ligue pour l'intégration scolaire (LIS), continued its agitation in Saint Leonard through 1969, culminat-ing on 10 September in a 'deliberately provocative march in support of unilingualism through the Italian neighbourhoods of Saint-Leonard' (Levine, 1990, 78). The march devolved into a riot of approximately 1,000 people: 100 people were injured, 50 were arrested, and the Riot Act was used to set curfews and restore order (ibid.). In the aftermath of the Saint Leonard riot, the government issued Bill 63 with a key pro-vision that guaranteed parents a choice in the language of instruction for their children. However, increasing francophone activism against immigrant anglicization and for the dominance of French in Quebec would see this bill replaced with future bills that would guarantee much stronger protections for the French language, culminating in the passage of Bill 101, the Charter of the French Language, in 1977.

The heated prominence of the Saint Leonard matter was linked not only to anglophone-minority language rights but also to the larger struggle of emerging Quebec nationalistic sentiments in post–Quiet Revolution Quebec. Thus, the first systematic call for a provincial, unilingual French-language policy was made in the early 1960s by the separatist political party RIN which had, as a special concern, the goal that all public education in Quebec would have French as the exclusive language of instruction (ibid., 53). RIN led many demonstrations even as they remained on the fringe of provincial politics through the mid-1960s, and some RIN members who wished for faster action formed the Réseau de Résistance, which eventually became the FLQ. Thus, alongside the activities of the RIN, the FLQ began to escalate their activities, coming into public prominence with the1963 bombing of a Canadian Army Recruitment Centre in which a night watchman was killed. Between 1960 and 1970, the FLQ was responsible for over 160 violent incidents, including bombings of English-owned businesses, banks, the Montreal Stock Exchange, and homes of English speakers – especially in the neighbourhood of Westmount – among other targets, at an average rate of one every ten days (Levine, 1990, 90). In total, eight people were killed and many injured as a result of these and other violent actions by the FLQ. The culmination of the FLQ's activities came about with the October Crisis of 1970, in which British Trade Commissioner James Cross was kidnapped and Quebec Labour Minister Pierre Laporte was murdered. The crisis led to Prime Minister Trudeau's implementation of the War Measures Act, the arrest of almost 500 people, and the deployment of federal troops in Montreal. Thus, the ongoing demonstrations, protests, and political activities over the place of the French language in Quebec fuelled the growth of the Quebec independence movement, and in 1967 René Lévesque formed the Mouvement Souveraineté-Association (MSA), which ultimately became the Parti Québécois in 1968. However, the events of the October Crisis also meant a loss of public support for violent means to attain Quebec independence and an increased support for the Parti Québécois, which finally came into power in 1976.

It was in the midst of this social and political ferment that calls for a royal commission on bilingualism and biculturalism began to emerge. At the beginning of 1962, with the Diefenbaker government still in power after four and a half years and rumours of a general election circulating throughout the country, the time was ripe for simmering political discussions regarding francophone discontent to be raised. In

Le Devoir on 20 January 1962, André Laurendeau, in what is now considered a seminal editorial (Smart, 1991, 2), criticized the federal government's Speech from the Throne for its 'silences on the major issues,' in particular the place of French Canadians in Confederation. Demanding an end to 'piece-meal concessions,' he called for a royal commission inquiry into bilingualism (Laurendeau, 1962). Gérard Pelletier was among those who saw Laurendeau's editorial as a crucial factor leading to the creation of the B and B Commission: 'It is extraordinarily rare for a newspaper article to persuade a government to take positive measures, but that is what André Laurendeau's editorial did . . . It called, for the first time, for a comprehensive approach to the problem' (Pelletier, 1989, R-9).

In his editorial, Laurendeau wrote that a royal commission should have three aims: to investigate the opinions of Canadians from coast to coast on the issue of bilingualism; to study how other countries like Belgium and Switzerland had dealt with similar questions; and to assess the situation of both languages in the federal public service (Laurendeau, 1962). The editorial sparked other calls for an inquiry, and on 17 December 1962 Lester B. Pearson, leader of the opposition, made a lengthy and significant speech in the House of Commons outlining the historical evolution of the relationship between what he called the 'two founding races' and stating that Canada was based on, among other things, a 'rejection . . . of the American melting-pot concept of national unity' (Canada, *House of Commons Debates*, 1962b, 2723). Pearson emphasized that 'we have now reached a stage when we should seriously and collectively in this country review the bicultural and bilingual situation in our country' (ibid., 2725). McRoberts writes that, although Pearson was uneasy with Quebec nationalism, he felt that only direct accommodation and recognition of Quebec's distinct status through dualism in the Canadian political order would hold the country together – and that a royal commission would be central to this effort (McRoberts, 1997, 39).

Prime Minister Diefenbaker rejected all calls for an inquiry, but when the Liberals were elected with a minority government in 1963, one of Pearson's first acts was to establish the Royal Commission on Bilingualism and Biculturalism. In her introduction to *The Diary of André Laurendeau*, Patricia Smart states that, alongside Pearson's conviction for the necessity of developing a new relationship with Quebec, the Liberals seized on the idea of the royal commission as a means of recapturing the Quebec vote they had lost to Diefenbaker in 1957 (Smart,

1991, 3). In his Speech from the Throne on 16 May 1963, anticipating the terms of reference to be announced, Pearson declared:

> The character and strength of our nation are drawn from the diverse cultures of people who came from many lands to create the Canada that is ours today. The greater Canada that is in our power to make will be built not on uniformity but on continuing diversity, and particularly on the basic partnership of English speaking and French speaking people. My ministers are determined that the partnership shall be truly equal. For that high purpose they are establishing, in consultation with the provinces, a commission charged to study, thoroughly but urgently, how the fundamentally bicultural character of Canada may best be assured and the contribution of other cultures recognized. (Canada, *House of Commons Debates*, 1963, 6)

The commission's terms of reference were then drafted in full by Maurice Lamontagne, president of the Privy Council (Morrison, 1989, R-8). These terms echoed Pearson's remarks on the nature of Canada as quoted above: 'To inquire into and report upon the existing state of bilingualism and biculturalism in Canada and to recommend what steps should be taken to develop the Canadian confederation on the basis of an equal partnership between the two founding races, taking into account the contribution made by the other ethnic groups to the cultural enrichment of Canada and the measures that should be taken to safeguard that contribution.'[8] With the terms of reference announced and approved by a majority of the provinces, an order-in-council on 19 July 1963 announced the creation of the commission and the appointment of ten commissioners, including co-chairmen André Laurendeau and Davidson Dunton.[9]

From the beginning, the B and B Commission was conceived by the government as a way of responding to the national unity crisis triggered by French-Canadian demands for full equality in Confederation. However, this was only one part of the historical context in which the commission was born and conducted its work. The 1960s were a period of great social unrest and fundamental change in attitudes, values, and social structures. This included a new sense of Canadian nationalism, as evidenced in the adoption of a new Canadian flag (1965) and the centennial celebrations of 1967 (with Expo '67 as their focal point); and the creation of a Royal Commission on the Status of Women (1968). As well, increasing visibility in Indigenous activism during this period – particularly against the White Paper and changes to the fabric of Canadian society stemming from the new immigration policy of 1962 – made the 1960s a time when established ways of organizing national belonging were coming into question, as the recognition and modes of inclusion of groups that had been historically marginalized were reworked and a rearticulation of a new national identity was occurring. The B and B Commission found itself at the intersection of these various struggles, with the result that its original model of a bilingual and bicultural Canada would be soon challenged.

3   Preliminary Hearings and Report

The preliminary stage of the B and B Commission consisted of both an investigative and a persuasive phase. The investigative phase included the preliminary hearings and regional meetings, and the persuasive phase involved the formulation, publication, and dissemination of the *Preliminary Report*. Central to this stage of the inquiry was its framing through the already delineated groups – other ethnic groups, founding races – as being centrally a problem about an equal partnership between the founding races, relegating concern with other ethnic groups to a marginal question of cultural contribution. Specifically, it was important to delineate the crisis in national unity as a problem between the founding races, and this was therefore the commission's main concern; it was required in order to establish the precise limits of the commission's mandate and its prescriptions for dealing with the public response to the alleged crisis.

Submissions by 'Indians and Eskimos' and 'other ethnic groups'[1] during the preliminary hearings reveal the counter-stories, deviations, and disjunctures to both the commission's terms of reference and its singular notion of a crisis in the history of the country. It is in these counter-stories and disjunctures that the fault lines of an emerging racialized hierarchy between founding races, Indigenous groups, and other ethnic groups can be detected. Moreover, it was in the preliminary stage of the inquiry that conflicts around these fault lines became visible. This was the moment when the established ways of organizing national belonging were being called into question, the moment when the commission had to heed petitions for new forms of recognition from French communities while also addressing the claims being made by Indigenous and other ethnic groups.

The establishment and maintenance of the 'founding races' formulation was a principal concern in this preliminary stage of the inquiry, for it was through this formulation that the white-settler nation's unisonance (Bhabha, 1990a) could be maintained, even though its essential character was portrayed as bilingual and bicultural. The 'founding races' vision was therefore the central point of tension in the inquiry's early days, with the commissioners being confronted by submissions from Indigenous and other ethnic groups that rested on a much different view of the country. The need to address this tension shaped the construction of the *Preliminary Report*.

Introductory Speeches

The commission's first meeting took place on 4 September 1963, and among its first public events were the preliminary public hearings of 7 and 8 November in Ottawa. From the start, there was a lot of interest in these hearings, with the one day initially allotted for them having to be extended to two days and two evenings (Canada, *Preliminary Hearing*, 1963, 13). These sessions laid the groundwork for regional meetings across the country in the following spring and summer, with locations ranging from Rimouski and Yarmouth to Regina and Winnipeg (Canada, *Preliminary Report*, 1965b). Hundreds of people attended each of these regional meetings, with daytime attendance ranging from 70 to over 300 people, and even larger crowds in the evenings of up to 800 (ibid.).

The exercise of defining the singularity of the problem that confronted the commission began in the preliminary hearings; in this persuasive phase of the inquiry, the challenge was to try and secure public consensus on the problem. The process began by attempting to anchor the terms of reference from the start. In their opening speeches at the preliminary hearings that launched these and all subsequent public meetings, co-chairmen Laurendeau and Dunton pointed to the importance and uniqueness of the terms of reference. Laurendeau stated: 'In many respects the Commission resembles all royal commissions ... in other ways this Commission is "pas comme les autres" ... this fact is derived from the very nature of the terms of reference, we are hence able to emphasize it' (Canada, *Preliminary Report*, 1965b, 177). Both Laurendeau and Dunton also specified clearly what they saw as the main concern of the terms of reference. Laurendeau led off: 'My colleague, Davidson Dunton, will tell you presently that in our opinion the central idea of the terms of reference is that of the equal partnership between the two founding races' (ibid.). He then went on to discuss the implications of the term 'biculturalism' in a detailed analysis:

> Implied in the word 'biculturalism' is the fact that in Canada there are two main cultures, each related to one of the principal languages, sharing much in common but each with many distinctive attributes. It will be an important part of our task to consider how these two main cultures may both develop vigorously under the concept of 'equal partnership.' At the same time, the Commission shall be concerned with the cultural contributions of other groups. The term 'biculturalism' in our minds does not carry the thought that the two cultures must be mixed, nor that individuals must necessarily possess both. But we do believe that it must imply an equality of opportunity for the individual as chiefly associated with one or the other of the two main cultures. (Ibid., 180)

In this lengthy exposition, the paramount question of the two main cultures was linked to the two main languages, with an added 'concern' for the cultural contributions of other groups. Yet, as it would be laid out in the final report, the ascendancy of the two main groups was retained by associating their cultures with the rights of the individual.

In the rest of his opening speech, Dunton outlined what the main questions for the commission would be, with only two of these fourteen questions addressing the other ethnic groups and none concerned with Indigenous issues (Canada, *Preliminary Report*, 1965b, 181). In Laurendeau's speech, he emphasized that the questions posed through the terms of reference underscored the need for extensive research; he also emphasized that the exact nature of the equal partnership needed to be determined (ibid., 178). In Laurendeau's opinion, this question was best answered by the public: 'And who can tell us this, if not the Canadians?' (ibid.). In their speeches, both Dunton and Laurendeau attempted to fix the terms of reference, already identified as something quite different from those of other royal commissions and hence worthy of special emphasis. By reiterating that the main issue before the commission was the relationship between the two founding races, they attempted to specify the primary objective both at the public hearings and in the commission's research agenda. In fact, the task of securing public consensus on a singular problem began even before the public hearings, and was also necessary in order to make the accumulating research relevant to the eventual report.

Laurendeau ended his speech by anticipating the overarching 'truth' of the *Preliminary Report*, the problem of a national crisis: 'The Canadian government, in setting up the Royal Commission on Bilingualism and Biculturalism clearly indicated its belief that we are in a state of emergency – an emergency that can jeopardize the very existence of Canada' (Canada, *Preliminary Report*, 1965b, 179). Such a statement was taken as proof, particularly in the media, that the commission from the very beginning had set out to manufacture a crisis (Wardaugh, 1983, 40).

Hearings

During the preliminary hearings of 7–8 November 1963, the commission's mandate was debated at length by the public, with the result that 'the Commissioners were able to grasp the attitudes of several thousand Canadians throughout the country as they discussed the questions raised by the Commission's terms of reference' (Canada, *Book I*, 1967, 175). As this debate proceeded, patterns of critique emerged that would become typical of the ensuing public discussions and submissions. Over the course of the preliminary hearings, seventy-six different organizations and individuals were heard by the commissioners (Canada, *Preliminary Report*, 1965b, 25). Throughout, conflict over the terms of 'the problem' surfaced repeatedly, particularly from members of the other ethnic groups. Dr J.A. Wojciejowski, representing the Canadian Polish Congress, began by questioning the commission's name: '[T]he very name of the Commission suggests that Canadian culture is or should be bicultural ... it seems to me that as far as culture is concerned, we cannot limit a culture in a mechanical way to one or two or three or four elements ... culture is something ... where no ethnic group has a majority. Uni-culture is impossible and multi-culture is a necessity' (Canada, *Preliminary Hearing*, 1963, 183–4). Wojciejowski's view that any attempt to divide culture into discrete components would be futile led to the suggestion of multi-culture, foreshadowing the calls for multiculturalism that would come from the other ethnic groups during the public hearings.

This caused Commissioner J.B. Rudnyckyj to question and caution Wojciejowski: 'Do you think that in the framework of our terms of reference it is possible to work with the concept of multiple bilingualism and multiple biculturalism? ... You know we have to stick to those two and we cannot go beyond the terms of reference' (Canada, *Preliminary Hearing*, 1963, 185). Despite Wojciejowski's critique of the limits of biculturalism, Rudnyckyj re-emphasized the institutionally, jurisdictionally, and epistemologically bound parameters of the investigation in an effort to retain the singularity of the problem to be investigated by the commission. In short, the commission, in Rudnyckj's view, could operate only within the terms of biculturalism and bilingualism, making 'multi-culturalism' and 'multi-lingualism' impossible. However, he did offer a creative solution to the problem, positing 'multiple bilingualism' and 'multiple biculturalism' instead. The saliency of Rudnyckyj's suggestion became clearer during the course of the inquiry as his personal position on bilingualism and biculturalism emerged and crystallized into a dissenting opinion at the end of *Book I* of the final report.

Numerous other opinions contesting the terms of reference were shared during these preliminary hearings. A common concern was the contrast between the terms 'other ethnic groups' and 'founding races,' which seemed to imply, as stated by Dr I. Hlynka of the Ukrainian Canadian Committee, 'a division of Canadian citizens into two categories ... first and second class citizens' (Canada, *Preliminary Hearing*, 1963, 84). Hlynka went on to state that his organization rejected any principle which would tend to 'recognize or to imply the superiority of one group of Canadians over another, whether it be on the basis of their ethnic origin, their culture, or the so-called prior historic right, because this means a return to a colonial status from which it has taken so long to emerge' (ibid., 83).

'Prior historic right' was a particular problem for the 'other ethnic groups.' For example, MP Robert Thompson, 'appearing as a private individual' (Canada, *Preliminary Hearing*, 1963, 64), stated that the commission had to determine whether the British North America Act made any concessions to French Canadians or whether it meant to offer a general guarantee of cultural preservation for all minority religions and ethnic groups in Canada. This was 'a matter of great concern,' he said, 'not only to all "new Canadians," who have settled in Canada since the original Confederation Statute was passed, but also to the Indigenous Indian and Eskimo populations, to whom a choice of allegiance between "French" and "English" cultures is bound to appear both unnecessary and meaningless' (ibid., 68). Here, Thompson was clearly maintaining the boundaries between the 'Indian and Eskimo' populations, the 'French' and the 'English,' and the other ethnic groups, the latter being referred to as 'new Canadians.' This triggered the following exchange between Commissioner Rudnyckyj and Thompson:

COMMISSIONER RUDNYCKYJ: In what chapter of the British North America Act, and in what paragraph of our terms of reference do you find the term 'New Canadian' and if you do not, why did you use this rather confusing term?

MR. THOMPSON: For the same reasons, I suppose, you use the words 'biculturalism' and 'bilingualism.' They are not in the dictionary. Unfortunately this is the only way one can well express the name of those who have come to Canada since Confederation and are not part of the true original founding nations and cultures. I wish there was a better word, and I would appreciate your suggestion if you have one.

COMMISSIONER RUDNYCKYJ: If the German group came two hundred years before Confederation, is this a newcomer group?

MR. THOMPSON: I would say that 'new' in French and English could all be thrown outside in saying that we are all Canadians, because that is the only hope of our nation continuing as a nation. I used it only as a descriptive, distinguishing adjective. (Canada, *Preliminary Hearing*, 1963, 175–6)

This exchange signalled the complications that were emerging as the commission attempted to set the basic terms of discussion. By maintaining that the problem confronting the commission, and the country, was one of *bi*-culturalism/lingualism, the commission was having to contend with the implied hierarchical location of groups that did not fall into either *bi* category – specifically, in this case, what had been lumped together as 'the other ethnic groups' in the terms of reference. As confirmation of how complicated this discussion of nomenclature was becoming, Laurendeau subsequently became embroiled in similar confusion about the terminology 'new Canadian' in his exchange with B.M. Belash, of the Ukrainian Professional and Businessmen's Club in Winnipeg, about Canadian radio broadcasts in the German language:

MR. CO-CHAIRMAN LAURENDEAU: You are speaking of the homes of new Canadians in terms of 25 per cent?

MR. BELASH: Pardon me, I am not speaking of new Canadians, I am speaking of third generation Canadians.

MR. CO-CHAIRMAN LAURENDEAU: Excuse my use of that expression, this is just a way of speaking.

MR. BELASH: I think it is a wrong way of speaking, if I may say so.
MR. CO-CHAIRMAN LAURENDEAU: Yes . . . (Canada, *Preliminary Hearing*,
   1963, 229)

In equating 'other ethnic groups' with 'new Canadians,' Laurendeau
was echoing the remarks made by Robert Thompson that Commissioner
Rudnyckyj had criticized. This indicated the extent to which the commissioners themselves were unsure about their own terminologies.

Towards the end of the preliminary hearings, the commission heard
from Mrs. Saul Hayes, president of the National Council of Women
of Canada – an umbrella organization representing many women's
groups across the county at the local, provincial, and national levels,
including many from 'ethnic groups' 'such as the North American
Indian, Polish, Italian, Jewish, Chinese, Negro, Ukrainian and Greek'
(Canada, *Preliminary Hearing*, 1963, 446). Hayes followed Hlynka's lead
when she stated that 'the terms of reference have implications that give
rise to the basic objection of dividing Canada into a primary group of
First Citizens and a secondary group of citizens who *may* qualify as
Canadians, under certain conditions' (ibid., 448). She then focused on
the hierarchical implications of the term 'new Canadians,' arguing that
the phrase was originally used to describe those who came to Canada
after 1947; however, through misuse, it had now obtained a secondary
meaning: those who arrived in Canada after 1759 but were not of French
or Anglo-Saxon origin. She continued, 'According to this, it would follow that if a person came from England in 1960, he is Canadian, but if
a Pole or a Ukrainian or a Jew traces his origin in Canada to his great
grandfather in 1799, he is a "new Canadian"' (ibid., 448). Here again,
the prior history claim of the founding races is contested by a critic of
the term new Canadian, who demonstrated that other non-English and
non-French groups could also make a claim of prior history. However,
Hayes went further, making explicit the hierarchy that resulted from
this opposition: a hierarchy of 'Canadian' and 'new Canadian' paralleled by the hierarchy of 'founding races' and 'other ethnic groups.'
This hierarchical disjuncture between race and ethnicity was one of the
central points of disagreement over the terms of reference. Although it
would be minimized in the *Preliminary Report*, the commission devoted
an entire section of *Book I* of the final report to explaining its position
on each of the terms of reference, with particular attention given to race
and ethnicity. The range of discussion on this issue that occurred during the preliminary hearings of 7 and 8 November 1963 were a preview

of the anxieties that the terms 'founding races' and 'other ethnic groups' would provoke for the duration of the inquiry.

When Hayes ended her presentation, Commissioner Royce Frith laid out the dilemma, as he saw it, with regard to the use of race and ethnicity in the terms of reference:

COMMISSIONER FRITH: One of the points you have raised has been raised frequently and poses to me, not as a member of the Commission but as a Canadian, a constantly recurring dilemma. It is caused by the fact that if we speak of the two principal races, or the two founding races, or the two principal peoples, we find that the person who says that has been criticised for overlooking the other ethnic groups. Now, the word 'ethnic' means racial, so we say then we will call them 'other ethnic groups' – or we will call them 'Polish-Canadians,' for example. Then they will say: 'Do not call me a Polish-Canadian; I am a Canadian, but do not overlook me.' We ask 'What about "new Canadian"' – 'No, that won't do, either.' What will do, in your experience? How can we find a word to describe a fact?

MRS. SAUL HAYES: Mr. Chairman, perhaps I could suggest to Mr. Frith the complication which you have pointed out, I think one can find right in the terms of reference themselves. When you say that 'ethnic' means racial, there is the distinction apparently intimated by the term used – the 'two founding races' and referring to the 'other ethnic groups.' Well, if the words are interchangeable, I do not know why they use two different words to describe the same meaning, right within this phrase, within the terms of reference itself ... The leaving of this term of reference strikes me as a kind of *a priori* conclusion – that, whatever the findings of the Commissioners should be, this is a conclusion that they must, by the very terms of reference, arrive at. Doesn't it beg the whole question? (Canada, *Preliminary Hearing*, 1963, 452)

In this exchange, Commissioner Frith positioned himself not as a commissioner but as a Canadian; one who is constantly stumped by the seemingly conflicting demands of 'them' or the 'other ethnic groups.' As noted in chapter 1, Ashforth discusses how commissions of inquiry are constructed as independent by the appointment of people seen to represent different interests and who will, once appointed, strive to consider the common good (Ashforth, 1990, 9). By speaking not as a commissioner but as a Canadian, Frith recognized both his inability to represent all the different interests of the various commissioners – some of whom did represent new Canadian groups – and his own location in the Canadian versus 'new Canadian' hierarchy. In this way,

he was able to retain his commissioner's authority to question Mrs
Saul Hayes at the same time as he spoke for the 'common good' of all
'Canadians' against the demands of the new Canadians or other ethnic
groups. However, this did not deter Hayes, who again pointed to the
contradictions of the terms of reference, revealing the a priori conclusion built into the inquiry based on this differentiation between ethnic
and racial groups.

Mr M. Garber, who made a presentation at the preliminary hearings
on behalf of the Canadian Jewish Congress, gave one of the strongest
criticisms of the term 'two founding races.' From the outset, Garber
made it clear that he was there only to address the terms of reference.
The particular term of reference to which he took greatest exception
was the one that used 'the word "race,"' which 'can be stretched into
"racialism" and . . . is reminiscent of the suffering of the smaller groups
wherever this word is emphasized' (Canada, *Preliminary Hearing*, 1963,
258). Garber went on to make the argument that the English and French
culture of Canada is the property not only of the 'original founders' but
also of those who subsequently immigrated to Canada (ibid., 260). He
made this argument on behalf of 'the 260,000 people that I represent,'
drawing on prior history not to make a claim as a founding people but
rather to make the case that 'we have had roots in this country for over
200 years' (ibid.). Based on this argument, Garber said, 'we strongly
urge . . . that at least this loose document be so amended that that reference to races of ethnic groups be eliminated altogether' (ibid., 261).

After Garber's lengthy presentation, he offered, in an exchange with
the commissioners, one of the most pointed repudiations in the preliminary hearings of the use of the word race in the terms of reference:

MR. CO-CHAIRMAN LAURENDEAU: Thank you, Mr. Garber. Of course, as you
know, we are not free to change the terms of reference. The most we can
do would be to transfer your remarks to the government. I do feel, having
listened to you, that the really important work in this field is 'biculturalism'
and not 'biracialism.'

MR. GARBER: Yes, but the suggestion is that maybe that is not what this means.
Yet, we are trying as lawyers to read what it says. Not everyone will have
the explanations which you have made to me. I have made the same objection in the Prime Minister's office, and he was horrified. He said, of course,
it was not meant to mean that. I cannot go to Canada's 19 million people
and tell them that what it says is not what it means. I do not think it should
be there at all. You are not talking about a partnership between two races,

because there is no partnership on that basis. There is partnership between cultures.

COMMISSIONER GAGNON: The fact that you are representing the Hebrews means something.

MR. GARBER: That does not seem to be the point. When you say, 'Other ethnic groups,' that means that those that are founding groups are also ethnic groups. We would like to see it state a partnership between the two cultures. I think the number of people who have come here after 1867, or who were already here in 1867, are rather unhappy with the statement that is made, suggesting that in 1867 Canada was only represented by Anglo-Saxons and French Canadians when also at that time there were 10,000 people who were neither Anglo-Saxons nor French Canadians. I say that the statement is wrong to the extent that today, and certainly in the future, the majority of people probably will be neither Anglo-Saxons nor French Canadians. (Canada, *Preliminary Hearing*, 1963, 262)

Laurendeau, although comprehending the problems involved in using the term 'race,' as outlined by Garber, had to once again reaffirm the institutionally, jurisdictionally, and epistemologically bound parameters of the investigation in order to maintain the formulation laid out in the terms of reference. Similarly, with respect to Garber's claim that this was to be an inquiry based not on race but on 'culture,' Commissioner Jean-Louis Gagnon attempted to explain away this approach as being the result of Garber 'representing the Hebrews' – a point that Garber succinctly dismissed as irrelevant. This exchange is ironic in that it foreshadows the path that the inquiry itself would take in *Book I* of the final report, where race is de-emphasized in favour of language and culture. Garber's point – that the term 'other ethnic groups' inherently suggested that the founding groups were themselves ethnic groups – added to the growing evidence of the contradictions within the terms of reference. His reminder that the non-Anglo-Saxon and non-French-Canadian presence would continue to grow into the future until it embraced the majority of the country's population would be an argument, and in some cases a fear, that would resurface throughout the inquiry.

At the end of Garber's presentation, Commissioner Rudnyckyj tried to find common ground with Garber within the limits of the terms of reference. The way he did this was consistent with his position as a well-known Ukrainian activist and professor of Slavic studies at the University of Manitoba, who had been selected as a commissioner in a bid to construct the royal commission as independent by 'the appointment of people seen to represent different interests' – in this case, Ukrainian Canadians. Unfortunately, the tactic he used in his exchange with Garber involved race:

COMMISSIONER RUDNYCKYJ: Would you submit the view that Canada was founded by one race, the white race?

MR. GARBER: White?

COMMISSIONER RUDNYCKYJ: The white race: Jewish, English, French and other people?

MR. GARBER: Well sir, when I was a student at McGill we did not have a true definition of the word 'race.' At that time I think the theory was that race is determined by your head measurement. There is a term for that. After I heard that lecture I measured my head. I was round-headed, so I really belonged to the Latin race, or the Mediterranean race. It is a dangerous word to use. Some people have used it and as a result have caused a great deal of trouble throughout the world from time to time. It is a word not to be used. (Canada, *Preliminary Hearing*, 1963, 264–5)

Commissioner Rudnyckyj had begun this exchange by attempting to find a single commonality between the founding groups, in this case the 'white race,' since, in his opinion, this commonality had the benefit of being porous enough to contain both the 'founding races' as well as Jewish Canadians. His strategy, although seeking to broaden the 'two founding races' formulation beyond English and French, still served to re-inscribe the white-settler underpinnings of the nation. Garber deftly exposed the slippery construction of race by recalling an earlier era's resort to the absurdity of craniology as the basis of racial categorization, and, in so doing, he also made clear that he would not rescind his repudiation of the term race. Co-chairman Laurendeau brought this dialogue to a rapid conclusion by interrupting the final exchange between Rudnyckyj and Garber, perhaps because the focus had been too long on the idea of 'race.' The confusion over the term race would not be dispelled easily, and in the end the commissioners would have to jettison this term before they could begin to write their final report.

There were two main strategies that those designated as 'other ethnic groups' employed in their campaign to gain inclusion into the two founding groups. The strategy of the Canadian Jewish Congress, as outlined by Garber, was to dismiss designations of race and ethnicity as irrelevant to the inquiry – race because of its inherent and dangerous racialism and ethnicity because all groups could be deemed ethnic. Instead, the focus was shifted to culture, but here the integrity of biculturalism was maintained, for it was a model of porous biculturalism where immigrant groups could make either of the bi-cultures 'their own property' (Canada, *Preliminary Hearing*, 1963, 260). Thus, although there was a bid for inclusion, it was into the one of the two 'founding' cultures – 'We say we are in favour of the two cultures' (ibid., 261). There was no claim made on the basis of being a separate founding group. This was in contrast to the second strategy – the argument of 'prior history' – which was best expressed by the Ukrainian community.

The Ukrainian community was probably the most vocal and well-organized 'other ethnic group' that made submissions and presentations to the royal commission. The most common basis for the Ukrainian bid for inclusion was through the claim of prior history, an idea that was utilized in order to make the explicit assertion that the Ukrainians, too, were a 'founding race.' This was exemplified in B.M. Belash's opening remarks to the commissioners: 'Canadian Ukrainian citizens feel that they are too a founding race since to a large extent it was the Ukrainians that did the work of building the railways, and it was the Ukrainians who found [*sic*] these settlements in the most inaccessible parts of Western Canada ... That is why a superficial interpretation of the term "founding races" is completely in error' (Canada, *Preliminary Hearing*, 1963, 220). Here, claims for inclusion into the 'founding races' built on the progressive transformation of the Canadian wilderness by the concerted efforts of other Canadians. This strategy of inclusion was parallel to Commissioner Rudnyckyj's earlier efforts to include the Jewish group in the founding-races category by naming them as 'white.' Similarly, Belash did not repudiate the notion of founding races, nor did he try to draw out the contradictions between the terms race and ethnicity as used in the terms of reference; rather, he judged the interpretation of the term 'founding races' to be superficial and incomplete. These different strategies for inclusion led to different claims for languages other than English and French, as well.

The Ukrainians' position on language was tied directly to their assertion that they were another founding race. The first language claim was a redefinition of bilingualism based on the historical evolution of the word in the province of Manitoba, as exemplified in the words of Mr. Belash: 'a clause from the Laurier agreement of 1887 reads as follows: When ten of the pupils in any school speak the French language or any language other than English as a native language, the teaching of such pupils shall be conducted in French or such other language and English upon a bilingual service' (Canada, *Preliminary Hearing*, 1963, 220).

Subsequently, Belash contrasted the strong wording 'shall be conducted' of the Laurier-Greenway agreement in Manitoba with the less emphatic 'may ... employ one of more competent persons to give instructions in any language other than English in the schools ...' in the Saskatchewan School Act, which led him to conclude that 'Manitoba recognized this right as a birthright of the citizens of Manitoba' (Canada, *Preliminary Hearing*, 1963, 220). He then went on to underline the implications of the historical 'right' to bilingualism in Manitoba for the present: 'The bilingual public schools of Manitoba from that date, 1887, were not English or French only but also English-German, English-Ukrainian and English-Polish ... Bilingualism of the western variety is very much alive even today' (ibid., 221).

In short, Belash re-inscribed the historical claim for bilingualism in Manitoba and also presented the unique Western definition of bilingualism. This call for a redefinition of bilingualism was the second important aspect of the Ukrainian language claim; in Belash's words, 'I would indeed suggest a re-examination of the meaning of the word "bilingualism" and a redefinition in its true unqualified sense; "bi" meaning two, and "lingualism" pertaining to language' (Canada, *Preliminary Hearing*, 1963, 227–8). Thus, the Western interpretation of bilingualism became different from a bilingualism referring only to English and French: 'We can admit that there is bilingualism, but there is a dual bilingualism: The French-English bilingualism of the federal government ... provided by the B.N.A. Act, and the actual diverse personal bilingualism of, I would say, the majority or at least half of Canadians' (ibid., 226).

Both of these claims about bilingualism were reinforced by Commissioner Rudnyckyj in his questions to Belash at the end of his presentation. After establishing Belash's expertise in this area – 'You are, apparently, a specialist in respect of bilingual schools in Manitoba' (Canada, *Preliminary Hearing*, 1963, 232) – Rudnyckyj adopted a line of questioning that allowed Belash to reiterate his earlier historical claims about the history of bilingualism in Manitoba:

COMMISSIONER RUDNYCKYJ: Would you suggest that the western Canadian interpretation of the word 'bilingualism' is the oldest Canadian interpretation and understanding of this word?

MR. BELASH: Considering the fact that the two languages of eastern Canada were [*sic*], I would say yes.

COMMISSIONER RUDNYCKYJ: They were bilingual before the British North America Act existed.

MR. BELASH: Yes but actually the first record I have found of this appearance of the word 'bilingualism' is in the Laurier-Greenway Act of 1887.

COMMISSIONER RUDNYCKYJ: You think that is the oldest use of the word 'bilingualism' in the western Canadian interpretation?

MR. BELASH: It is possible that in the schools of Manitoba, and I refer to the Mennonite schools before 1897 the word may have been used. Manitoba is still part of western Canada so I can only answer your question in the affirmative.

COMMISSIONER RUDNYCKYJ: In your submission to this Commission would you include a brief in respect to the history of that term?

MR. BELASH: Yes, that could very well be done. (Canada, *Preliminary Hearing*, 1963, 233)

This exchange demonstrates that commissions of inquiry can also be thought of as a 'theatre of power ... ritually played out before a public audience,' where the commission 'interrogates society on behalf of the State ... within a framework of codes and rules for representing true knowledge' (Ashforth, 1990, 9). Just prior to the back-and-forth between Rudnyckyj and Belash, Laurendeau had completed a lengthy and adversarial exchange with Belash about radio and television broadcasting in languages other than French or English. Thus, the subsequent interrogative interaction between Rudnyckyj – both a commissioner and a Ukrainian activist and professor of Slavic studies – and Belash served to ritually reinforce the truth of Belash's earlier claims to a historically unique Western bilingualism. Through this interrogative performance in the 'theatre' of the inquiry, the truth of this claim was maintained before the public audience. Further, by ensuring that the history of the term would be submitted in a brief by Belash, Rudnyckyj guaranteed that this claim would have to be considered by the commission – and that these principles would be enshrined in Rudnyckyj's own, dissenting Separate Statement appended to *Book I* of the final report.

The Ukrainian claim to language was also based on a territorial principle. That is, Belash built his argument for a unique Western bilingualism on the grounds that 'Winnipeg is a place where you can do business in Ukrainian if you wish' (Canada, *Preliminary Hearing*, 1963, 221). He elaborated: 'It is possible for a person in Winnipeg to spend a day making purchases, visiting the doctor, dentist and lawyer, attending a concert or recital or meeting, go to church on Sunday, using no other language but Ukrainian. I have made purchases at Eaton's in Winnipeg using only Ukrainian' (ibid., 221–2). Here, Belash locates the quotidian in a particular space, Winnipeg, from where he extrapolates this normalized everyday experience to all other Prairie provinces. Therefore, a particular space within the nation was demarcated as the naturalized place for languages other than English or French, and this argument was bolstered by that place's demographics: 'Ukrainians are still the second largest ethnic group,' and 'Germans are more numerous now than French in Greater Winnipeg' (ibid., 223). For Belash, the facts of this particular territory within the nation were a direct challenge to the hegemony of English and French bilingualism and biculturalism as set out in the terms of reference: '[E]ach of the ethnic groups – has a particular language and culture to contribute to the composition of the yet undeveloped unique culture which we shall one day call Canadian ... it would be wrong to penalize a person of other racial origin in Manitoba ... We must consider the languages spoken in the individual province' (ibid., 222–3). Thus, an English-French bilingual and bicultural hegemony was directly challenged by the demographic reality of the demarcated territory – in this case, the provincial space.

By staking out this unique territory, Belash was also able to construct a Ukrainian person who has a 'racial origin in Manitoba,' a notion that paralleled the territorially based French claim for founding-race status in Quebec. However, as noted earlier, founding-race status for the Ukrainian community was based on a claim of prior history, which Belash linked explicitly to the Ukrainian claim for language recognition: '[W]hen you consider the fact that now we have third generation Canadians, and my children are fourth generation and speak Ukrainian ... To Canadians who speak this particular language, having learned it in Canada rather than elsewhere, from our parents who also learned the language here this is a Canadian language' (Canada, *Preliminary Hearing*, 1963, 231). In this statement, all the bases of the Ukrainian claim for founding-race status came together: prior history, the territorially demarcated provincial 'milieu,' and Ukrainian language use and generational linguistic reproduction. Founding-race status was claimed through a 'Canadian' language; a language that had become Canadian through its historical naturalization and reproduction within a particular territory. By establishing a claim based on historical and territorial precedents, Belash was attempting to parallel the French assertion of founding-race status, with the implication that other groups who could not make this particular claim were to be excluded: 'Supposing we are not third generation Canadians but individuals who came over from another country this year, or last year – perhaps some time since the end of the war – bringing into this country a language from the other country, we would have to consider it a foreign language in spite of any personal feeling' (ibid., 231). Therefore, Belash outlines the Ukrainian bid for founding-race status by differentiating Ukrainians from recent immigrants and their languages and by emphasizing the 'Canadian'-ness of the Ukrainian language – the language of a people with an established Canadian historical presence within a particular demarcated territory, and a language now Canadian through its historical use and current everyday viability.

The implications of a claim constructed in such a way for other groups was not lost on representatives such as Garber of the Canadian Jewish Congress, who explicitly addressed the Ukrainian bid for linguistic parity with the founding races: 'We are not at all interested, for the moment, in the position of the Ukrainians. Our approach is entirely opposite. We have educated people in Hebrew, but we consider that our private reserve. We will ask the Canadian government to make Hebrew the third language in Canada, and we are quite prepared to pay for it' (Canada, *Preliminary Hearing*, 1963, 261). This position was consistent with Garber's earlier statement that the Canadian Jewish community he was representing could see itself making either of the bi-cultures 'their own property' (ibid., 260); thus, although there would be a request to make the Hebrew language the 'third language of Canada,' that language would also remain self-funded in their own private schools, separate from the public, officially recognized English and French languages.

The Ukrainian community's comprehensive petition for founding-race status was made for the Ukrainian community alone. However, other organizations were also present to make founding-status demands on behalf of the other ethnic groups. For example, Walter Bossey, director of the Institute of the Canadian Ethnic Mosaic Confederation, explained that his organization did work on behalf of the 'non-English, non-Scotch, non-Welsh, non-Irish, non-French, Canadian population' (Canada, *Preliminary Hearing*, 1963, 458) – or, more specifically, 'The national institute provisionally represented seventeen nationalities, called ethnic groups' (ibid., 460). To support his claim on behalf of all the other ethnic groups, he began with the example of his own family: 'My grandchildren and children, we are now fifty Canadians. My oldest son, born in Canada, married a war bride – English, in my family. A second son married an Irish teacher in Montréal. A third son married a

Jewess, a first comer to Canada of family ... and so on (laughter). Who are we now? ... "We are Canadians!" ... This is the mosaic ... a multi-cultural one' (ibid., 461). Drawing on the expansion and gradual hybridization of his own family, Bossey defined Canada as multicultural and a 'mosaic.' This allowed him to use population statistics to develop his argument for the representation of other groups in Confederation:

MR. BOSSEY: Let you look [sic] for a few seconds at the statistics of 1961. Population 19,000,000. British, 43%, French, 30%; 74% together. 26% left ... What are you going to do with the rest? Who are they? ... What are you going to do with these five million Canadians. Are you going to make Confederation of your own two groups, and you will only say to us: 'What contribution you make; how many sewers you take out for us, and open restaurants, you Greek and others?' 'And you Ukrainians, you make such nice farms; how much you dig for us.' Is that right? Think of my boys, one in Japan was in the Navy. Another was making forty 'ops' over Germany. I have been in the Army and serving during the Second War. What is wrong with us? Why? My accent? Well some people like my accent.

Again, demographic data is used by another ethnic group to argue for recognition. Similar to the argument used by the Ukrainian community, Bossey made the claim of historical nation-building by referring to the labour of different groups and also his and his sons' war service, forcing once more the question of how these contributions were any less important than or different from those of the founding races: 'What is wrong with us?' The only possible difference that Bossey did mention was a linguistic accent, which suggests his recognition of a Renanian rooting of immutable differences in language. When Bossey was cut off by the co-chairman of the inquiry, he came to his substantive suggestions on constitutional reform: 'We are going to insist and do whatever is possible, so that in this new assembly for the new Constitution, it will be an assembly of the Canadian mosaic ... In other words, I say that should there be a proportion, a standard, for each 25,000 of population, one representative. That would mean we are going to have an assembly of 800 Fathers of Confederation' (Canada, *Preliminary Hearing*, 1963, 466). Bossey's formula for constitutional reform would give recognition to the new Canadians as a collective third group. The contradiction in his argument – making the case for the inclusion of other ethnic groups on the basis of historical nation-building contributions, yet calling the other ethnic groups 'new Canadians' – went unremarked. So did another inconsistency: arguing that the lines between the different groups had become harder to distinguish through the generations, while also calling for every ethnic group to have representation by origin only. Nevertheless, Bossey was clear that the mechanism for the equitable inclusion of other ethnic groups in Confederation required constitutional reform.

This call for constitutional reform was echoed by Nelson Clarke of the Communist Party of Canada. Beginning with the assertion that the word 'race' as used in the terms of reference was unscientific (Canada, *Preliminary Hearing*, 1963, 511), Clarke commented that there seemed to be two distinct sets of questions in the terms of reference – those having to do with constitutional relations, and those having to do with language and culture (ibid., 511–12). Warning the commission that both questions could not be 'compressed into a study of language and culture' (ibid., 513), he pushed for a detailed consideration of all the terms of reference. In particular, he was concerned about what he saw as the substantive constitutional questions regarding the organization of the Canadian nation: 'Are Canadians one nation, or do the French and English comprise two nations?' 'Should the British North America Act now be replaced with a new constitution?' (ibid., 512). However, this dichotomization of language and cultural issues against constitutional issues missed Bossey's point that issues of language and culture are in fact constitutional concerns.

Another group, the National Indian Council of Canada, which was the only Indigenous group at the preliminary hearings, also made a bid for founding-race status. Representing the council, Mrs Ethel Brant Monture stated:

> Mr. President, gentlemen. I represent the National Indian Council of Canada. We respectfully submit that Canada is a tri-lingual country. Our imprint is indelibly on this land. Through the years we have added at least the colour. We were told at the first hearing of this Commission we would be invited to be a part of it [sic], that we would not be asked for representation. We feel until we are taking our full share at all levels we are in many ways a wasted people. We ask for your friendly consideration of this request. Indians possess a culture quite distinct from the biculturalism of French Canadians through which is woven a pattern of Canadian rights. (Canada, *Preliminary Hearing*, 1963, 144)

In this excerpt, Monture began by making the claim for founding status through language by declaring Canada to be a trilingual country, even though it was unclear of which specific Indigenous language she was speaking. Nonetheless, language was the basis of her case for a distinct but equally founding culture: an Indigenous culture with an indelible imprint on the land. Indigenous groups were not included in the terms of reference and were ultimately excluded from consideration in the final report, despite the myriad submissions received and the large volume of research material collected on the subject. Nevertheless, this did not prevent Indigenous groups and representatives from making a range of submissions to the commission. Despite efforts to exclude Indigenous concerns from consideration, these claims and issues were set out in petitions to the commission which attracted considerable media coverage.

While the preliminary hearings proved to be a venue for Indigenous and other ethnic groups to resist the founding-races hegemony as laid out in the terms of reference, the official function of the hearings was to define and limit the singularity of the problem under investigation. However, achieving public consensus on this would continue to challenge the commission through the rest of the public hearings. This was foreshadowed in Co-chairman Dunton's closing remarks: 'A number of people have spoken about definitions and terms and meanings in the Order in Council. Some confusion may be cleared up by a careful reading of statements made at the opening of the hearings yesterday ... some probably will not become completely clear until our reports' (Canada, *Preliminary Hearing*, 1963, 547). After sitting through the preliminary hearings, Dunton was well aware of the difficulties posed by much of the terminology in the terms of reference, but his comments optimistically suggested that the publication of the reports would clear up these difficulties. He finished by stating: 'Even if people perhaps disagree with some of the phrases in the terms of reference, we hope they will still come forward with their views, in any case, since we are extremely anxious to have all those different views' (ibid., 548). One wonders whether he ultimately came to regret this invitation.

The Preliminary Report

The *Preliminary Report* was published on 1 February 1965, its findings being based on the hearings of November 1963 and the regional meetings of March-June 1964. It was a surprise best-seller, selling 5,000 copies within twenty-four hours of its release, and, as Laurendeau recalled in his diary, 'the event caused a stir from sea to sea' (Smart, 1991, 30).

The report was a material representation of the findings of the inquiry as 'the aspect of State as auditor is symbolized materially by a Commission's published Report, representing the product of a search for the truth'; in this case, the 'truth' of the hearings and attendant evidence organized into book form (Ashforth, 1990, 9). The findings of the *Preliminary Report* were summarized in the commissioners' opening remarks – 'they have been driven to the conclusion that Canada, without being fully conscious of the fact, is passing through the greatest crisis in its history' – and book-ended by the opening sentences of the final chapter: 'All that we have seen and heard has led us to the conviction that Canada is in the most critical period of its history since Confederation. We believe that there is a crisis' (Canada, *Preliminary Report*, 1965b, 13, 133).

The *Preliminary Report* inaugurated the second phase of the inquiry: the persuasive phase. The investigative phase continued concurrently through 1965, however, since after the report's publication the commission began regular public hearings which ended that December (Canada, *Book I*, 1967, xv). The report's main function was to persuade the public of the existence and particular nature of a national crisis. In his textual analysis of the report, Chua, drawing on the work of Dorothy Smith, unravels how the idea of a 'crisis' was embodied as a textually constructed reality that in turn made reference to the world external to the text, which then became available to the reader (Chua, 1979, 47–8). Thus, the report was necessarily an occasioned construction resulting from the 'contextual organizational practices of the reporters in their practical accomplishment of the description of a social situation' (ibid., 48). These organizational practices, as constitutive features of the documentary reality, included 'the reporters' interpretation and organization of the publicly expressed, and often contradictory, opinions regarding the situation to be described' (ibid.). Chua claims that there were three organizational practices through which the national crisis was formulated: identifying the problem, managing conflicting opinions, and characterizing the problem as a national crisis.

After Laurendeau and Dunton had set out their formulation of the problem in their opening speeches, the submissions from the public in the ensuing preliminary hearings and regional meetings made it clear that not everyone shared the commissioners' outlook. Thus, with the publishing of the *Preliminary Report*, the persuasive phase of the inquiry began; organizational practices were mobilized to manage conflicting opinions in the constitution of a national crisis – and to persuade the reading public of its existence.

The Legitimacy of the Authors and the Validity of the Evidence

In the *Preliminary Report*, the first thing that needed to be established was the legitimacy of the report's contents. One way to accomplish this was to demonstrate the impartiality of the commissioners and the range of the evidence collected and collated.

In describing the inquiry as a theatre of power, Ashforth details the characteristics of the legitimate inquirers: 'Public inquiries mediate between State and Society ... they venture out from the official spaces of State to inspect conditions with their objective gaze ... a Commission is expected to be impartial and independent of sectional interests in Civil Society. Commissioners are frequently appointed because they represent interests' (Ashforth, 1990, 9). The venturing out from official spaces can be seen in the first words of the *Preliminary Report's* preamble: 'Ten Canadians traveled through the country for months, met thousands of their fellow citizens, heard and read what they had to say' (Canada, *Preliminary Report*, 1965b, 13). Similarly, the first paragraph of the postscript to the report stated: 'This ... is a presentation of interim opinions ... which were freely arrived at by ten Canadians belonging to the two cultures or coming from circles integrated with one of the cultures' (ibid., 143). At the very start and the very end of the *Preliminary Report*, the reader was reminded that the commissioners were just 'ten Canadians' and hence independent of the state – as they should be – as well as members of the larger public. Emphasizing their diversity and impartiality, the commissioners confirmed their objectivity by assuring the public that that they left the precincts of official Ottawa to inspect the varied conditions of Canadians everywhere. All of this was necessary to secure public consensus on the commissioners' findings.

The legitimacy of the report was also based on the validity of its evidence. The range of evidence collected and collated into the report was detailed carefully in its opening pages, which listed the range of meetings, hearings, interviews, letters, and media materials that informed the report under the heading 'Evidence.' The report continued: 'Thus, what we refer to here as "the evidence" consists in the main of the opinions expressed before us' (Canada, *Preliminary Report*, 1965b, 16). However, a few pages later, pointing to the large number of questions provoked by the terms of reference, the commissioners stated: 'We therefore had to establish from the very beginning a very large field of research. We could not undertake this research ourselves, for we had neither the time nor the competence to do so. We had to entrust it to experts, especially since these questions . . . have seldom been studied in depth' (ibid., 22).

There was a tension between, on the one hand, the commissioners' desire to portray the *Preliminary Report* as a faithful compilation of the thoughts of Canadians, and the inquiry's requirement for facts on the other. This was also evident in Laurendeau's opening remarks at the preliminary hearings, where he had suggested both the need for extensive research and the need to ask Canadians for answers; he had emphasized the latter, however, since he was aware of the political legitimacy that came with representing the report and its conclusions as built on the opinions of Canadians. The same awareness was visible from the very start of the *Preliminary Report*, as in the opening paragraph of its preamble: 'The ten do not now claim that they are relying on this as a scientific investigation, nor do they have solutions to propose at this stage. All they say is this: here is what we saw and heard, and here is the preliminary – but unanimous – conclusion we have drawn' (Canada, *Preliminary Report*, 1965b, 13).

Therefore, in the opening act of the persuasive phase – the publishing of the *Preliminary Report* – the commissioners were engaged in a careful balancing act between mobilizing research and expertise and assessing the 'truth' of popular opinion. In order to maintain the legitimacy of the evidence upon which the report was based, the commissioners had to show that they were representing popular opinion by reiterating that the report was a compendium of all they had been told; and yet, that their access to research and expertise allowed them to retain their authority as independent (albeit state-appointed) inquirers, and thus authorized them to interpret and represent popular opinion as authors of the report.

The Documentary Reality of a National Crisis

Upon publication, an inquiry's report becomes the authoritative statement pertaining to political action (Ashforth, 1990, 7). Nowhere is this point made more clearly than in the preamble of the *Preliminary Report*: 'We simply record the existence of a crisis which we believe to be very serious. If it should persist and gather momentum it could destroy

Canada. On the other hand, if it is overcome, it will have contributed to the rebirth of a richer and more dynamic Canada. *But this will be possible only if we face the reality of the crisis and grapple with it in time'* (Canada, *Preliminary Report,* 1965b, 13, emphasis in original). Thus, the call for action was intimately bound up with identifying the singular problem: the national crisis.

The process through which the B and B Commission's *Preliminary Report* came to be the authoritative statement pertaining to political action required more than just the establishment of the commissioners' legitimacy as authors and the validity of the evidence upon which the report was based. The challenge was also to textually construct a documentary reality of a national crisis in the world external to the text, and to make this reality available to the reader of the text in order to present a convincing case that there was a singular crisis between the two founding races in the nation (Chua, 1979, 47–8). This was achieved through the interpretation and organization of the publicly stated, and often contradictory, opinions expressed at the hearings (ibid.). Accordingly, in the *Preliminary Report,* the commissioners were careful to manage conflicting ideas; specifically, opinions from other ethnic and Indigenous groups were turned into unit items, seen to be in conflict or contradiction with each other. These units were then juxtaposed against other opinions, which were arranged in such a way as to resemble collective speech, thereby giving credence to the latter and weakening the claims of the former.

Other Ethnic Groups

Chua demonstrates how, in the *Preliminary Report,* disparate accounts by various French-Canadian groups testifying that a national crisis existed were organized into collective speech by retaining only the French identity and the geographical location of the speakers (Chua, 1979, 53). Specifically, statements made by French Canadians at regional meetings in different geographical settings were reorganized into an account that 'collect[s] these specificities under the auspices of Canada, and ... display[s] these locations as constituting Canada' (ibid.). In this way, a collection of statements was transformed into a qualitatively different speech through the reorganization of various abstracted opinions into a collective French-Canadian opinion (ibid.). Conversely, Chua discusses how locality, ethnicity, and language can also be used to constitute each negating opinion as one unique item, thus rendering collective opinion impossible (ibid., 54). In the *Preliminary Report*, this was most easily done with the opinions of other ethnic groups, who, because of their ethnic, linguistic, and geographical diversity, could be presented as fragmented. Reflecting the strong role played by the Ukrainian groups in rejecting the idea of two founding races, the *Preliminary Report* often invoked the geographical specificity of the prairies as a place from where strong 'third force' sentiments were emanating: 'On several occasions the expression "third force" was used to emphasize that these otherwise dissimilar groups have in common the characteristics of being neither British nor French' (Canada, *Preliminary Report*, 1965b, 37), and, 'The desire of these groups to be seen as a special element in Canadian life was strongest on the Prairies. Elsewhere, solidarity with English or, in some cases, French Canada, was more often emphasized' (ibid., 51). In direct contrast to the strategy by which geographically disparate French-Canadian speech was organized into a collective opinion, these two quotes demonstrate how the report emphasized the geographic fragmentation in the opinions of other ethnic groups by localizing a particular opinion as strongest in the prairies – as opposed to a placeless 'elsewhere.' Related to this was the ongoing effort by the report's authors to underscore the dissimilarities between the various other ethnic groups, to emphasize their fragmentation, and hence to continually undermine their self-characterizations as a third force or third element in the nation.

The other ethnic groups' self-identification as a collective third force or third element was one of the main challenges to the founding-races formula. Since the idea of a national crisis hinged on this formula of two founding races, the organizational practice of the report with respect to other ethnic groups was most frequently to demonstrate their lack of cohesion and consistency. Lack of cohesion was indicated by vague attributions of opinions; for example, 'some people were in favour of recognizing not only French and English in the teaching system, but other languages as well' (Canada, *Preliminary Report*, 1965b, 67). This opinion, like many others that might have negated the singularity of a national crisis, was said to be held by 'some people,' whose lack of a clear identity made it difficult for them to cohere into a collective voice. Negating opinions were also characterized as anomalous unit items, which were easy to dismiss: 'Once the disquieting idea of "second-class citizenship" had been aired and the strongest possible protest lodged against it . . . ' (ibid., 52). Here, the person who lodged the protest is unclear – perhaps it was the commissioners – but the clear implication was that, once the protest had been lodged, this opinion was rescinded and relegated to the past.

Presented opinions, particularly those on language, were also dichotomized in the report in order to minimize their negating impact: 'A comparatively [*sic*] few, who live in groups where their own language is commonly used, speak little or no French or English. Of the great number that habitually use one of these languages in their working lives, some are anxious to maintain their own language ... others are content to see their children grow up just like Canadians of British or French origin' (Canada, *Preliminary Report*, 1965b, 126). Again, vague, contradictory attributions such as 'some' and 'other' are used to imply that other ethnic groups, no matter to what extent they are integrated in Canadian society, cannot have complex desires for linguistic and/or cultural maintenance, including varying degrees of multilingualism.

Other claims made by various ethnic groups were handily erased from the report by relegating them to further study: 'It should be understood of course that we shall be continuing our study of these claims in our final report. The question we are asking ourselves here is somewhat narrower: what role do the other ethnic groups play in the crisis which is threatening to tear Canada apart today?' (Canada, *Preliminary Report*, 1965b, 126). Here, not only was the scope of the question narrowed to the point that all other opinions could be deemed irrelevant for present consideration, but the question itself was constructed in such a way that the 'role' of other ethnic groups was restricted to the part they played in a de facto crisis; the result was a limited representation of claims made by other ethnic groups in the hearings.

Ethnic groups were also atomized by their ethnicity and language in order to demonstrate their lack of collectivity in speech and opinion: 'It is difficult to describe the character of a segment of the population that is so diverse: each ethnic group has its own original language and culture. And even within one group, because of factors of geography or individual characteristics, many divergences are to be found' (Canada, *Preliminary Report*, 1965b, 126). Although the ranges of geography and individual characteristics were in fact proof of Canadian collectivity in the case of the founding races, for the other ethnic groups, diversity atomized and hence negated their opinions. Also, diversity of ethnicity and language could then become the justification for understanding absences and differences of particular ethnic groups as challenges to the collectivity of their opinions: 'Moreover, some of these groups did not present themselves to us at the regional meetings. We met very few Canadians of German or Dutch origin, relatively few Poles, Italians or Finns, but many Ukrainians. Finally, among those who participated in the discussions, reaction differed greatly from one minority to another' (ibid., 126–7). In this statement, not only are the absences to the collectivity indicated, but the supposedly disproportionate representation of Ukrainian opinion is specified in order to emphasize the fragmentation of other ethnic groups.

In the penultimate section of the *Preliminary Report*, the commissioners analysed the range of opinions presented as they tried 'to weigh what we have heard, and to look behind the views expressed' (Canada, *Preliminary Report*, 1965b, 109). With respect to other ethnic groups, their presentations were again described in such a way as to atomize their identity: 'Many people of other than British or French descent consider themselves part of either English-speaking or French-speaking Canada ... there is a considerable number who though they regularly use one of the official languages, and are largely integrated in the life around them, still wish to conserve and foster their particular heritage of language and culture. A few Canadians speak neither English nor French. Their problems are real, but not central to our study' (ibid.). Furthermore, the range of opinions from the various ethnic groups, including those challenging the terms of reference, were subsequently subsumed into the two dominant groups; and those who spoke neither of the two dominant languages were decisively excised from all consideration in the report. This was yet another dismissal of the other ethnic groups' collective claims and laid the groundwork of the commission's strategy for dealing with these groups in the final reports.

The two brief sections of the report that dealt directly with the other ethnic groups both concluded with summary statements about their lack of cohesion and consistency: 'A varied range of views was offered to us, bearing witness to the efforts being made to work the other ethnic groups into a really Canadian context ... But we could not say that the other ethnic groups proposed a clear, consistent and definite formula' (Canada, *Preliminary Report*, 1965b, 127–8). Curiously, where the lack of unifying values was seen as a barrier to collectivity among other ethnic groups, the same characteristic in each of the founding races, insofar as the report tracked the wide range of opinions in the English and French communities, seemed to present no barrier to collective representation in the report.

Indigenous Groups

If the dominant interpretation and organization of other ethnic groups and their opinions in the report showed them to be lacking cohesion and consistency, the treatment of Indigenous groups and their issues showed them to be peripheral to the report and its concerns. That said, in its first chapter, the report was also careful to acknowledge the special status of 'Indians' and 'Eskimos': 'The Commission cannot forget that there is in Canada a native population, not large in number it is true, but one which has its traditions and its rights ... Their position and future prospect would have to be the object of special study' (Canada, *Preliminary Report*, 1965b, 22). The marginal position of Indigenous groups in the report was a reflection not only of their absence from the terms of reference but also of their last-place position – a short paragraph at the end of five pages – in the instructions given for preparing briefs for the commission: '[T]here is also a prior contribution that all the others followed: that of the first inhabitants of the country, Eskimos and the Indians. They make up the oldest group, and in comparison, all the English and French-speaking peoples would appear to be New Canadians. The Commission recognizes clearly that it has a duty to give special attention to the problems of the Eskimos and the Indian in our present world' (ibid., 187). In both these excerpts, the 'special' or exceptional status of the Indigenous groups is emphasized, particularly in terms of their unique 'problems' and as objects of study, an approach that served not only to peripheralize but also to pathologize them. The exceptionality of the Indigenous groups also operated to remove them from founding-race parity with the English and French, thus negating one of the strongest possible challenges to the dualism of the founding races and the crisis therein.

Although the report acknowledged the traditions and rights of Indigenous groups, Indigenous claims to language rights, like those of other ethnic groups, were presented as fragmented and inconsistent. Throughout the commission, 'Indians' and 'Eskimos' were lumped together as one unit and their issues were discussed always in tandem; however, in discussions of language claims, the consistent demands by 'Eskimo' groups for language support were juxtaposed against what was characterized as the inconsistent claims for the same support by the Indians: 'In Victoria, an Indian chief stated that after doing everything to cause the extinction of the Indian language in that region by taking drastic steps to exclude it from the schools, Canadians are now asking that it be exhibited for the tourist trade, even though it is hardly spoken now. "When my wife, my brother and myself die, no one will speak my people's language any longer"' (Canada, *Preliminary Report*, 1965b, 67). This statement, which clearly outlined Indigenous concern with the death of Indigenous languages, was followed up by:

> As far as the maintenance of the Indian languages is concerned, the Commission has noted that opinion is not unanimous. In part this is explained by the variety of Indian languages, each of which may have its local dialects. In these conditions, English very naturally becomes the lingua franca of the Indian band and all the more so since they see the knowledge of that language as an economic necessity: 'The whole world speaks English,' most of the chiefs told us at a meeting of the Indian-Eskimo Association in London. On the other hand, the Eskimos we met were practically all in favour of keeping their language. (Canada, *Preliminary Report*, 1965b, 67)

In this part of the report, the impact of the first statement is curtailed by citing supposedly contradictory opinions from other chiefs. Although English was naturalized as a lingua franca, and the support of English by a vague number of chiefs derived from its instrumental capacity as an 'economic necessity,' the desire for language retention as part of the cultural survival of Indigenous peoples was never mentioned. Inconsistent positions on the part of the 'Indians,' preceding as they did the clear and consistent message from the 'Eskimo' communities about their desire for language retention, created the impression of a lack of cohesion within the Indian and 'Eskimo' grouping, which had an overall effect of diminishing the strength of the 'Eskimo' claim.

Further contradictions among the Indian groups were highlighted in the discussion of bilingualism by presenting a lack of support for French/English bilingualism as the effect of age. Thus, statements such as, 'The older chiefs present voiced their concern that certain changes might affect their status: "Our treaty was written in English and was signed under the British flag. If we change the language, the treaty becomes worthless,"' were positioned against other statements such as, 'Younger members of the group showed interest in this matter, but one of them who belonged to the National Indian Council recognized that there was no doubt whatever, in his mind, about French being the official language of Canada' (Canada, *Preliminary Report*, 1965b, 128). This comparison of older and younger Indian opinions was spurious at best; about two weeks before the publication of the report, Kahn-Tineta Horn, a twenty-three-year-old Mohawk activist and the National Council of Indians' 1963 'Indian Princess of Canada' ('Kahn-Tineta Horn Critical,' 1965), made remarks that directly refuted such a position on bilingualism at a talk given at the University of Toronto: 'Indian rights are based on the fact that "we were here first"; the French-Canadian has no rights, and English-speaking Canadians have already made far too many concessions to those who speak French' (Shepherd, 1965, 1). Although these remarks were not part of the submissions to the B and B Commission, the newspaper article covering Kahn-Tineta Horn's remarks on the exploitation of the Indians – 'Indian cheated by white man, says Mohawk model' (ibid.) – was part of the research material collected for the commission. Further, Kahn-Tineta Horn would later make a controversial submission to the commission and garner more media coverage.

Ironically, the only unanimity of opinion in the report with regard to the 'Indians' and 'Eskimos' came from the 'white' audience: 'We found great sympathy in "white" audiences for the plight in which Canada's two Indigenous peoples find themselves, as the relentless march of North American industry and technology moves into territories once exclusively their own. We were impressed with this unanimity of views' (Canada, *Preliminary Report*, 1965b, 50). In this careful construction, white audiences are portrayed not only as uniformly sympathetic to Indigenous problems but also as innocent – since New World industry and technology, and not white-settler colonialism, are blamed for the loss of Indigenous territories. This paragraph, appended to the end of a section presenting Indigenous claims as contradictory, underscores the collectivity of speech from the white audience as opposed to 'Indian' and 'Eskimo' inconsistencies.

The peripheral positioning of the Indigenous groups can be seen throughout the report. The only extensive information on Indigenous demographics was given as an extensive footnote in the second chapter, and, even there, Indigenous opinions were labelled as inconsistent, hence their collective voice was undermined before any submissions were even discussed: 'As to the problem raised by their integration into Canadian life, with relation to their conflict which causes opposition between the "two founding races," not all of them would react in the same way' (Canada, *Preliminary Report*, 1965b, 37). Towards the end of the report, in a final chapter entitled 'The Crisis,' the peripheral position of the Indians and Eskimos was explicitly outlined: 'In this conflict which divides the two societies by setting them one against the other, Indians and Eskimos are in a position apart' (ibid., 128). With the tangential place of Indigenous people in relation to the national problem thus confirmed, the discussion that couched this crisis as mainly a problem of French and English relations could continue.

Ethnic Origin versus Mother Tongue

In the *Preliminary Report*, opinions from both the Indigenous and other ethnic groups that challenged the singularity of the problem as an English-French national crisis were consistently organized as fragmented, contradictory, and peripheral. In this way, the collectivity of these groups was undermined in the report, strengthening the construction of the documentary reality of a national crisis. However, the collectivity of groups, in particular the other ethnic groups, was also challenged through the mobilization and use of statistics, specifically ones drawn from the 1961 Census of Canada.

In the hearings, as described above, many of the claims made by other ethnic groups were based on their demographic size. Quite early on in the report, the basis for these types of demographic claims was challenged. On one occasion, for example, a Winnipeg speaker was said to be guilty of exaggeration when he said that 'we are the third element of the population of this country, of which I think our proportion today is almost one-third' (Canada, *Preliminary Report*, 1965b, 50). In a footnote to this sentence at the bottom of the page, census statistics were cited: 'The 1961 Census of Canada establishes at 13.5 p.c.[2] those Canadians whose mother tongue is other than English or French, while those of non-French, non-British origin constitute 28.5 p.c. of the population. Of course, this 'third element' is composed of many different linguistic groups' (ibid.).

It was here that the distinction between ethnic-origin statistics and linguistic groups was first flagged in the report. This distinction became a key element in the debate on demographic claims, particularly for the other ethnic groups. Later in the report, the import of this point was expanded upon:

> In the game of numbers and percentages in which the participants engaged, Canadians of ethnic origins other than British and French appeared to occupy a strategic position. Thus some English-speaking participants like to emphasize [their] ... imposing fraction of the population, which the latest Census sets at 13.4 per cent according to mother tongue and 26.8 per cent according to ethnic origin ... When they looked at the country as a whole they often included in the 'English' group all Canadians not of French origin – a procedure which clearly reduces the importance of the 'French' group, and thus makes majority rule more imposing. (Canada, *Preliminary Report*, 1965b, 100–1)

There was a range of ways in which various groups mobilized census data to their advantage: the English used the other ethnic groups to inflate their numbers in order to increase their majority; the French excluded the other ethnic groups in order to highlight their vulnerability; and other ethnic groups mobilized the figures not only to demonstrate their demographic clout but also to make or oppose claims for rights at the local level. Census data was also used to show that no groups could make a majority claim:

> Others called attention to the fact that no group, strictly speaking, has a majority in the country. Thus, the population of British origin, which was 60.5 per cent of the whole in 1871, was no more than 43.8 per cent in 1961. Hence, from the ethnic point of view, the Canadian population is made up of more or less important minorities; this was suggested to us at regional meetings. It therefore follows, from this point of view, that the majority rule could not be legitimately applied in our country. (Canada, *Preliminary Report*, 1965b, 101)

This assertion by other ethnic groups that no group could make a majority claim based on ethnic origin is countered by a footnote at the bottom of the page: 'It is important to point out ... that the mother tongue of 58.4 p.c. of all citizens was English' (Canada, *Preliminary Report*, 1965b, 101). Therefore, claims made by other ethnic groups as to their large demographic significance, based on a collective non-British and non-French origin, are again countered through the census data on linguistic groupings.

Under the stipulations of the terms of reference, having to consider groups other than the French or English introduced the actual problem of how to define these groups. The commission was clear as to how it would tackle this issue, using census data to serve its own conclusions. In the Working Paper of December 1963, which was given out for the use of all of those preparing briefs for the commission, section 12 addressed the question of 'other' cultures. There, a footnote with a table stated:

> To put the problem in its proper perspective, we must keep in mind the respective importance of each of these groups. As languages and cultures are in question here, we believe it necessary to utilize the statistics relating to *mother tongue* and not to ethnic origin. In the *1961 Census of Canada* (Population, Official Language and Mother Tongue, Catalogue: 92–549), in terms of mother tongue the Canadian population divides as follows:

Total population:	18,238,247
Mother tongues:	
English	10,660,534 (58%)
French	5,123,151 (28%)
Others	2,454,562 (14%)

> 'Others' is broken down into several linguistic groups of which the principal ones are (over and above 100,000):

German	563,713 (3%)
Ukrainian	361,496 (2%)
Italian	339,626 (2%)
Dutch	170,177 (1%)
Indian and Eskimo	166,531 (1%)
Polish	161,720 (1%)
Others	691,266 (4%)

> (Canada, *Preliminary Report*, 1965b, 186)

The same section maintained the centrality of race: 'The mainspring (l'idée-force) of the terms of reference, and consequently of the Commission, is the idea of "an equal partnership between the two founding races"' (Canada, *Preliminary Report*, 1965b, 186). In relation to the two founding races, the idea of 'race' was not supplanted, as it was in relation to 'other' groups, by the categories of 'languages and cultures' and 'linguistic groups.' The hierarchy between the two founding races and other ethnic groups was therefore upheld, with other ethnic groups being designated as linguistic groupings.

Numerically, the distribution of the population based on ethnic origin looked significantly different from the one based on mother tongue:

Distribution of the Population by Ethnic Origin, Canada, 1961

Canada	18,238,247
British	7,996,669 (43.84%)
French	5,540,346 (30.37%)
Other Ethnic Origin	4,701,232 (25.75%)

(Canada, *Preliminary Report*, 1965b, 192)

Comparing the census data based on ethnic origin with that based on mother tongue is instructive: mother-tongue distribution decreased the numbers in the 'other' category when compared to the ethnic-origin category. Thus, by defining the other ethnic groups as fragmented linguistic categories when the same was not specified for the two founding races, claims made on the basis of the other ethnic collectivity could be contested (as in, they are only 14 per cent of the population, not 26 per cent) or disregarded (as in, they are just a collection of small linguistic groups – German 3 per cent, Ukrainian 2 per cent, Italian 2 per cent – and so on).

In fact, while the report drew a clear distinction between mother-tongue and ethnic-origin data, and cited census data to support its position, the census itself was not as categorical. It defined mother tongue as 'the language first learned in childhood and still understood' (Canada, *Preliminary Report*, 1965b, 191). Its definition of ethnic group, on the other hand, was more complex: 'Ethnic group: is traced through the father. The question asked was "To what ethnic or cultural group did you or your ancestor (on the male side) belong on coming to this continent?" The language spoken at that time by the person or his paternal ancestor was used as an aid in the determination of the person's ethnic group' (ibid.). Language, in other words, was a concrete feature in the determination of ethnic origin. As well, 1961 was the first time that the census posed the question of ethnic origin; before then, questions on origin had been couched in terms of *racial* origin.

By the end of the Second World War, genetic research had begun to show decisively that there was no biological foundation for the concept of 'race' (Bourhis, 2003, 17). One of the best-known challenges to the census's methodology on this point came from Norman B. Ryder, who was a demographer acting as a consultant to the Dominion Bureau of Statistics (DBS) (ibid.). Ryder analysed the results of the 1941 census racial-origin question and found that there was an array of interpretations as to what exactly the question was asking, resulting in a wide range of categories of responses: 'The detailed origins table for 1941 presents the following types of answers: colour (Indian, Negro); language (Czech and Slovak, Ukrainian); religion (Jewish, Hindu); and birthplace-cum-nationality (Austrian, Belgian). Most of the origins listed could refer either to a language or to a birthplace' (Ryder, 1955, 466). As well, on comparing the mother-tongue and racial-origin data gathered from the 1921, 1931, and 1941 censuses, Ryder determined that the origin questions did not exclude all those who did not belong and did not include all those who did.

Based on these analyses, Ryder concluded that the 'prime source of unsatisfactory statistics on origins has probably been the ambiguity of the term "origin"' (Ryder, 1955, 469). He therefore suggested that 'the identification of an ethnic group ... is a complex sociological task about which we still know rather little ... But a firm foundation for such inquiries can be provided by sorting the population into linguistic elements. In the transmission of cultural heritage, language is of such pre-eminent importance that it qualifies as a necessary condition for inclusion and exclusion' (ibid.). Hence, Ryder emphasized a strong and linguistic orientation in the origin question because it gave 'a unique and relevant criterion' (Beaud and Prévost, 1996, 3) to the difficult study of ethnic groups. Specifically, he recommended that the origin question be partnered with the one concerning mother tongue: 'After asking an individual: "What language did you first learn to speak?" the census-taker would then inquire further, "What language did your father first learn to speak?" ... The answer, unlike those given to the question of origins, would refer to the individual's experience, both personally and through his parent, with the culture to which the language concerned gives its name' (Ryder, 1955, 477–8). Although Ryder's construction of the origin question was not adopted by the DBS wholesale, it did influence how information on ethnic origin was to be elicited in the 1961 census – that is, it suggested using a question on the language spoken by the person or his/her paternal ancestor upon arrival on the continent to aid in determining the answer to the question about ethnic origin: 'To what ethnic or cultural group did you or your ancestor (on the male side) belong on coming to this continent?'

Faced with the criticism that it had mistakenly used the word race to distinguish groups whose differences were not necessarily biological, and contending with the fact that Nazi war crimes had cast opprobrium on the term itself (Beaud and Prévost, 1996, 3), the DBS had been forced to rethink its collection of racial-origin statistics. The result was that, by 1961, the question on origin had shifted from one explicitly about racial origin to one of 'ethnic or cultural groups,' with language embedded as a concrete determining criterion. This complicated link between language and ethnic origin meant that it could be mobilized to define groups and make or challenge their claims. Thus, in the *Preliminary Report*, mother tongue and ethnic origin were overtly separated in relation to other ethnic groups even though a tangible linguistic trace remained in the question of ethnic origins.

The Beginning and End of the Preliminary Report

The *Preliminary Report* ended with a postscript drawing a parallel to the 1837–8 Rebellions in Lower and Upper Canada, which eventually led to the publication of Lord Durham's report: 'The present crisis is reminiscent of the situation described by Lord Durham in 1838: "I found two nations warring in the bosom of a single state"' (Canada, *Preliminary Report*, 1965b, 144). In Lord Durham's original report, this statement was followed by: 'I found a struggle, not of principles, but of races' (Lucas, 1970, 16). An *Ottawa Citizen* article with the headline 'Two Soliloquies' stated that Lord Durham's famous dictum 'finds a modern counterpart in the Laurendeau-Dunton Commission' ('Two Soliloquies,' 1965).

Thus, there was a parallel between the two reports, not only in the sense that each perceived a national crisis, but also that in each case the crisis was one between the founding 'races.' Durham's usage of the word race was akin to 'nation,' the more commonly used term in this era. Further, in his introduction to *Lord Durham's Report*, Gerald M. Craig writes that, although Durham spoke often of the English and French 'races,' he 'considered it possible for other *people* to join this race, if English become their first language and if they became thoroughly imbued with an "English character"' (Craig, 1963, vii, emphasis added). Although both Durham's report and that of the B and B Commission referred to the dominant groups in terms of 'race,' whether or not the usage of 'race' was completely parallel in the two documents would not be clarified until *Book I* of the final report was published, approximately two years after the publication of the *Preliminary Report*.

As well, the title that the commissioners had desired was not used. The original title of the report was to have been 'The Canadian Crisis,' but Pearson intervened when the report came to cabinet, saying that the title was too 'sombre in tone' and that 'it is important that the present title should not gain currency' at a time when Quebec was wrestling with a constitutional amending formula ('Cabinet Concerns 30 Years Ago Mirror Today's Problems,' 1996). Furthermore, Finance Minister Walter Gordon believed that 'there would undoubtedly be strong reaction in the rest of Canada to further concessions to Quebec,' a reaction that would be fuelled by a report entitled 'The Canadian Crisis' (ibid.). In his diary, Co-chairman Laurendeau detailed his attempt to explain to Pearson the reasoning behind the commission's selection of the title: 'He listened politely to what we had to say about the title: that it corresponds rigorously to the content of the volume, that the experience on which the report is based being unusual for a royal commission, we could allow ourselves to draw attention to it in our title, and finally that the title helped make it clear that this was not the final report' (Smart, 1991, 129). Yet, despite Laurendeau's best efforts, 'none of these arguments made much difference with Mr. Pearson: he seemed to be a little obsessed with Mr. Diefenbaker' (ibid.), which referred to Pearson's fear that Diefenbaker would use the commission's report to prove how the Liberals had manufactured a crisis (ibid., 127). In the end, the federal government's anxiety about national unity took precedence over the commission's wishes and the report was eventually published under the less inflammatory title of *A Preliminary Report of the Royal Commission on Bilingualism and Biculturalism*.

The publication of the *Preliminary Report* made this textually constructed reality of a national crisis available to all and symbolized an invitation to public discussion. This public discussion, an element of the persuasive phase of the inquiry, was crucial to securing public consensus on the existence and nature of the national crisis. And, to a considerable extent, the shape it would take was foreshadowed by the media coverage following the *Preliminary Report*'s publication.

Media Reception

Tabled in the House of Commons on 25 February 1965 by Prime Minister Pearson, the *Preliminary Report* received considerable media coverage. Its dominant theme was widely echoed, with headlines across the country proclaiming the existence of a national crisis on the following day. Some of the headlines included 'Nation Faces Split: Report' (Winnipeg *Free Press*); 'Serious Danger Found to Canada's Existence' (Charlottetown *Guardian*); 'We Face Breakup' (Edmonton *Journal*); and 'Canada's Unity Said in Danger' (Regina *Leader-Post*).

The possibility of a national crisis in Canada received considerable international press coverage, which reported on the shock that the *Preliminary Report* had invoked in Canadians: 'The Preliminary report of the Royal Commission on Bilingualism and Biculturalism is plainly intended to shock Canadians into a realisation that the country faces a crisis threatening its very existence' ('Report on Canada,' 1965); 'Last week [Canadians' complacency] was shattered by the authoritative interim report of the Royal Commission on Bilingualism and Biculturalism' (Canada, 1965); 'An editorial in the New York Times has described the report as the "worst shock Canada has had in many a year"' (Canada Correspondent, 1965). In each of these articles, the focus was again on the dominant crisis as formulated by the report, with no mention at all of other ethnic or Indigenous groups.

On 27 February, the Montreal *Gazette* reported that Quebec media's initial reaction to the report was positive. It cited an editorial by Vincent Prince in *La Presse* with the headline 'A Brutal and Clear Diagnosis' and an editorial in the *Montréal Matin*, both published on 26 February, as supportive overall of the diagnosis of a national crisis (Ferrabee, 1965c). Quebec City's *Le Soleil* welcomed the report as 'lucid and frank' and *La Presse* greeted its findings as 'giant steps towards unity and justice' (Sloan, 1989, R–19). *Le Devoir*, the very paper that had run Laurendeau's seminal editorial piece calling for the creation of a royal commission on bilingualism and biculturalism, also 'warmly welcomed the 1965 Report' (ibid.).

The *Gazette*'s own comments on the report in an article on 26 February focused almost solely on the English-French crisis, with no mention of other ethnic or Indigenous groups. Only the last entry in a list of sixteen 'Highlights' of the report referred to 'immigrants from other than Britain of France [who] tend to integrate with English-speaking society and view equal partnership with suspicion' (Ferrabee, 1965b). Clearly, the Quebec media, English and French alike, was focused primarily on issues related to the national crisis of the two founding races, and other ethnic groups were deemed to be important only to the extent that they were allegedly integrating predominantly into the English-speaking society and were suspicious of any equal English-French partnership.

However, outside Quebec, there was a wider range of opinion as to the degree to which there existed a national crisis between the two founding races. Support for the report's main findings could be found in the Toronto *Telegram*, which declared that 'the differences dividing the nation *have become increasingly obvious*,' and the Kitchener-Waterloo *Record*, which stated that the *Preliminary Report* 'has not pulled its punches, but instead given us the straight goods about our social, cultural, political and constitutional condition, especially as it is affected by the nation's French-English duality' (Ferrabee, 1965c, n.p.). More muted was the Peterborough *Examiner*, which began, 'Quebec needs rescue of a kind perhaps, but the very fact that it can contemplate separation discloses that its economic state is by no means desperate,' and then continued, 'but the thing Quebec must have is the genuine support of the rest of the country' (ibid.). Challenging the report's findings were such papers as the Windsor *Star* ('the French-speaking people are apt to blame English-speaking people for the troubles of their own making and with the remedies largely in their own hands') and the Calgary *Herald* ('The preliminary report . . . seems rather heavily weighted with sympathy toward the French-Canadian point of view, and tends to make English-speaking Canada largely responsible for the strains to which Canadian confederation has been subjected during the past two years') (ibid.). Other papers deemed the conclusions of the report alarmist, examples being the Edmonton *Journal* ('The central conclusion of the Royal Commission . . . probably will be considered alarmist by the great majority of Canadians') and the Vancouver *Sun* ('The first report of the Royal Commission is a cry of wild alarm') (ibid.). The diversity of media opinion on the *Preliminary Report*, in all probability, reflected the diversity of opinion across the country.

Besides directly engaging with the report's conclusion that Canada was faced with a national crisis, many newspaper articles explored the idea that the commission had a built-in bias (something that Pearson himself had feared), which made the postulation of a national crisis inevitable. The Manchester *Guardian*, citing Laurendeau's opening remarks at the preliminary hearings, stated: 'The Commission is vulnerable to the charge that it approached its problems with strong preconceptions' ('Report on Canada,' 1965). Others went further, with, for example, Don McGillivray of the Ottawa *Citizen* citing both the bilingualism of all the commissioners and the terms of reference as the source of the inquiry's preconceptions: 'The terms of reference do not ask the commission to tell what should be done. The commission is told what should be done ... the commission is asked to tell how to do it' (McGillivray, 1966, n.p.). These charges echo some of the concerns outlined in an earlier article in the *Citizen*, published as the preliminary hearings opened: 'The Dunton-Laurendeau commission starts off with a built in bias toward the idea that French Canadians are getting a poor deal out of Confederation as it exists today. The terms of reference, the backgrounds of the 10 commissioners, the "crisis" atmosphere of their appointment – all combine to slant the commission in one direction' ('Two Soliloquies,' 1965). Similar statements would be made throughout the inquiry.

To some extent, on the day after the report's publication, the media covered the issues brought up by the other ethnic groups. For example, the Ottawa *Citizen* stated: 'Quebec's success in bringing the focus of national attention to bear on its special grievances sometimes frightens the other third of Canada. This fear that other ethnic groups might be forgotten in the developing dialogue between Canadians of French and English origin was coupled with a strong affirmation of their importance to Canada' ('Two Soliloquies,' 1965). Also, the Toronto *Telegram* carried a short article entitled 'And Those in Between?' on the other ethnic groups, which began with the statement 'What does the Bi-Bi Commission have to say about the 6,000,000 Canadians who aren't British or French in origin?' and then covered some of the larger issues raised ('And Those in Between?' 1965). And, under the headline 'West Seen Rejecting Biculturalism Issue,' the Winnipeg *Free Press* featured a very short article which detailed some of the claims for inclusion made by other ethnic groups ('West Seen Rejecting Biculturalism Issue,' 1965). Nevertheless, although there was a certain amount of reporting on the issues raised by other ethnic groups, the coverage of the supposed national crisis was much more extensive.

The publication and public reception of the *Preliminary Report* was a crucial element in the persuasive phase of the inquiry, and, despite the strong textual construction of a national crisis, the media varied in its assessment of the report's conclusion. As well, coverage of the issue and causes of built-in bias, as well as the concerns of other ethnic groups, varied across the country. However, while the report's authors, through the organizational and ordering practices they had followed, were able to focus the public discussion to a large degree on their main conclusion of a national crisis between the founding races, claims made by the other ethnic groups could not be completely overshadowed. Indeed, the publication of the report initiated a country-wide public debate, as reflected in the media. In the main, a public consensus was secured that a national crisis involving the two main groups did, in fact, exist. Yet claims challenging the singularity of the problem, particularly by the other ethnic groups, were also noted and circulated in this debate.

Concluding Summary

In the preliminary stage of the inquiry, imposing and securing public consensus on the singularity of the problem was the main object of the commission. From the start, this singularity was structured by the terms of reference; the preliminary stage of the B and B Commission was a site for contestation over the terms of reference and for organizing this singular crisis between the two founding races. During this stage, there emerged various strategies of resistance by Indigenous and other ethnic groups to the racialized hierarchy that was being installed through the commission's terms of reference – strategies that ranged from seeking entry into the white-settler category by building claims for founding-race status to rejecting the hierarchicalization of the terms of reference and advocating instead a model of 'multi-cultures.'

In response to the *Preliminary Report*'s singular notion of a crisis between two founding races – a crisis textually constructed through the ordering and organizational practices of the report's authors – disjunctures and counter-stories appeared. These revealed the fault lines of the racialized hierarchy which the terms of reference attempted to set into place between founding races, other ethnic groups, and Indigenous groups – as in, for example, the treatment of census data on mother tongue and ethnic origin, or the fragmentation of 'Indian and Eskimo' demands in order to atomize collective bases for claims. As the commission attempted to engineer a new formulation of a bilingual and bicultural 'unisonant' nation, with white-settler social cohesion as the central focus, the establishment of a singular crisis became the first step in consolidating the centrality of the founding races with the marginalization of other ethnic groups and the erasure of Indigenous concerns.

That said, following the publication of the *Preliminary Report*, an invitation for the public to engage with the report led to a mixed outcome. Media coverage makes it clear that, while a public consensus on the singular problem of a national crisis between the two founding races did emerge, this consensus was not complete: contesting claims and debates regarding the extent of the national crisis continued to circulate. Despite the commission's attempts to secure the singularity of the crisis, the counter-stories of Indigenous and other ethnic groups would resurface during the public hearings, ultimately forcing the commission to reconsider the terms of reference by shifting the focus away from race and ethnicity and onto language and culture. As well, during this preliminary stage of the inquiry, language was mobilized as a basis for both making and challenging claims, a development that foreshadowed the emerging importance of language and culture in organizing relations between the founding races and other ethnic groups. It was perhaps inevitable that, at this historical juncture – in the wake of Duplessis and in an era marked by a decisive move towards secularism in Quebec – the Pearson government would embrace language and culture as a basis of inclusion and equality for the French people. Nonetheless, what is clear is that an emphasis on language and culture, as reflected in the B and B Commission's terms of reference, would usher in a new chapter in Canadian history; one that would see complex negotiations and outright disagreements around fundamental issues of national identity, and eventually a shift towards language as a defining feature of Canadian nationhood and belonging. In short, the debate over the commission's terms of reference and the idea of a national crisis in this preliminary phase of the inquiry was the opening salvo that set the tone and emerging patterns for the B and B Commission's ensuing work.

4 Public Hearings and Research

In the preliminary stage of the royal commission, the singular problem of a national crisis between the two founding races was the subject of disagreement between the commission and Indigenous and other ethnic groups – disagreement that revealed the fault lines of a racialized hierarchy installed through the terms of reference. This formulation of belonging was necessary in order for the commission to engineer a unisonant yet also bilingual and bicultural white-settler nation; but resistance to the consolidation of this hierarchy meant that public consensus could not be assured. This chapter examines the next stage of the inquiry. Since it covers a substantial amount of material, the chapter is divided into three parts.

Part one deals with the public hearings, the briefs that were submitted, and the issues that were raised as causes for concern to the groups involved. During the course of the public hearings, groups continued to challenge the hegemonic formulation of the terms of reference by building on patterns of critique and resistance from the preliminary hearings – and in this process a yet-unspecified notion of multiculturalism became a point around which the location of Indigenous and other ethnic groups could be debated. The public hearings were the site where various groups manoeuvred within the terms of reference to push for a shift from *bi* to *multi*-cultural belonging, even as the exact meaning of multiculturalism remained ambiguous. As well, public-hearing submissions and research 'facts' confirmed that race and ethnicity were still contentious terms for organizing belonging; thus, language, as the proxy for issues that resist resolution on their own terms (Harpham, 2002, 65), emerged in concert with multiculturalism as the terrain on which to advance and limit substantive claims from other ethnic groups. This marked a turn in the inquiry, with the commission shifting from race and ethnicity to language and culture as the bases for organizing a new formulation for a bilingual and bicultural white-settler nation.

Part two deals with the shift in the location of Indigenous groups in relation to the commission. Originally excluded from consideration in the inquiry through their absence in the terms of reference, this decision was overturned towards the end of 1963. Indigenous groups were then invited to submit briefs, and considerable research resources were devoted to determining the situation of 'Indians and Eskimos' in Canada. However, as the research agenda on Indigenous groups proceeded, the commission began to organize the 'facts' on Indians and Eskimos in order to develop a rationale which would again exclude them from consideration. This re-exclusion emerged out of the challenge that Indigenous groups' claims for founding-group status presented to the commission's quest for white-settler cohesion based on the two founding races.

Part three deals with the expansion of the commission's research program, which, like the public hearings, was a continuation of the investigative phase. During this stage of the inquiry, the research program of the commission expanded and, through arm's-length expertise, served the important purpose of conferring upon the commissioners the authority to contest or reinforce findings from the public hearings when they came to produce their final report. Thus, the centralization of knowledge – achieved through the legitimization of some fact against other facts in order to justify features and forms of policy (Corrigan and Sayer, 1985, 124) – would give rise to the final report of the commission, and then culminate in the Official Languages Act of 1969 and the Multiculturalism Policy of 1971.

Part I – The Public Hearings: Submissions, Briefs, and Reports

Immediately after the publication of the *Preliminary Report* in February 1965, the commission began the regular public hearings that were to inform the writing of its final report. There were fourteen sessions of public hearings across the country from March to June and November to December 1965, with each session lasting from one to four days. These public hearings differed significantly from the preliminary hearings in that first briefs were to be prepared according to guidelines set out in the Working Paper of December 1963 (Canada, *Preliminary Report*,

1965b, 183), and then discussions at the hearings were to be focused on the issues raised through the briefs. As was outlined in the preface to *Book I* of the final report, the regional meetings were understood to be informal and exploratory in approach; in contrast, the official hearings would be an opportunity for precise questioning and a thorough discussion of the issues where the commissioners could work from a close study of the briefs (Canada, *Book I*, 1967, xvi). Thus, the range of discussion possible during the public hearings was, to a large extent, prescribed and narrow, although the commission did hold a few supplementary private meetings as well (ibid.).

The public hearings, then, were constrained not only by the necessity of submitting briefs but also by the guidelines for brief preparation. In the diary that he kept during the commission, Laurendeau recalled the constraints of the briefs in comparison to the relatively 'freer' expressions of 'real feelings' at the preliminary hearings and regional meetings: 'It's true that several briefs bring new and interesting element to the debate; but they express opinions that groups have reached over time, often through compromise, in such a way that the representatives are bound by their texts and aren't in a position to say much more' (Smart, 1991, 131).

During the public hearings, groups and individuals submitted 404 public and 4 confidential briefs to the commission (Canada, *Book I*, 1967, 177). An overview of these briefs reveals the wide array of groups and individuals represented: through the briefs, a picture of 'multiculturalism' emerged that was intrinsically linked to language and consequently raised a number of issues around language education and schooling. The Canada Ethnic Press Federation played an active and important role in keeping the various communities informed about the submission of briefs, and the reactions to them from other communities; it also played a significant advocacy role. Of the briefs that could be considered to be from other ethnic groups, roughly half were submissions from the Ukrainian community. Nevertheless, smaller groups that had been less active in commission activities to date, such as the Japanese community, also submitted briefs, as did the Polish, German, and Italian communities. Most other racialized (that is, non-white and non-European) groups, such as the Chinese communities and black communities – though not any of the South Asian communities – commissioned research reports, studies, or essays such as 'The Chinese in Canada' and 'Negro Settlement in Canada.' A number of briefs were submitted by other groups, such as the Canadian Labour Congress, the United

Church of Canada, and the Imperial Order Daughters of the Empire, underscoring that although calls for briefs were apparently publicly distributed, the resultant imbalances in representation reflected the built-in partialities already identified in the terms of reference.

The Emergence of 'Multiculturalism' and
the Importance of Multilingualism

Patterns for making claims and contesting the terms of reference that were set during the preliminary phase of the inquiry became blueprints and starting points for subsequent petitions for inclusion by other ethnic groups during the public hearings. For example, the variety of monikers used for other ethnic groups during the preliminary hearings – 'third force,' 'third element,' and 'New Canadians,' among others – although still in circulation – began to coalesce around the term 'multicultural-ism,' which came to encompass many of the ideas and values that characterized the positions of other ethnic groups. Multiculturalism started to signify such strategies for inclusion as claims relating to prior history and population size. Although deployed in various ways by different groups, the term began to acquire a range of meanings across which the location and inclusion of other ethnic groups could be discussed.

The Social Study Club of Edmonton, a group that described itself in its brief as 'nearly all old-timers in the Province of Alberta,' began its submission by establishing its historical claim:

> In those early days of Alberta, we were all 'homesteaders' who had come to Canada because the title to 160 acres of good land could be obtained if one was, or intended to become, a British subject . . . At least that was the hope; and we traded work and mingled in play with Tony, Mike, Slim, Pete, Alfonso, Mac, Irish, Ole or Jack; and we always understood one another sufficiently well, without bothering about bi-lingualism . . . and it was this diversity of nationalities, with their different languages, handicrafts and customs that provided the background for the attractive kaleidoscope which was the beginning of a representative and distinctive Canadian culture. (Social Study Club of Edmonton, 1964, 1)

The theme of 'homesteading' in the West was a strategy similar to the claims for belonging made by the Ukrainian groups during the preliminary hearings, but a new element was the fact that the Edmonton group dismissed bilingualism as something unnecessary for communication among immigrants. Instead, 'diversity' – linguistically and otherwise – was invoked as part of a 'distinctive Canadian culture,' an idea that would re-surface time and again in subsequent discussions about multiculturalism and national belonging in relation to other ethnic groups.

Building on the soon-to-be-familiar claim that Canada was a land populated by immigrants, the Edmonton group's brief then commented on the goals of the inquiry:

> Now, it seems, a campaign is to be attempted to compensate for alleged economic injustices with an artificial form of bi-culturalism which will try, through an artificial bi-lingualism, to overcome an economic problem with a cultural remedy. We say *artificial* because bi-lingualism has not been adopted spontaneously. This effort is following an unnatural course rather than recognizing the actual fact that a multi-culturalism has already been adopted spontaneously by the people themselves. (Social Study Club of Edmonton, 1964, 4)

Although theirs was a relatively short brief, the Edmonton group's sub-mission signalled the emergence of new, important discourses around multiculturalism, among them the naturalization of multiculturalism and its identification as a distinctive Canadian culture. Also, the link between multiculturalism and language was established, though here mainly to point to the artificiality of bilingualism and the concomitant spontaneity of multiculturalism.

The link between multiculturalism and language was also consid-ered by the Mutual Co-operation League of Toronto, which described itself in its brief as a 'multicultural and multilingual body.' Beginning with a reference to the 1961 census data, the league argued that 'there is neither one race nor language in this country forming a clear major-ity ... For these reasons, we consider the advancement of bilingualism as insufficient in scope, and that of biculturalism as limited in vision' (Mutual Co-Operation League of Canada, 1964, 1). Claiming a distinct 'lack of enthusiasm for "bilingualism,"' the league proposed a demo-graphic basis for language education: 'With respect to the inherent right of a human being to preserve his identity and heritage, we propose that children from any community of our member group, with at least 500 souls in a compact area, should be able to receive instruction in their own language of at least 2 weekly periods from first grade of public school, and treated as regular subject of the school curriculum' (ibid., 2). However vague the delineation of 'compact area,' in all other aspects the brief was quite clear about the specificities of multilingual schooling. Nor was it unique in this respect: many of the briefs submitted for the public hearings linked multilingual schooling with multiculturalism.

The Canadian Mennonite Association also took up multiculturalism and multilingual schooling. In its brief, the association warned that English-French biculturalism would push other minority cultures into third place. These groups, it said, 'would not be opposed to having French or English taught as an additional language in the public school, but they would resent it crowding out their language now placing second' (Canadian Mennonite Association, 1965, 3–4). For the Canadian Mennonite Association, bilingualism and biculturalism were useful only insofar as they moved 'society from a monocultural status to multilingualism and multiculturalism' (ibid., 3). Thus, the group concluded with the following suggestion to the commission: 'It is our hope, that, while the Royal Commission must address itself to a specific problem indicated by its name (Bilingualism and Biculturalism), the larger frame of reference will be multilingualism and multiculturalism' (ibid., 4). Here, the example of multilingual schooling was not used to point to the dangers of bilingualism and biculturalism, as other groups did; instead, the association argued that bilingualism and biculturalism were just stepping stones to the ideal of multilingualism and multiculturalism.[1] The notion of multiculturalism as the teleological endpoint of a model society would surface again in the course of the public hearings. Meanwhile, with all languages, including French, regarded as equal, and with the teaching of them being publicly supported, demographic factors were used as the basis of claims for multilingual schooling.

Another group that advocated multiculturalism and multilingual schooling was the International Institute of Metropolitan Toronto. This was a community-wide voluntary agency that worked with new immigrants – specifically providing settlement services – and had a representative membership of 'people of fifty-six national backgrounds' (International Institute Canada, 1964). Based in Toronto, the institute was able to stake its expertise in multiculturalism on the changing nature of the city. Changes in the composition of the city – the proportion of British and French residents, for example, dropped from 72 per cent in 1952 to 56 per cent by 1961 – heralded an inevitable cosmopolitanism, a point the brief expanded upon:

Culture is a developing concept and in a world of easy mobility, no society can maintain a static culture nor are cultures linked in an absolute way to

political allegiance. A new idea of citizenship is developing which transcends culture and language. The homogeneity of the people of the nation states of past generations is no longer possible in the modern world.
A country in which the majority of the people adhered to the same culture, language and religion and political affiliation has never been true of
Canada. Therefore, we have an opportunity to demonstrate to the world
the idea of a multicultural country with a common loyalty and citizenship.
(Ibid., 2)

Similar to the brief from the Canadian Mennonite Association, the
International Institute's brief saw bilingualism and biculturalism as
only a part of the whole which was multiculturalism, underscored by
the demographic shifts from a monocultural to multicultural society.
By emphasizing that cultural pluralism was built into the British North
America Act, the argument could be reiterated that bilingualism and
biculturalism were just a passing phase on the road to the ideal of a
multicultural society.

The Role of the Canada Ethnic Press Federation

During the commission's public hearings, the ethnic media also played
an active role. It kept various communities abreast of developments
in the inquiry, especially as they pertained to the other ethnic groups.
As well, the ethnic media reported on reactions to these developments
among other ethnic groups, which allowed the commission to moni-
tor opinions at the grass roots. The ethnic press, as the 'only nation-
wide organization of "other ethnic" groups in Canada,' also advocated
on behalf of other ethnic groups by submitting a substantive brief to
the commission (Canada Ethnic Press Federation, 1964). Commission
researchers therefore made an extensive collection of ethnic-media articles and their summaries by government departments, such as those
produced by the Department of Citizenship and Immigration's Foreign
Language Press Review Service.

A working paper prepared for the commission by R.F. Adie, 'The
Other Ethnic Groups and Mass Media,' stated that about 80 per cent of
all ethnic publications in Canada were in languages other than English
or French; 10 per cent were in English or French; and the remaining
10 per cent were in a 'mixed' category, which meant English or French
and another language (Adie and Krukowski, 1966). Adie found that
there was a conflict within the function of the ethnic media that led to

both integration and segregation: 'It aids in the assimilation of the immigrant into his [sic] new social environment; and it retards such assimilation. It is the greatest single source of information on the new country, while at the same time the maintenance of the inherited language, and the publication of homeland and group news, tend strongly to perpetuate a consciousness of difference' (ibid., 54). This alleged contradiction, of course, informed how the commission read the ethnic press.

In its brief, the Canada Ethnic Press Federation never directly expounded upon multiculturalism, but, as one of the largest representatives of other ethnic groups, it did engage with the many tenets associated with that idea. An overarching theme in the brief was that the 'Unity of Canada transcends every other consideration.' It next clarified this point: 'At the same time it emphasizes that the very diversity within that unity gives it strength and makes it exemplary' (Canada Ethnic Press Federation, 1964, 19). Although the phrase 'unity in diversity' was a common one throughout the commission, it was invoked in a variety of contexts. For example, in the brief from the Anglican Church of Canada, the words of Jacques Cartier were cited to indicate early Canada's unity despite the diversity of the founding races – this was done without considering any other ethnic groups at all (Anglican Church of Canada, 1965). However, the Ethnic Press Federation's conception of unity in diversity was much more in accordance with the ideal of multiculturalism. Describing their notion of a 'constructive diversity,' the federation stated: 'Unity with diversity must be accepted as a basic principle of Canada ... It is not open to either of the parties to the original pact to make unilateral changes. Through immigration the original terms have been modified but the purpose of that variant is to add strength and provide additional hue and color to a tripartite national entity' (Canada Ethnic Press Federation, 1964, 9). The organization also argued strongly for multilingualism beyond English and French, linking language preservation to cultural retention (ibid., 15). As well, the federation made a strong case for maintenance of the 'language of origin.' Even though the working paper on the ethnic media argued that the ethnic press served to maintain 'the inherited language,' and hence impeded integration and promoted segregation, the federation clearly argued the opposite, asserting that preservation of one's language of origin could in fact aid in integration.

Finally, the brief made the case for multilingualism and multilingual schooling. Using a dictionary definition of bilingualism, the federation interpreted the commission's statements on bilingualism to develop its idea of 'factual bilingualism,' defined as 'where one of the languages is neither English nor French.' Decrying the restricted meaning of 'bilingual' in Canada as only that of English and French, the federation suggested that 'Canadians of other than English-French extraction, may select one of Canada's official languages and retain their language of origin as their other language and hence be unofficially bilingual.' Citing the by now well-known statistics that 14 per cent of the population had a mother tongue other than English or French and that 26 per cent of the population were of non-British or non-French origin, the brief continued, 'They are all at various stages in the selection of English or French as their mother tongue. Hence it is reasonably fair to say that these people are factually bilingual' (ibid., 8). Thus, with mother-tongue and ethnicity statistics informing the federation's notion of unofficial bilingualism, a 'factual bilingualism' rested on the idea that bilingualism could be a step en route to multiculturalism. Having made the case for the preservation of the language of origin and the existence of factual bilingualism, the federation's brief moved on to argue that, on the basis of this, languages other than English and French 'have a status in Canada and in some way recognition must be given to them' (ibid., 9). This recognition meant multilingual schooling beyond English and French, both at the high school level and, where numbers warranted, at the elementary school level (ibid.).

Other Perspectives on Multiculturalism:
Briefs Submitted by Ethnic Groups

Although many ethnic groups submitted only one brief, the variety of positions that were taken on the issues pertaining to multiculturalism meant that full, community-wide endorsement was rarely achieved. Dissension within the communities could often be traced through their conflicting statements to the commission or in the ethnic media. Such contention, for instance, appeared in the Polish, German, Japanese, Italian, Chinese, and Ukrainian communities, and the brief submitted by the umbrella organization of The Canadian Council of National Groups also reflected the wide range of approaches to the issues at hand.

For example, in the Polish community newspaper the *Alliancer*, the author of an article entitled 'Introduction of the Polish Language' wrote about unhappiness with the Polish brief, which was seen to contain mild and compromised demands with respect to the right to Polish-language education. Comparing the Ukrainian community's unequivocal demands to the timid Polish brief, the article suggested that the Canadian Polish Congress should make stronger demands for the introduction of Polish-language schooling before Polish cultural heritage in Canada disappeared (Bienkowska, 1965).

Similarly, in a German ethnic newspaper, the *Northwest*, an editorial critiqued the brief submitted on behalf of the German community by the Trans-Canada Alliance of German-Canadians ('Why Is the Voice of the German-Canadian So Weak?' 1965). Comparing in detail the German demands outlined in the brief to Ukrainian and other ethnic group demands already presented to the commission, the editorial found them to be overly modest. Although the brief did ask for the right to support the preservation of the community language – here the editorial interjects: 'As if this privilege had not existed all along!' – it did not ask for any concrete support beyond a request for the free use of Canadian school premises on evenings and weekends. The editorial ended with the statement that no culture could be preserved through self-denial; rather, if one wanted to preserve something, one had to be willing to fight for it (ibid.). In other community newspaper articles, it emerged that the overall position of the German community, although not supportive of preserving the language of origin, did look favourably on the idea of multiculturalism: 'Canada is not expected to become a Tower of Babel ... But to lay down the rule that Canada should have two cultures is illogical and outright wrong' ('Once Again: Two Languages,' 1964, n.p.). In supporting the idea of multiple cultures yet not of multilingualism beyond English and French, the German community adopted a stance that was controversial but not unique.

The Japanese-Canadian community took a position similar to the German community regarding preservation of language of origin. In a brief presented by the National Japanese Canadian Citizens' Association (NJCCA), English-French bilingualism was recognized and demands for 'ethnic language' preservation were modest and unspecified (National Japanese Canadian Citizens Association, 1965). However, the NJCCA's position on multiculturalism was quite different from that of many other ethnic groups. Although it did challenge the notion of two founding races – 'Canada, as a nation, is a nation of immigrants and encompasses more than the two "founding races"' – it advocated not multiculturalism but rather a pan-Canadian identity: 'We further believe that the emphasis should be placed, not on the multi-national or racial origin, not on the hyphenated Canadian, but on "Canadianism" – one and indivisible' (ibid., 3). It explained: 'The need for Canadianism is emphasized by the bitter experience of Japanese Canadians during the war years ... This segment of Canadian citizenry were forcibly moved, under escort, to ghost-towns or concentration camps. We believe that hyphenated Canadianism contributed to this injustice' (ibid.).[2]

The Nisei's (second-generation Japanese Canadians) move from a hyphenated to a pan-Canadian identity reflected their desire for assimilation (National Japanese Canadian Citizens Association, 1965, 3). Yet this desire for assimilation did not necessarily mean support for biculturalism. As the report stated, 'They were opposed to culture as a wall protecting groups from each other.' Drawing on their wartime experience, the Japanese Canadians 'said every time exclusive societies are formed, they invite discrimination. They said when a group of Chinese congregate in the back of a bus and chatter away in Chinese, they are inviting discrimination ... People who cling to their cultural background are harming themselves; this is the lesson they learned from what happened to them during the war' (ibid., 2). This example using Chinese people designated them as agents in their own harm and drew a parallel to the dangers that the Japanese saw in not 'assimilating.' The implications of this perspective on biculturalism are clear, as outlined in the next paragraph:

> It was against this background they saw the problem of biculturalism. They said it was their impression, which they had from the press, that French-Canadians are only working for French-Canadians, that they were only thinking of their own rights, never of others, and also they were not thinking in terms of their contribution to the country but only of their rights in it ... As one said, 'We're making a total effort; why can't French-Canadians do the same.' Implicit in much of what they said was the idea that they had suffered worse discrimination than French-Canadians and yet they were not prepared to sacrifice their cultural heritage on the altar of the general good of Canada. One had the feeling that, given their story, this idea was the necessary basis of their sanity and pride. (National Japanese Canadian Citizens Association, 1965, 2)

The idea that the French-Canadian cultural heritage should be sacrificed for the 'general good of Canada,' in the same way that Japanese Canadians were willing to sacrifice theirs, re-emphasized the overall promotion of a pan-Canadian identity by this community. Given its history and demographics, this group could acknowledge bilingualism as an already entrenched feature of Canadian identity, but not multiculturalism or biculturalism. 'They wish to be considered just as Canadians' (ibid., 2).

But there were variations to the community position outlined in the NJCCA brief. Members of the Manitoba Japanese Canadian Citizens Association, a chapter of the NJCCA, specifying that they were speaking on behalf of their association chapter only, submitted a short statement to the commission. Unlike the NJCCA, this group was more supportive of a position that could be considered multicultural:

> Each ethnic group by maintaining a part of their culture contributes to what might be called a 'Canadian culture.' This hybrid culture, we feel, should not be restricted to bilingualism. Although Canada was a bilingual and bicultural country at the time of the enactment of the B.N.A. Act, it is not necessarily true now. Manitoba certainly is not bilingual or bicultural at the moment. (Manitoba Japanese Canadian Citizens Association, 1965, 1)

This rejection of English-French bilingualism was in stark contrast to the NJCCA's position. Bilingualism and biculturalism were again seen as vestiges of the past and not indicative of the present provincial reality. Although the group did not use the term 'multiculturalism,' its statement was more reflective of multiculturalism than of the English-French bilingual alternative.

Another community that was noticeable for its lack of support of multiculturalism was Italian Canadians. In contrast to the long-established Japanese presence in Canada, the bulk of Italian immigration to the country was relatively recent. In response to an invitation to submit a brief, the Italian Aid Society, based in Toronto, wrote to the commission that it had decided not to make a written submission. But it went on to say that it fully endorsed the commission's terms of reference: 'We feel, that since Canada, as a result of Confederation is officialy [sic] a bilingual and bicultural country there should be no attempt to multiply the difficulties inherent in such a system by any suggestion that there should be special treatment afforded any other ethnic groups towards the perpetuation of the cultures, languages, customs, etc., of these groups' (Bagnato, 1963, 1). The group also stated that it would confine its request for support to efforts at integration, specifically ' ... to have multi-lingual staff employed in those departments and agencies with which many of our people have to deal ... This would be in an effort to expedite the handling of the problems of those who have not, as yet, mastered the English language' (ibid., 2). Government help for the community's efforts to learn the majority language of English, the group argued, would facilitate integration in Toronto, where settlement issues for Italian newcomers were considerable. In this context, the preservation of language of origin was not seen as a priority, given that a large segment of the Italian community still had a vital first language; rather, the community's main challenge was to overcome the lack of knowledge in the majority language which made settlement difficult, particularly in relation to accessing state services and employment.

However, for Italians in Montreal, represented in the brief presented by the Canadian-Italian Business and Professional Men's Association, the issue of preserving language of origin was important. Vincenzo Radino argued that a loss of the Italian language would mean a loss of contact with the original culture (Canada, *Transcripts of Public Hearings*, 1965a, 4273). Emphasizing language of origin as the medium through which familial and community connections would be maintained into the future, Radino felt that Italian was under threat and that, without support, 'it is definite that in 30 to 50 years we will not have a medium of communication between us' or between the generations (ibid., 4276). Thus, in the context of Montreal and Quebec, integration issues – while important – did not mitigate the need for the long-term preservation of the Italian language as a way to ensure the future viability of an Italian community; this need had primacy even though there was support for bilingualism. It would therefore seem that, for Italian Canadians, the perspective on community language issues varied by local context and settlement pressures.

Submissions from the Chinese community included a letter from the Reverend Andrew Lam of St John the Baptist Anglican Church in Fort Garry, Manitoba, and an essay by Foon Sien on the 'Chinese in Canada.' Lam's letter, a written recollection of the presentation made to Commission Co-chairman Laurendeau upon his visit to his Diocesan Committee, emphasized the barriers faced by the Chinese community in Canada. Lam described Chinese Canadians as an 'integral part of the population' and detailed the barriers to full citizenship experienced by the community (Lam, 1965).

The pressing problems faced by this community, as described by Lam, were all immigration-related; specifically, they were connected to the difficulties the Chinese confronted compared to other groups in sponsoring family members' immigration, and the challenges of emigrating to the United States, where their ethnic background prevented them from entering despite their Canadian citizenship. Lam gave voice to the 'hopes of Canadian citizens of Chinese descent that they be given assurance of full acceptance.' He stated that 'we, as Canadian citizens of Chinese descent, feel at times rather uncertain of the place we occupy in the eyes of Canada. Are we regarded as Chinese first and only second-arily as Canadians? Are we fully accepted as citizens even though we are not members of the two founding races or nations?' (Lam, 1965, 2). Given these concerns about second-class citizenship, Lam's letter ended with a reiteration of the plea for full acceptance of Chinese community members 'so that their individual contributions in their daily endeav-ors and the richness of their cultural heritage may add to fulness [sic] and strength of Canadian life' (ibid.).

Foon Sien's essay, seventy-eight pages in length, was submitted a few years after Lam's letter. An ex-employee of the War Service Department and also president of the Hoysun Ningyung Benevolent Association, which represented about half the Chinese population in Canada (Sien, 1967), Sien detailed the history of the Chinese in Canada, including the different types of racial exclusions suffered by the com-munity, with an emphasis on the barriers imposed through Canadian immigration regulations and practices over time. There were several references to language in the essay but these were focused mainly on how language, along with colour discrimination, was a barrier to so-cial interaction (ibid., 14). As in Lam's letter, the emphasis was not on the need for founding-race status, but on acceptance and equal rights as a fully recognized minority group. Sien used the mosaic metaphor to argue for equal inclusion: 'Bringing to this land only their strength, perseverance and determination, a deep philosophy of life, they [the Chinese] grew into this mosaic of Canada, and today they are one of the brilliant colours without which this rich tapestry perhaps would be insipid' (ibid.). Further on, Sien outlined the central role of the Chinese in building the Canadian Pacific Railway (CPR), and he pointed to this history as indicative of the 'strength, perseverance and determina-tion' and achievements of the community. Chinese participation in the building of the CPR not only reflected these laudable group charac-teristics but also became a prior historical and nation-building claim, similar to those made by the Ukrainians during the preliminary hear-ings. For the Chinese, this nation-building claim was the basis not for founding-race status and entry into the white-settler category but for recognition as an essential element of the Canadian mosaic. The for-mulation of a Canadian mosaic where the Chinese community could enjoy equal rights reflected closely the concept of multiculturalism that was advanced earlier by other ethnic groups. Preservation of language of origin was not an issue; rather, similar to the Italian community, Sien saw language as a concern only insofar as it was a barrier to full participation and citizenship in the larger Canadian community.

Ukrainian submissions far outnumbered those from any other ethnic group. The brief submitted by the Dominion Executive of the Ukrainian Self-Reliance League of Canada used the now-familiar tactic of disputing founding-race status for only the English and French by invoking Ukrainians' historical contributions to nation-building, thus challenging English-French bilingualism and biculturalism: 'Those pioneers of Ukrainian origin who broke the virgin prairies, cleared the bush, built the roads, worked the mines, were unquestionable "founders" in their own right . . . ' (Ukrainian Self-Reliance League of Canada, 1965, 5). The brief also contested the statistical manipulations of the commission researchers whereby 'the "other" groups are reduced to 14% of Canada's population by the simple expedient of using mother tongue rather than ethnic origin' (ibid., 2); the League took the position that other groups actually made up 30 per cent of the population since, as it explained: 'Although language is a primary facet of culture, it is not the whole of culture' (ibid.). The brief also argued in favour of other Canadian ethnic identities by outlining a more complex understanding of cultural identification: 'The fact remains that there are a significant number of people in Canada who feel themselves completely Canadian but do not want to, and see no reason why they should, try and pass themselves off as English or French' (ibid., 3).

This was the foundation upon which the brief argued for a territorial basis for rights:

> We see no reason why Canadians should accept any assumptions that there are constitutional differences between the French-Canadians and the 'other' Canadians outside the province of Quebec, except for the status of the French language in Parliament and in the Courts as guaranteed in the British North America Act. Indeed, all the 'others' are entitled to the same privileges outside of Quebec as are, or may be, extended to the French-Canadians in the future. (Ukrainian Self-Reliance League of Canada, 1965, 4)

In taking this stand, the League was countering what it called 'first and second class categories of people, discrimination, favouritism and inequality' (ibid.). From this it followed that equal rights for all groups, regardless of 'founding' status, could be ensured through demographic and territorial principles.

Although the brief argued that language was only one component of cultural identity, it did go on to make the case for the preservation of the culture – including language – of other ethnic groups as a way to contribute to the development of Canadian cultural values and preserve and perpetuate their heritage, especially since these were privileges demanded by French-speaking Canadians (Ukrainian Self-Reliance League of Canada, 1965, 10). Specifically, the League argued that 'the "others" seek no special status of favour; they merely seek equality for their cultural values and cherished traditions' (ibid., 8). Further, in the summary of its brief, the League asserted that cultural values were given substance through language maintenance (ibid., 11) and argued for equality in language use and teaching, but again along territorial lines (ibid., 10). This brief, though, had to make some careful manoeuvres in developing its case for multilingual language rights based on territorial principles. First, although it argued against mother-tongue data being used solely to determine ethnic identity, the substantive right that it demanded was language preservation. Also, the territorial principle for according these language rights was based in the larger space of 'English-speaking Canada,' even though the brief argued at the same time that there were no 'founding' races. Yet, despite these manipulations, the overall thrust of the brief was to argue against English-French bilingualism and for multilingualism and multilingual rights.

In making the case against biculturalism, the League began with the idea that, historically, the only principle of unity in Canada was diversity (Ukrainian Self-Reliance League of Canada 1965, 4). Its conception of unity in diversity was similar to the multicultural ideal advanced by the Canada Ethnic Press Federation, which, as we have seen, broke with any notion of biculturalism. The League's position in this respect had strong support from the *Ukrainian Women's World* newspaper, which stated, 'Since Canada is not merely bi-lingual and bi-cultural but multilingual and multicultural our principle is an absolute equality of all Canadians' ('Canada Is Ours,' 1965, n.p.).

Another group took up the idea of absolute equality for all Canadians, but with some fundamental differences. The Canadian Council for National Groups was a Toronto-based umbrella organization for a number of European ethnic groups, including the Polish Democratic

Association, the United Jewish Peoples Order, and the Association of United Ukrainian Canadians. Its brief began by citing figures from the 1961 census to make the case that Canada was a nation built through immigration and would continue to be so: 'The statistics show that 92 percent of our population is composed of immigrants and their descendants. With the exception of the native Indians and Eskimos, it can truly be said that "we are immigrants all" in Canada' (Canadian Council of National Groups, 1964, 16). Although the brief began with the familiar discourse regarding nation-building and the significance of immigration throughout Canadian history – the discourse through which many other ethnic groups constructed a claim for a particular mode of national belonging – the council's brief did not make the usual subsequent argument in favour of multiculturalism. Rather, it disputed what it called 'the doctrine of the third force' and the 'theory of the "mosaic"' (ibid., 13). Specifically, the brief asserted that the idea of the 'third force' – meaning the totality of the ethnic groups other than English and French – was 'false and misleading' (ibid.), while the notion of a mosaic was no better since 'it conceives of the ethnic groups as static and separate parts of English and French Canada – permanent little islands of immutable cultural values' (ibid.). The brief further argued that this line of thinking attempted to create the 'illusion of three equal partners – equating the parts (national groups) with the whole (English and French Canada)' (ibid.).

The brief did not embrace the argument that Canada is a multicultural nation, but neither did it support the principle of a bilingual and bicultural nation without qualification. Instead, it described Canada's history of racial and ethnic discrimination, particularly in relation to immigration and citizenship regulations, and focused especially on the denial of citizenship rights as a result of police and government blacklists based on 'suspicion of membership or membership [*sic*] in progressive and left-wing organizations' (Canadian Council of National Groups, 1964, 18). The brief argued that 'the denial of citizenship rights as a result of arbitrary political prejudice is, in a real sense, a denial of equality in the matter of all rights' and, while acknowledging that there had been a slight relaxation in the application of this policy, maintained that an end to such discrimination was a prerequisite to fulfilling the commission's mandate with respect to the other ethnic groups (ibid.). It suggested the need for a new constitution that would ensure 'the basic rights of all citizens regardless of their origin, colour and creed' while also guaranteeing self-determination and equality of rights for French and English Canada. The Council of National Groups highlighted three overarching rights: the outlawing of discrimination based on ethnic origin (to be enshrined in a Bill of Rights); the right to citizenship as a constitutional right; and the right of all national groups to cultivate the traditions and languages of their forefathers, as well as the right to voluntary association for this purpose (ibid., 25). The concern here with fundamental anti-discrimination protections echoed that of the Chinese community and recommended the recognition of Canada's bi-cultural duality only if coupled with an acceptance of the fundamental and equal rights of citizenship of all Canadians, including the right to preserve languages of origin.

The Canadian Council of National Groups understood that, with the increasing urbanization of the population, the 'tightly knit language communities were a phenomenon of large-scale immigration in a by-gone era'; and that each succeeding generation of Canadian-born children of immigrants would have English as their primary language, with the result that 'the language of the fore-fathers is lost' (Canadian Council of National Groups, 1964, 14). In its view, however, this was not a reason for giving up the fight. Multilingual schooling was again seen as the vehicle for language preservation, although, unlike those ethnic groups that recommended multilingual schooling at the elementary level, the council focused on high school and university 'where justifiable and practical' (ibid., 23). This suggests that differences in multilingual-schooling proposals depended on the importance each particular group gave to the preservation of their language of origin.

'We Are Canadian': Challenges to the Idea of Canada as a Multicultural Country

Another set of briefs directly challenged the idea that Canada was a multicultural country; they came from organizations as diverse as the Imperial Order Daughters of the Empire, the United Church of Canada, and the Canadian Labour Congress, among others. The Voice of Canada League, a clearly pro-English and anti-bilingualism organization, tackled the issue of other ethnic groups towards the end of its brief, after enumerating the multiple reasons why English-French bilingualism and biculturalism would not work in Canada. It argued:

1) CANADA is – without any question – A BRITISH DESIGNED COUNTRY. This is a SIMPLE FACT OF HISTORY
2) This is a key factor which has proven itself responsible for attracting so many from other countries

By now, the millions of Canadians whose ethnic origins must be regarded as other than either British or French – have come to Canada because of their belief in the soundness of our original constitution. They came because of their belief in an opportunity to become 'Canadians'

They – DID NOT come to Canada with the intentions of remaining forever identified with some 45 countries which have contributed to our population. They came with the full realization that – while remaining absolutely free to preserve interests in their traditional cultures – they would – nevertheless – expect to become 'assimilated' into the life of Canada. (Voice of Canada League, 1964, 4–5)

The league was not prepared to even consider the notion of a bilingual and bicultural Canada; rather, a British Canada was the only legitimate one, and all other ethnic groups should assimilate into it, while remaining free to preserve their traditional cultures. How these groups were to preserve their cultures was never specified – an omission that presumably removed them to the realm of private community concerns. Instead, the assimilation of immigrants into this British-based Canadian identity was seen as the only way to preserve Canadian unity: 'Let all of those of our multi-racial origin groups recognize they have an *obligation* to consider themselves as CANADIANS ONLY – without hyphenation of interests or loyalties in any form' (Voice of Canada League, 1964, 5). This was the classic pro-Anglo, anti-biculturalism, and anti-bilingualism stance, in which the desire of other ethnic groups for cultural retention had no place.

Another group with a solid Anglophilic background was the Imperial Order Daughters of the Empire (IODE), founded in Canada in 1900. The IODE was one of the largest Canadian national women's voluntary organizations, which at the time of the commission was raising and spending over a million dollars annually on education, emergency welfare, and other community services (Imperial Order Daughters of the Empire, 1964). However, unlike the Voices of Canada League, the IODE was supportive of bilingualism and biculturalism, particularly because it saw this foundational duality as something that differentiated Canada from 'the one melting pot' system of the United States (ibid., 10). Having recognized biculturalism and bilingualism as a bulwark against the United States, the brief went on to describe the danger of what might happen if Canadian duality failed: 'Should our "two melting pots" system disintegrate or fail, it is our belief that Canada would probably be unable to resist eventual "Americanization"' (ibid.). The role of bilingualism and biculturalism as a buffer between Canada and the United States was a common rationale that was used, particularly by Anglophone communities, throughout the commission in favour of including the French into the category of founding races. However, this inclusion did not extend to the other ethnic groups.

The IODE position on multilingualism and multiculturalism was quite clear: 'Canada is not a multilingual or multicultural society' (IODE, 1964, 10). Arguing against the 'hyphenated Canadian' form, the IODE believed that 'all native-born and naturalized Canadians should be dignified by being referred to simply as "Canadians"' (ibid., 8). It declared that all immigrants must learn at least one of Canada's two official languages as a requirement of citizenship, and, to this end, 'many I.O.D.E. chapters conduct their own basic English classes for immigrants' (ibid., 17). Acknowledging that immigrants may initially wish to speak their own languages, the IODE warned that this could lead to divisions: 'This would only serve to split or divide us into the same old discordant pattern of Old Europe. This Canada does not want' (ibid., 9). Although the IODE did recognize that immigrants wanted to and needed to learn the majority languages, especially for 'social and economic advantage' and necessity (ibid., 9), by invoking the fears of old world divisions or Balkanization, it understood any desire by immigrants to preserve languages of origin as a threat to Canadian unity. Specifically, it was the preservation of ethnic languages that was seen as a potential threat to being 'Canadian' – and this fear of fragmentation was a common trope in the rejection of multiculturalism and the promotion of assimilation.

The Canadian Labour Congress (CLC), founded in 1956 and representing more than 1,200,000 trade-union members at the time of the commission, also submitted a brief. In it, the congress stated its position unambiguously with respect to the inquiry: 'A working class institution representing . . . workers in every part of Canada from a variety of ethnic and other backgrounds, we are firmly committed to preserving Canada as one united country' (Canadian Labour Congress Canada, 1965, 9). The CLC supported biculturalism and bilingualism as a way to address the economic inequalities of French and English Canada, as 'Quebec has for generations been a low-wage area' (ibid.). The brief also argued that Canada's bilingual and bicultural nature had meant that it had 'never subscribed to the melting pot theory' (ibid.), which presumably differentiated it from the United States. In relation to other ethnic groups, the CLC was supportive of cultural preservation, stating: 'We believe no obstacle should be placed in the way of these groups in their legitimate endeavours to preserve language and traditions which are dear to them.' This decisively moved other ethnic groups into the realm of private community concerns, as the brief went on to make clear: 'We do not subscribe to a polyglot Canada.' There then followed the rationale for not extending official recognition to ethnic languages: 'Those who have come to Canada as immigrants must have done so with full awareness that they were leaving one environment to enter another and that this would require adjustment to the use of a new language ... They cannot therefore ask that their particular language of origin should be entrenched in Canada as it was in the country they came from' (ibid., 10). The first implication of this is that immigrants chose freely to come to Canada, and that these 'choices' were fully informed as to what rights they would retain and under what circumstances, among other things. As well, there is the implication that the desire to learn a majority language is incompatible with the wish to preserve one's language of origin. Coupled with this is the assumption that language learning is an unproblematic and natural phenomenon for immigrants. This notion that there is an embedded and informed choice in immigration that precludes the right to ask for any formal recognition of other cultures, or any shift in the national status quo, would be frequently heard in arguments pertaining to multiculturalism and multilingualism during the inquiry.

The United Church of Canada, although critical of any notion of founding 'races' and preferring the French version of 'peuples' in its brief, was still in favour of bilingualism and biculturalism. In addition, with respect to multiculturalism, the church did recognize that 'Canada is ethnically and sociologically multicultural ... politically, however, Canada is, at least to some degree, bilingual and bicultural' (United Church of Canada, 1964). In particular, this meant that 'the British and the French did the founding, and others did not' (ibid., 13). The brief went on to explain:

> When people of these other origins came to Canada, they came to a political community which was already established, whose institutions had been shaped by the French or the British, or both, who had been here first. This was one of the given facts which even the early German immigrants to Lunenburg County, Nova Scotia, or Waterloo County, Ontario, faced and had to accept. They had not the slightest prospect of setting up a German law, German political institutions, German as an official

language. The same is true of later arrivals, such as the Ukrainians in the Prairie Provinces. This is no reflection on the Germans or the Ukrainians or anyone else. It does not for a moment deny, or minimize, the·immense contribution they have made to Canada, economically, politically, culturally. But this contribution, however great, does not give their law or their language the same constitutional position as the law and language of the English and French. (Ibid., 14)

Thus, an ethnic and sociological multiculturalism was trumped by the prior claims of those two peoples 'who had been here first.' Here there was a convenient bifurcation between the sociological and the political in order to maintain the prevailing position of the English and French. Sensitive as it was to the sociological reality of other ethnic groups, the church supported the 'teaching of the languages of the "other cultures,"' but only 'as [an] optional cultural subject in high school and university where a substantial group of citizens so desires' (United Church of Canada, 1964, 5). Of course, marking these languages as optional subjects at higher levels of education emphasized the peripheral importance of language preservation for other ethnic groups.

The *Montreal Star* submitted a brief to the commission on behalf of the English minority of Quebec. Locating itself within the province in relation to the nation – 'we are in the distinct position of being a daily voice in a community which is a minority in the city and province which we serve, while, at the same time, we belong to the English-speaking majority in Canada as a whole' – the *Star* also saw itself as the representative of the English in Quebec: 'It has occurred to us that THE MONTREAL STAR does, in a sense, represent a "community" voice' (*Montreal Star*, 1965, 1). Conceding the legitimacy of the French communities' claims and concerns, the brief went on to outline the fear held by English-speaking families in Quebec of becoming aliens in 'their own land' (ibid., 4). In relation to other ethnic groups, though, the brief was unequivocal: 'We suggest also a strict proviso against multilingualism.' The *Star* described the dangers of extending rights similar to those of the English and French to other groups:

It would be in our judgment, however, a grave mistake to provide special linguistic, legal and constitutional privileges to other racial minorities. It may well be true that, in the three prairie provinces for example the proportion of Ukrainian, German and Polish minorities is greater than that of the French minorities in those provinces. This seems to us a matter of small concern. Almost all of them, in their origins as immigrants, chose the English side. They have all made a great contribution to it and have deepened and enriched English Canadian culture. To deliberately splinter them now by providing six or eight languages of instruction, for instance, instead of two, would be to destroy or to delay the emergence of any real Canadianism. We can, for historical and traditional reasons, create a bicultural state. We should not deliberately set ourselves to the construction of a Tower of Babel. (*Montreal Star*, 1965, 7)

Embedded in this statement was the idea that providing other ethnic groups with rights equal to those of the English and French would threaten social cohesion, or what the brief went on to describe as 'that basic degree of homogeneity essential to our future' (ibid., 7). The Tower of Babel metaphor was used here and often throughout the hearing to signify threats to social cohesion, highlighting the increasing salience of language in Canadian unity. As well, and once again, the notion that immigrants choose to immigrate – predominantly to 'English' Canada – was invoked to thwart any claims for equivalent rights.

Thus, during the course of the B and B Commission's public hearings, multiculturalism emerged as a way to break with the hierarchy installed through the terms of reference for the other ethnic groups. The claims made for a multicultural instead of bicultural mode of inclusion were based on a variety of strategies, many of which had already been advanced during the course of the preliminary hearings; these included historical, demographic, and territorial claims. Nevertheless, what multiculturalism meant in practice remained unspecified, with a wide range of definitions being advanced on all sides of the debate. Multiculturalism was posited as a naturalized Canadian trait or as an expansion beyond the two founding races' conceptions of 'unity in diversity,' and bilingualism and biculturalism were seen as just stepping stones to the ideal of multiculturalism. Yet multiculturalism was also understood to be a threat to social cohesion and pan-Canadian identity, be that a singular Anglo-centric or a bicultural Canadian identity, and also as a compromise to the Canadian dualism seen to be a bulwark against the United States.

In many of these discussions, language emerged as the substantive element for advancing and demarcating the boundaries of other ethnic groups' rights and inclusion. This came through such issues as multilingualism; formal versus private multilingual schooling; the level at which multilingual schooling would begin, if at all; the inevitability of factual bilingualism; the positioning of majority-language learning as incompatible with preservation of one's language of origin; and the invoking of metaphors such as the Tower of Babel and 'little Europe' as threats to white-settler social cohesion. Different ethnic groups and factions, for a variety of reasons specific to the history and conditions of their particular communities, positioned themselves differently in relation to these issues. Another feature of these discussions was assumptions about immigration: that immigrants chose to come, knew the socio-cultural and political context before arriving, and thus forfeited the right to ask for any formal recognition of their cultures and languages. This notion of choice would become an important element in the commission's attempts to locate the other ethnic groups.

Part II – 'Indians and Eskimos'

As we have seen, although the commission's terms of reference did not mention Indigenous groups, these groups did make presentations to the inquiry in its preliminary phase and their issues were discussed in the *Preliminary Report*. Moreover, in a working paper for Study Group 'D' of the commission, dated December 1963, it was clearly stated that 'The Commission recognizes that it has a duty to give special attention to the problems of the Eskimo and the Indian in our present world' (Study Group D, 1963, 2). The need for special attention to Indigenous issues in the royal commission was backed by public demand and taken up in the media to such an extent that even a year later the *Montreal Star* reported, 'The commission widened the horizons of its massive investigation in response to public demand,' and 'the consensus was that Indians and Eskimos have been largely ignored until now, and that the bicultural commission would be an appropriate vehicle to reverse the trend' ('Eskimos Enter Culture Study,' 1964, n.p.).

Not surprisingly, then, Indigenous groups were again represented in the public hearings of 1965. Just prior to the submission of briefs, the Indian-Eskimo Association, an umbrella group representing eighty organizations with about one thousand members in total, held its very first provincial conference in London, Ontario, on 20–22 November 1964. Commissioner Gagnon was present at the conference, as was the commission research and liaison officer, Ilona M. Varjassy. The commission records contain a summary report of this conference that was prepared by Varjassy. Although the 'problems of bilingualism and biculturalism were not discussed' directly during the conference, issues felt to be germane to the inquiry were addressed and the participants' views on them were recorded by Varjassy and included as part of the materials used by the commission in the writing of the report (Varjassy, 1964b). Varjassy's conference summary and evaluation include a précis of presentations made by such people as Daniel G. Hill (the director of Ontario Human Rights Commission); statistical information about Indigenous groups, their incomes, and their population distribution throughout the country; and personal interpretations of presentations during the conference.

A theme that surfaces often in this summary is that the problems facing Indigenous communities are so overwhelming that the concerns of the inquiry are irrelevant to them: 'The social and economic problems of the Indians are so great, deep and bitter that the cultural and language problems must wait until they realize them' (Varjassy, 1964b, 3). But there is more to it than that. The report continues:

> If one brings up the question of B and B while chatting with Indian chiefs their reaction generally seems to be indifferent or negative. But then one learns that a good part of the reserve-Indians, over 200,000, have yet to learn ... that they are not only members of a band but citizens of a nation, that equality means more than a treaty signed a long time ago, that they too are living in the 20th century and not in the 19th, or 18th. They are yet to learn that useful employment is the first step to dignity and self-sufficiency. (Ibid.)

In Varjassy's mind, then, the irrelevance of the inquiry for Indigenous groups stems not just from the magnitude of their challenges but also from their being rooted in the past. These two factors, along with fragmentation among Indigenous groups 'by language, differences, inertia, poverty and distance,' would constitute the commission's main rationales for excluding these groups from the scope of its inquiries (Varjassy, 1964b, 3).

The issue of fragmentation, in particular, was highlighted in the conference summary (as it was in the *Preliminary Report*) in order to underscore that Indigenous people did not make up a unified group. This argument was mobilized particularly in relation to language, as the summary stated: 'They could not agree on whether they want to preserve their own language or not. Most of them thought that it would be useless because only in Ontario there are six different Indian languages spoken' (Varjassy, 1964b, 5). The idea that a surfeit of languages makes it pointless to try to preserve them echoes the argument used in the *Preliminary Report* to reject efforts at Indigenous language preservation. Also, the cultural concerns of Indians contrasted starkly with those of other groups: 'This problem fundamentally starts with the fact that the Indian culture was not designed for western civilization, and although it contributed to Canadian culture – the Indians themselves became more and more a marginal group as the Western civilization progressed in North America' (ibid.). Here, the 'cultural problem' of Indigenous peoples is deemed exceptional, with its pathology located in a 'culture' that is seen as incommensurate with progressive Western civilization. This argument pre-figures the rationale of the White Paper on Indian policy which the government would develop a few years later. All of this led to the following conclusion:

> The Canadian Indian problem is so complex that an inquiry into the existing situation of this large and important group should be handled by a special Royal Commission ... Although it should be desirable to deal in depth with the Indian problem, it seems unrealistic to hope that the Royal Commission on Bilingualism and Biculturalism can keep up this responsibility. The Commission has only a limited time for its inquiry, also is limited by its terms of reference. (Ibid., 5–6)

This argument would again appear in *Book I* of the final report and would continue to concern the government throughout the 1960s. However, as Alan Cairns states, when the suggestion of a Royal Commission on Indian policy was raised by Gordon Robertson – at the time the Clerk of the Privy Council – in the late 1960s, Trudeau and Jim Davey (one of his trusted advisors at the time) both feared that 'Natives might argue convincingly that they be regarded as "citizens plus"' through such a commission, and so the matter was dropped (Cairns, 2000, 165).

Despite this, the same conference led to a decision on the part of the Board of Directors of the Indian-Eskimo Association to submit a brief to the B and B Commission. That brief began with the statement that the Indians and Eskimos are '*first* citizens,' which make them 'more Canadian than any other groups that have arrived since European settlement' (Indian-Eskimo Association of Canada, 1965, 2). They resented having their situation compared to that of new immigrants, even if they shared some of the same challenges (ibid.). In their case, preservation of cultural heritage was stated to be 'not a privilege but a right, guaranteed by solemn treaty,' and this right had to be accepted by the public if Canadian 'citizenship' was to have any meaning for Indians and Eskimos (ibid., 3). After outlining the problems confronting Indigenous communities – poverty, loss of culture, lack of self-government – the brief summed up the goals of native peoples as '*equality of opportunity*' and 'an opportunity to share in *all* the benefits of Canadian life without loss of identity' (ibid., emphasis in original). Concretely, with respect to the inquiry, this meant that issues of bilingualism were once again of marginal interest: 'It is little wonder that the current discussions concerning Bilingualism and Biculturalism are seemingly remote from their sphere of interests. For example, for them the problem of "language" is one of retaining their own native languages and acquiring facility in either English or French' (ibid., 2).

The commission's public hearings came at a bad time for another Indigenous group, the National Indian Council. Some months before, Varjassy had prepared a confidential memorandum for all the commissioners about a private meeting that she, as the commission's representative, had had on 26 November 1964 with Wilfred Pelletier, executive director of the National Indian Council and editor of the *Thunderbird*. In this memorandum, Varjassy noted that Pelletier's legitimacy as a leader of the council was in question. Claiming that disapproval of his appointment – not election – as executive director of the council had 'deep roots in the Indian society,' the memorandum went on to state that Kahn-Tineta Horn and Richard Pine, the Garden River chief, 'are trying to form another Council which would really represent the Indian people' (Varjassy, 1964c). By the following year, this dispute was being discussed in the mainstream media, with the Regina *Leader-Post* reporting Kahn-Tineta Horn's criticism of the National Indian Council 'as being controlled by non-Indians' ('Kahn-Tineta Horn Critical,' 1965). Pelletier's political difficulties were thought to be the reason he was reluctant to submit a brief to the commission. However, Kahn-Tineta Horn did submit a brief, and it attracted a lot of attention.

Speaking on behalf of the Caughnawaga reserve in Quebec, Kahn-Tineta Horn's brief expressed concern that if 'the province of Quebec should separate from Canada ... the Iroquois in Caughnawaga, St. Regis and Oka would be swallowed up in a "foreign" nation' (Horn, 1965, 17). Outlining the colonial history of the Iroquois and the French, the brief concluded that there was no future for the French language in their community: 'After 300 years of close contact virtually no Iroquois speak French and it is obvious that we do not want to and are never going to . . .' (ibid., 16). As well, the brief declared:

WE INDIANS ARE AGAINST ALL POLITICAL 'ISMS.' We are opposed to Facism, Communism, Capitalism, and we are particularly suspicious of political 'bilingualism.' We support anyone's right to freely choose to speak two or twenty languages but we reject the implied legislative attempt to force us to accept more than one official language. Indian legend says that 'to speak with two tongues is to tell a lie.' The title of this Commission should be corrected. It creates the false impression that there are actually such things as 'bilingualism' and 'biculturalism.' Canada's culture is the sum total of all the ways of life of all its people, and although there are supposedly many sub cultures, there cannot be 'bi culture.' (Ibid., 7)

Although biculturalism was dismissed, it was bilingualism that was most strongly repudiated, again highlighting the importance of language as the substantive measure of culture: 'WE INDIANS WILL NEVER SUBMIT TO BEING FORCED TO SPEAK ANOTHER LANGUAGE after our own Indians [sic] language and English if we choose (or in some cases French)' (Horn, 1965, 8). The brief was clear that the Indian languages were of paramount importance, but it acknowledged that English, or in some cases French, was necessary as another language. It also anticipated the common criticism of Indigenous linguistic fragmentation: 'If having more than one language unites and enriches, then Indians with 200 different language dialects should be the wealthiest of all. However, we know it is a barrier to understanding and unity and to overcome these barriers, Indians long ago developed one language – the Sign Language which was known by all Indians' (ibid., 4). The brief ended by restating the incompatibility of English-French bilingualism with the Indigenous community and its colonial effect: 'We will resent and resist any legislative force to make us take on another language because it is our right and because it is destructive and undemocratic . . . Anyone attempting to impose on us their "bilingualism" means to us the end of culture and languages of our ancestors and indicates their lack of respect for our way of life and our People' (ibid., 17).

There was another brief from the Caughnawaga reserve, this one from John Curotte, chairman of the Caughnawaga Defence Committee. The brief began with an overview of European colonial history in

Canada before challenging the notion of founding races, on the grounds that 'the "founding races" were the Indians, and the others could be called the "invading races," or the second coming races or whatever fits' (Caughnawaga Defence Committee, 1965, 4). The brief also contested the idea of bicultures: 'It must be recognized that the white society in Canada cannot have biculturalism if this means "two" cultures. The white society has one culture – "The Pursuit of More Possessions and Power." Canadians of British, French, Hebrew, Italian, German, Ukrainian ancestry may deny this, but the general principle is the same for all ethnic white groups' (ibid., 2). Thus, the brief collapsed all white ethnic groups into one, contesting the notion that biculturalism was even possible. It then went on to suggest a form of multi-cultures instead:

> If 'equal partnership' is to exist, it cannot forget the superior claims of Indians, and if the difference in population between 13 million English to 5 million French (a difference of 8 million) is to be overlooked as unimportant, then the difference in population between 5 million French and 350,000 Indians (a difference of 4,650,000) must also be overlooked. 'Equality' of groups which are so uneven in numbers should also include Indians and bring into it 'multi' instead of 'bi.' (Caughnawaga Defence Committee, 1965, 4)

This sense of 'multicultural' was quite different from the multicultural of other ethnic groups; it was 'multicultural' specific to Indigenous peoples. The committee's reconfiguration of 'multicultural' introduced yet another complexity in how the term was being deployed throughout the public hearings, underscoring again the term's lack of precision.

The brief addressed the issue of bilingualism as relevant for Indigenous communities:

> As to two languages, it has long been accepted that Red Men are entitled to their own original ancient language which precedes that of the languages of the Western world by thousands of years. However, the Red Man welcomes, for the purpose of survival in the world of competition, a second language which has proven to be the English language despite some 320 years of association with the French language which was the first white man's language heard by the Iroquois in about 1645. It is clear that we are part of a Two Language World. (Caughnawaga Defence Committee, 1965, 3)

The history of Indigenous communities and their languages creates a prior claim to their original language, with the second language being for merely utilitarian, work purposes. The brief reiterated this point: 'We have sought to preserve the traditional language of the Oneidas, Cayugas Onondagas, Senecas, Tuscaroras and the Mohawks ... In the outside world, whether it is in South America, United States, Canada or anywhere our men are working in steel work the language is English. Our choice of "bi" or two languages is natural, normal and practical' (Caughnawaga Defence Committee, 1965, 8). In essence, the brief was advocating the idea of a factual bilingualism for this Indigenous community, a concept that had already surfaced in the public hearings. It ended by taking a position against bilingualism, noting that 'Iroquois reject any change in the language conditions of the country and, as it is our right as warriors who were never conquered, we do so proudly' (ibid., 9). In conclusion, it can be said that, although this brief uniquely raised the idea of 'multi-cultures' in the context of Indigenous cultures, its emphasis on language for both cultural and economic survival and its resistance to English-French bilingualism made its positioning in relation to the commission similar to the submission of Kahn-Tineta Horn.

Another submission, addressed specifically to Commissioner Laing, was from a non-Indigenous person. It was a memorandum written by A. McPhedran, the assistant general manager of the Bank of Nova Scotia in Calgary. An attached covering letter indicated that the memorandum was in response to a request for information on the education of Eskimo and Indian children in the Northwest Territories. Basing his information on a short stay in the Territories, which included a visit to a local residential high school, McPhedran noted: 'I'm sure that you will appreciate that this is far from a thorough study of the problem as I was only in the area about 24 hours' (McPhedran, 1964). He praised the modernized, clean layout of the school but decried the culturally irrelevant curriculum and the segregation of students of Catholic and Protestant backgrounds. Focusing on the disjuncture between the school's modern conveniences and the 'primitive' environments of the students' family homes, the memorandum insisted that there was a need to rethink the purpose of residential-school education:

> At the age of six the child is taken by the authorities from his home, be it igloo, tent or shack and flown into Inuvik where they come face to face with modern living comforts, such as running water, electricity and movies. It must be remembered that in their own environment they have only

lanterns and other primitive conveniences. Is it reasonable to believe that after they have finished their schooling that these children will go back to cutting ice from the lakes and hauling it for miles for drinking and cooking purposes and putting up with other inconveniences? Will these boys turn out to be trappers, as their fathers are? If not, what can we do with these people if we are going to educate them? We must find a place for them in the southern society ... It seems to me that it is most important that there be a continuing research into the problem of educating primitive people, but equally important is the research into what we are going to do with them after they have been educated. (McPhedran, 1964, 1–2)

His language and analysis reflected a civilizing and missionary attitude towards the Inuit. Although McPhedran questioned the purpose of residential schooling, it was not because of the colonial relations and practices that were entrenched at these schools in relation to Indigenous students; rather, the concern was utilitarian in nature and reinscribed the colonial positioning of Indigenous people and their ways of life as 'primitive.' This then was the rationale for assimilation and cultural erasure.

The inquiry also commissioned an extensive research report. Entitled 'Indians and Eskimos of Canada: An Overview of Studies of Relevance to the Royal Commission on Bilingualism and Biculturalism,' and written by Frank G. Vallee, it was an extensive two-volume, 300-plus-page document. The report began by stating that the inquiry had decided not to commission a full report on 'Eskimo and Indian matters' because research in these areas was already underway or completed, mostly by the Department of Northern Affairs and Natural Resources. Accordingly, the commission decided to limit its own research commitment to a review of studies whose findings were pertinent to its terms of reference (Vallee, 1966). A substantial part of the report concentrated on the history and sociocultural life of Indigenous peoples, with an anthropological and legal perspective on the issues. The report focused on language usage within Indigenous groups as an 'indicator of cultural distinctiveness' (ibid., 68), and it began with the idea that people of Indian and Eskimo ancestry could not be considered as an ethnic group:

One reason that we cannot consider the people of Indian and Eskimo ancestry as an ethnic group equivalent, say, to the French-Canadian, English-Canadian, Ukrainian-Canadian, and the like, is that there is no one language which serves as a symbol of distinctive identity at the national level. Students of language classify Indian languages into linguistic groups or stocks ... For Canada, such a classification yields ten Indian and one Eskimo language groups or stocks. (Vallee, 1966, 68)

This statement echoes Renan's model of linguistic racism, which conflated ethnic groups with language groups or stocks. There was an inherent contradiction here in using language to signify ethnicity since, if the distinction was between language 'stocks' or families, then languages such as French and Italian would in fact belong to the same language group (Romance) – and, as such, the French and the Italian groups could not be considered separate ethnic groups. The report made this distinction based on language stocks because it was advancing an argument that, owing to the range of Indigenous language groups, there could be no mutual intelligibility across these groups and hence the Indians or the Eskimos could not be considered as discrete ethnic groups (Vallee, 1966, 69). This analysis not only saw the linguistic diversity of the Eskimo and the Indian communities as a barrier to their unity as an ethnic group, but it also reinforced the dominance of English and French, since they were deemed the lingua francas for these communities. Although the report conceded that 'the chief aim of the census language question was to discover which of the official languages – that is English or French – the people of Canada speak,' it still drew upon census data to come to its conclusion that only about 19 per cent of Indigenous peoples spoke neither English or French and thus had an Indigenous first language, whereas 'the great majority of Indians in Canada speak English' (ibid., 71). In the rest of the report, Indigenous language diversity was identified as a problem of language maintenance, education, and interaction with government services. The research report's position on Indigenous languages was one where the linguistic diversity of Indigenous languages was a problem, and it reinforced the primacy of the majority languages as a way to circumvent the problems of this language diversity.

Not only did the inquiry commission a research report on Indigenous groups, its members also went on an Arctic tour to meet with the Eskimos. Varjassy prepared a background report entitled 'The Canadian Eskimos' to provide Information on the Canadian Arctic for a proposed visit of the Commissioners (Varjassy, 1964a). This report was highly anthropological in its tone and content. Beginning with a section on pre-European contact, it also included material on the 'Eskimo Language,' but this was mainly a description of structural linguistic features and again anthropological in tone. Education accounted for an extensive portion of the report, and here again the issue of language arose:

> The language of instruction used has been English because in the areas concerned, English has been the main language outside Eskimo ... It has been federal policy that education in the Eskimo language is not feasible as there are very few qualified teachers who can speak Eskimo. In any event, it is a language that would not help in providing for employment or leading, ultimately, to higher education since it has virtually no written literature and is not readily adaptable to modern concepts or activities. (It has, for instance, no numbers beyond twenty). The Department of Northern Affairs, however, has a great interest in the Eskimo language for its cultural values and has fostered the development of new orthography which will in time serve to render the Eskimo language of greater use and support to the Eskimo people. (Varjassy, 1964a, 16)

The division between the cultural value of a language – as something pre-modern that must be preserved – and the utilitarian function of language – as something that must be modern, that is, Western and written – is posited in order to create the justification for English-language instruction. This anthropological emphasis in the report, and the colonial lens through which the report viewed the language and educational issues of the Inuit people, speak to the perspective through which Indigenous issues were informed and considered by the commission.

While the public hearings were underway, Indigenous issues were making headlines in the mainstream media. On 22 November 1965, towards the end of the commission's hearings, the Indian-White Committee of Kenora organized a 400-member march to the town council to present a brief detailing the demands of the local and neighbouring Indigenous communities. Among other issues, the brief described the poverty and job discrimination suffered by Indians, the wage inequities, the lack of access to emergency medical care, and the need to extend the trapping season. This incident garnered a lot of media attention and also prompted a series of articles on Indigenous issues in various newspapers, as well as editorials and commentaries.

Many of these articles drew parallels between the plight of Canadian Indigenous peoples and that of black Americans in the U.S. South. For example, an editorial in the Toronto *Daily Star* declared that 'to compare the plight and resentments of our Indians to the problems of

Negroes in Mississippi and Harlem is not far-fetched' ('The Shame of Our "Mississippi" Indians,' 1965, n.p.). Media interest in Indigenous issues during the public hearings resulted in these issues being linked to the inquiry, which, for its part, displayed considerable interest in them as well (Woodbridge, Morrow, and Hepner, 1965). The media glare on Indigenous issues, and the ensuing public demand for including Indigenous issues in the inquiry, also meant that the commission would have to carefully consider how it would deal with Indigenous issues in the final report, if at all.

In summary, multiculturalism also surfaced in relation to Indigenous issues, and, given some of the briefs that Indigenous groups presented and the claims they made during the public hearings, the question of 'Indians and Eskimos' obviously had to be settled before the final reports could be written. Indeed, the prominence of Indigenous issues in the media and public demand during the public hearings meant that the commission could not ignore Indigenous concerns. Indigenous communities also insinuated themselves into the inquiry by submitting briefs during the course of the public hearings – briefs that revealed certain patterns of resistance to the hierarchy presented in the commission's terms of reference. Also, Indigenous groups stressed the universality of Aboriginal Sign Language to refute arguments about the fragmentation of Indigenous languages, and they promoted a model of multiculturalism organized around the inclusion of the 'multi-cultures' of Indigenous groups, short-circuiting many of the claims made by other ethnic groups and marking Indigenous peoples as distinct from immigrant communities. Indigenous claims for cultural preservation were emphasized as not just privileges but concrete treaty rights.

The idea that bilingualism and biculturalism were irrelevant for Indigenous groups was argued not just by Indigenous communities but also by the commission. However, for the commission, this irrelevance grew out of pathologies located in Indigenous peoples themselves – that is, the commission felt that 'Indians and Eskimos' were rooted in a pre-modern and pre-literate past which was incompatible with modern Canadian life and community. In addition, linguistic fragmentation was perceived to undermine any group claims. The claims advanced by Indigenous groups, however, challenged the founding-races model of the terms of reference directly; therefore, in order for the commission to maintain the social cohesion of the bicultural and bilingual white-settler nation, its rationale for excluding

Indigenous groups from its consideration had to be based on their pathology and exceptionality.

Part III – The Research Program of the Inquiry

Just as the commission had mobilized research resources on Indigenous groups, ultimately developing rationales for excluding Indians and Eskimos from the inquiry, research resources were also extended to other topics in the inquiry as had been promised right from the start of the commission. In the *Preliminary Report*, the commissioners had stated that a 'very large field of research' would be required in order to carry out the project of the inquiry and inform the writing of the final reports (Canada, *Preliminary Report*, 1965b, 22). However, the duration and expansion of the research program generated considerable political and public controversy. The research program was a crucial part of the inquiry because it provided the commissioners with the authority to contest or legitimate findings from the public hearings and submissions – an authority that would become very useful in the production of the final reports. This authority emerged from the arm's-length relationship between the commissioners and the experts who provided the required information, since the expertise of the researchers bestowed a scientific and objective 'truth' on their material and analysis. In this way, the experts furnished the commissioners with the authority to address any submissions or findings which challenged their formulation of a bilingual and bicultural white-settler nation.

The research phase expanded during the public hearings and continued on until the final reports were being produced, with many of the research reports being published in their own right. There were almost 150 official research reports in total as well as a multitude of confidential reports, letters, and summaries. The magnitude of the inquiry's research component was well known at the time because of controversy over the costs that this work involved – controversy that was widely covered in the media. For example, Don McGillivray, a reporter for Southam News Service, wrote an article entitled 'Most Controversial Inquiry in History' in which he stated: 'One of the basic criticisms the commission must meet is that it has cost too much, in time and money . . . One of the most time and money consuming aspects has been the research program which has grown far beyond the original plans' (McGillivray, 1966b, n.p.). The issue of the inquiry's costs was also brought up often in the House of Commons, with perspectives on the matter varying from party to party. During budget deliberations on 21 April 1966, Jean Marchand, then minister of Citizenship and Immigration, responded to the media coverage of the cost of the royal commission to date: 'It was said that it was the most expensive commission in the history of confederation ... it is possible that this figure will reach between $4 and $7 million ... There is no need to be scandalized by such heavy expenditure' (Canada, *House of Commons Debates*, 1966a, 4121). Marchand went on to assure the House that most of the funds – between 75 and 90 per cent – were allotted for research or the secretariat. He further assured that the salaries paid to the commissioners represented no more than 5 per cent of the funds allowed to the commission for its work. As an ex-member of the commission himself, Marchand was best positioned to defend its expenditures; he argued that it was polarization across the different regions of the country and the issues raised by the terms of reference which required the commission to embark on such a vast research program in order to seek out the 'deep-rooted causes of uneasiness in Canada' and offer solutions 'acceptable to Canada as a whole' (ibid., 4123).

In response, E. Nasserden, a member of the Conservative opposition, underlined the division between the opposition and the government regarding the inquiry:

What he [Jean Marchand] has said was that this has been one of the most costly commissions in the history of Canada. He has tried to justify the action of the government, action taken in the face of opposition put forward during the period when this matter was first under consideration. I say to you, sir, that this commission has ignored the hopes and aspirations of more than one-third of the population of Canada, those of ethnic origin other than French or English, the two founding races of Canada. We on the opposition side of the House of Commons believe that rather than emphasize the differences that exist between Canadians in one part of this country and those in another part, the primary objective of a government that is striving for unity should be to bring Canadians together on those things that they have in common. We believe that the place to do that is at the conference table with positive suggestions rather than negative ones and questioning of the differences that exist between one part of the our nation and the other. (Canada, *House of Commons Debates*, 1966a, 4123–4)

Significantly, although Nasserden believed that the other ethnic groups had been ignored by the commission, his solution was not their inclusion; rather, he suggested a common pan-Canadian identity in place of the inquiry's 'negative' emphasis on the differences between Canadians. By implication, then, the commission's various research projects also served to emphasize these 'differences.' And so the battle lines were drawn. For the Liberals, the commission's research held the promise of revealing and solving the problems of unity, while for the opposition this research merely served to reinforce the perceived differences between Canadians and thereby exacerbate the country's disunity. These arguments, picked up in the media, were echoed by many members of the public.

Public knowledge of the breadth of the commission's research program also served to bestow a scientific legitimacy on the inquiry, since the accumulation of research allowed it to speak with authority – particularly when it agreed or disagreed with positions taken in briefs presented during the public hearings. Furthermore, this scientific legitimacy emanated from the fact that it was not the commissioners but 'experts' who carried out the research. Nikolas Rose and Peter Miller note: 'The complex of actors, powers, institutions and bodies of knowledge that comprise expertise have come to play a crucial role in establishing the possibility and legitimacy of government. Experts hold out the hope that problems of regulation can remove themselves from the disputed terrain of politics and relocate onto the tranquil yet seductive terrain of truth' (Rose and Miller, 1992, 188). In the case of the B and B Commission, the experts were either civil servants or contracted researchers, and specialist academic and political opinion was also sought. Thus, by having experts produce the research, a distance between the commissioners and the research was introduced, conferring legitimacy on the inquiry's findings. In the inquiry, the disputed terrain of politics was the complex realm of the hearings, whereas the 'truth' emerged out of the scientific accumulation of facts by the experts. The distance of experts from the 'disputed terrain of politics' authorized them to approve and reify the truth or knowledge – in this case, the knowledge about people, languages, and other related research topics.

In addition to the research areas already discussed, one of the commission's major undertakings was the study of other countries with more than one official or national language, such as Switzerland and Belgium. South Africa was another multilingual country that especially interested the commission. A report on the introduction of Afrikaans into the English-language-dominated South African public service, entitled 'Afrikaans in the Public Service,' was translated by the Canadian Secretary of State Translation Bureau and circulated to all the research supervisors. The report gave an overview of the challenges and successes of introducing Afrikaans into a predominantly English-language-based public service after the 1925 recognition of Afrikaans as 'an official language of the Union' (Marais, 1965, 1).

In addition to this translated report, Professor W.H.O. Schmidt, head of the Department of Educational Psychology at the University of Natal, Pietermaritzburg, South Africa, submitted a five-page document and was invited to spend a few days in Ottawa with the commission. Schmidt offered a comprehensive comparison between the bicultural and bilingualism problems in Canada and those of South Africa, based on his observations and conversations with sundry Canadians during his travels through the country. He outlined what he saw as the main challenges involved in introducing bilingualism and biculturalism in Canada, as well as the necessity of instituting countrywide English-French bilingualism in order for the French-Canadian population to maintain its cultural viability – for this, he suggested a 'radical change in the legislation' which would guarantee French parents the right to the education of their children in their mother tongue in all provinces (Schmidt, 1965). Schmidt went on to discuss the problems of 'other minorities,' too:

> In my discussions with Canadians I have heard it said again and again that the English-French relations are complicated by the fact that any language rights relating to the education of children which are granted to the French inhabitants of predominantly English provinces would have to be granted to the 'other minorities' as well; if this were done, the unity of the nation would be endangered (I heard the term 'balkanization' being used). (Ibid., 4)

This statement leaves no doubt that the commission was mobilizing expert opinions which bolstered the link between linguistic rights for other minority groups and the familiar spectre of 'balkanization.'

In order to accentuate his point, Schmidt compared the immigrant situation in Canada with that in the United States. 'The U.S.A., it can legitimately be said, would not have produced a unified American nation, if immigrants had all been granted the right to instruction through the medium of the mother tongue; it is the emphasis on a common language and a common American way of life that has made the U.S.A.

great' (Schmidt, 1965, 4). By highlighting his status as an 'observer from outside,' Schmidt emphasized the objective expertise that enabled him to compare immigrant situations in both countries and conclude that, if Canada was to be as great a country as the United States, it should also proscribe mother-tongue instruction for immigrants. Lest this be read as suggesting that such instruction should apply to French-Canadians as well, Schmidt was quick to point to the exceptionality of their case:

> The position historically and psychologically – of the French Canadians – seems to me very different from that of any of the immigrant groups. They are not 'another minority,' except in a strictly numerical sense. The immigrant who left Germany or Poland or Italy or the Ukraine, because he saw better opportunities in North America or because he wanted to escape from an intolerable situation, came in the full knowledge that he would be starting a new life and giving up his old way of life; he knew the price he would have to pay, and he was prepared to do so. To the French Canadians, as far as I know, this does not apply: he [sic] entered into a partnership. (Schmidt, 1965, 5)

Thus, the French were different from the 'other minorities' by virtue of their history and 'psychology.' Once again, the idea that immigrants chose to come, and that they did so fully informed about the nature of their new country, echoes earlier arguments against language and culture preservation rights for other ethnic groups made during the public hearings.

A different type of academic contribution to the commission was formed by the various reports on conferences. One such conference report that was included in the commission's research concerned the Lake Couchiching Conference of 1965, entitled 'Our Changing Canadian Community' (Bertrand and Burgis, 1965). In this report, issues that were seen as germane to the inquiry were highlighted and recorded. For example, a presentation, entitled 'Values in Conflict,' by Professor David Gauthier of the Department of Philosophy at the University of Toronto was summarized in great detail in the report. In his presentation, Gauthier discussed what he saw as the three main minority groups in Canada – 'the French Canadians, the ethnic minorities and the natives' (ibid., 5) – and asserted that one of these groups, the ethnic minorities, 'do not have an Indigenous life within the Canadian environment and in that respect are quite different from the French

Canadians' (ibid.). With respect to the Indigenous peoples, Gauthier was even more dismissive, arguing that their efforts at cultural survival were futile:

> For the native Canadian, treaties and reserves were bad mistakes. A way of life has been artificially preserved which has no real relationship to our modern community. Therefore the Indian cannot satisfy his wants in the Canadian situation and therefore is frustrated. We are only subsidizing his frustrations or his alienations or ennuyance because no other form of satisfaction is opened to the Indians. He is presently in a state of 'ennuyance' or in a state of not having any values, the solution here is one of assimilation. (Bertrand and Burgis, 1965, 6)

In this summary of the presentation, expert terminology ('ennuyance') was mobilized in order to explain Gauthier's assimilative agenda for Indigenous communities, foreshadowing the arguments of the government's White Paper on Indian policy.

The commissioners also eagerly sought academic expertise from linguists. A memorandum from commission co-secretary Neil M. Morrison to the commissioners outlined the possibilities of a visit by professors Einaar Haugen of Harvard University, Joshua Fishman of Yeshiva University, and Werner F. Leopold of Nebraska University – at the time, these professors were all recognized as specialists in the area of bilingualism and linguistics, and they are now regarded as founding members of the field of study known as Language Policy and Planning. Since these three distinguished academics were already coming to Canada as part of the planning committee for an international linguistics conference, they were also invited to meet with the commissioners and research staff (Morrison, 1966). The importance of expert opinion in the area of bilingualism was emphasized particularly by Professor and Commissioner Rudnyckyj, who was the sole commissioner with any expertise in languages and linguistics. In a memorandum to his fellow commissioners and inquiry staff, which contained excerpts of a speech he had given at the University of North Dakota on the subject of 'Formulas in Bilingualism and Biculturalism,' Rudnyckyj extensively cited the work of these three linguists (Rudnyckyj, 1965). For example, he referred to Haugen's idea that one's degree of 'bilinguality' does not necessarily correlate to one's degree of biculturalism: 'A bilingual speaker of English and Norwegian in America is not necessarily bicultural' (ibid., 6).

Haugen, according to Rudnyckyj, explained further that although there may be high correlation between the lexical content of language and culture, the syntactical, phonological, and morphological aspects of language did not necessarily reflect culture directly (Rudnyckyj, 1965, 6). Thus, 'some of the problems raised in connection with bilingualism will prove to be almost entirely problems of biculturalism, involving attitudes to the people who speak the languages rather than the language themselves' (ibid., 7). In this way, Rudnyckyj drew on linguistic expertise in order to underline the idea that bilingualism did not necessarily coincide with biculturalism, even if the two were often confused, and that this confusion required attention to social issues broader than just linguistics: 'Linguists will find it helpful here to create liaison areas between themselves and the social sciences' (ibid., 6). The importance of distinguishing between bilingualism and biculturalism, and the possibility of uncoupling one from the other, was a central element in the evolution of the commission's notion of 'multiculturalism within a bilingual framework.' In his separate statement for *Book I* of the final report, Rudnyckyj would address this theme as he elaborated his particular vision of a language policy for Canada.

Another form of expertise, which the inquiry drew upon heavily, was political expertise. Private meetings with high-ranking government officials from various departments took place and confidential records of these meetings were included as part of the inquiry's research material. For instance, on 11 October 1965, a private meeting between representatives of the Department of Citizenship and Immigration – including the deputy minister, Claude Isbister; the assistant deputy minister, Charles A. Lussier; and the director of the Citizenship Branch, Jean Lagasse – and the co-chairmen of the commission, Laurendeau and Dunton, was organized by the commission co-secretary, Neil Morrison (Stinson, 1966). In a 'Summary of Discussion,' Lagasse discussed the department's policy regarding the integration of other ethnic groups, explaining that branch policy had been to facilitate the continuation of culture as long as people wished to preserve it. Integration, to his mind, was actually language assimilation, and did *not* mean loss of culture; 'Culture outlasts language,' he stated. He elaborated that it was possible to think of oneself as being a Cree even if one had lost the ability to speak Cree. Therefore, the branch supported the learning of English by immigrants, but opposed 'engineering the loss of immigrant cultures' (ibid., 2). Based on this logic, the loss of languages of origin and the concomitant support for dominant languages could still be congruent with integration as long as there was no 'engineering the loss of immigrant culture,' whatever that meant in concrete terms. The department pro-vided support for English-language training for immigrants as a result of provincial requests in 1954, which involved the federal government paying 100 per cent of the costs of textbooks and 50 per cent of teach-ers' salaries, except in British Colombia and Quebec where there were no such agreements (ibid., 3). This support was seen as commensurate with the goals of immigrant integration, or 'language assimilation.'

The integration of immigrants was an ongoing concern of the depart-ment. Deputy Minister Isbister observed that, under present policies, there were highly concentrated groups developing in certain centres (for example, Italians in Toronto), causing him to wonder if integration was operating rapidly enough. As well, he shared his fears that racial and cultural differences were the source of violence and serious antago-nisms in many parts of the world where concentrated groups lived side by side; therefore, in the light of rapid urban growth in Canada, the question was if new or different policies were needed as immigration changed the country's character (Stinson, 1966, 2).

Isbister's anxieties about the changing character of the white-settler society as a result of the growing number of urban immigrants – and the challenges this posed for integration – foreshadowed the linkages the commission would make in its final reports between other ethnic groups and the ameliorative possibilities of the integration of 'racial and cultural differences.' The importance of integration with respect to issues of immigration was reinforced in another summary document produced by commission researchers that described, in detail, the re-sponsibilities and organization of the Department of Citizenship and Immigration:

> Within the Department of Citizenship and Immigration, the Immigration Branch, the Indian Affairs Branch and the Citizenship Registration Branch are responsible for the administration of the Immigration Act, the Indian Act, and the Canadian Citizenship Act, respectively ... It will be noted, then, that two major areas of concern for the Branch are immigrants and Indians. The main objective is to encourage and assist the effective integra-tion of these groups into the Canadian and the urban community respec-tively. (Canadian Citizenship Branch, 1964, 2)

Indigenous and immigrant groups were therefore linked through the federal government's concern over the 'effective integration' of both groups, echoing Isbister's worries about 'racial and cultural differences' – be they immigrant or Indigenous differences.

Around this time, Quebec was in the process of developing its own immigration policy and the commission researchers obtained a short summary of the announcement of this initiative. In a commission-produced research document summarizing issues relevant to the inquiry, an overview of the goals of Quebec's immigration service noted that the immigration advisor to Pierre Laporte, at the time Quebec's cultural affairs minister, had suggested studying 'means of integrating new Canadians into the French-speaking environment of Quebec' (Canada, Quebec Immigration, n.d.). The Lesage government announced the creation of a Quebec Immigration Service on 10 February 1965. Yves Gabias, the provincial secretary in the former Union Nationale government, stated that the purpose of this service would be to 'assist the integration of immigrants into Quebec's French-speaking community' (Hawkins, 1988, 214). In both these announcements, the integration of immigrants was seen as a primary component of the new immigration policy. Although in the case of Quebec the intended integration was into the 'French-speaking community' instead of into an English-speaking milieu, the idea that integration required learning a dominant language – and the lack of stated support for the preservation of languages of origin – demonstrated a similar 'language assimilation' model of integration in both Canadian and Quebec immigration strategies.

Concluding Summary

During the course of the public hearings, multiculturalism acquired a salience, albeit across a range of meanings, in relation to other ethnic groups, while language emerged as the key issue around which these groups' claims for inclusion were assessed. Though the commissioners engaged with these various interpretations and meanings of multiculturalism and language as they prepared to write their final reports, the authority to contest or reinforce these interpretations and meanings could only be conferred though the research program of the inquiry.

The continuation and expansion of the research program generated considerable political and public controversy. The research program was a crucial part of the inquiry because it provided the commissioners with the authority to contest or legitimate findings from the public hearings and submissions, an authority that would become very useful in the production of the final reports. This authority emerged from the arm's-length relationship between the commissioners and the experts who provided the required information, since the expertise of the researchers bestowed a scientific and objective 'truth' on their material and analysis. In this way, the experts furnished the commissioners with the authority to address any submissions or findings which challenged their formulation of a bilingual and bicultural white-settler nation.

Expert knowledge was mobilized to confirm the argument that immigrants 'chose,' fully informed, to come to Canada and in so doing forfeited all rights to language and cultural preservation. Over the course of the inquiry, this discourse about immigrants became a rationale for understanding – and eventually regulating – immigrant linguistic and cultural rights. Expert academic knowledge was also used to confirm the fossilization of Indigenous groups in an anti-modern past of treaty rights and reserves in order to justify the logic of assimilation. In this way, language and identity were elided through a selective historical lens in order to provide a rationale for the eventual exclusion of Indigenous groups from the inquiry and to erase the claims for substantive recognition of multilingual rights from other ethnic groups. Highly sought-after academic opinions from linguists were also mobilized in order to develop a rationale for distinguishing between bilingualism and biculturalism; this was an important element in the evolution of the idea of multiculturalism within a bilingual framework. Finally, political expertise introduced the theme of integration, which came to be defined as linguistic assimilation; a way to ameliorate the 'problem' of racial and cultural differences – both Indigenous and immigrant – at the federal and provincial levels. Again, this particular understanding of integration would become prominent in relation to other ethnic groups in the commission's final report, and would eventually dominate policy discourse.

Therefore, the patterns of resistance to the hierarchy of founding races that first became apparent in the preliminary hearings were built upon during the public hearings, leading to the emergence of an unspecified notion of multiculturalism and language as the terrain on which Indigenous and other ethnic groups could negotiate claims for inclusion. This was part of the shift from race and ethnicity to language and culture that the commission would advance, in its final report, as the basis for building a new bilingual and bicultural white-settler nation. However, as the next chapter will show, this shift to language and culture in no way refuted the racialized hierarchy of the terms of reference; rather, racial differentiation was shifted onto the terrain of language and culture. As the investigative phase of the inquiry drew to a close, these developments laid the groundwork for the final phase of the commission – the persuasive phase – where the publication of the final report would usher in policies and legislation aimed at creating a new formulation of the Canadian nation.

5   Book I: The Official Languages

This chapter addresses two important developments that made language and culture central to the evolution of a national policy of multiculturalism within a bilingual framework. First, the contradictory mechanism by which language and culture operated to reinscribe the disavowed racial and ethnic hierarchies of the terms of reference are traced through the introductory and paradigmatic 'blue pages' of *Book I* of the final report. This contradiction became visible in the disjunctures and discontinuities that were revealed as bilingualism and biculturalism were defined and the terms anglophone and francophone made their first appearance. The specific relation between language and culture that emerged in the blue pages suggested that the openness of language was foreclosed by a 'bicultural' notion of culture, which reinstalled the original, racialized hierarchies between founding races and other ethnic groups.

Second, this chapter discusses how the establishment of equal relations between the English and French groups required the Other; that is, Indigenous groups and other ethnic groups – whose claims were erased and marginalized, respectively, by the royal commission – were necessary for the commission to organize the new bilingual and bicultural white-settler nation. This is illustrated in the way the commission treated census data to make the case for a particular model of English-French bilingualism. As well, the white-settler foundations of this new *bi*-nation were entrenched when some of the 'guiding principles' in the development of Canadian bilingualism were adopted from South Africa's example of erasing Indigenous languages through the imposition of a hegemony of colonial languages. The recommendations suggested in *Book I* of the final report quickly gave rise, in the interests of national unity, to the Official Languages Act, but anxieties regarding social cohesion and the Other were also a driving force in the emergence of this legislation. Finally, Commissioner J.B. Rudnyckyj's thwarted attempt at the end of *Book I* to develop a racialized classificatory system to reconfigure the inclusion of the third force into the white-settler category underscored the entrenched limits of the founding-races hierarchy and the vexed place of the Other, despite the shift to language and culture as the new terrain for organizing inclusion.

Tabling *Book I*

The publication of *Book I* of the final report, entitled *The Official Languages*, was a watershed moment for the commission. It was the culmination of close to four years of work and heralded the publication of further volumes. The report textually reified all the research and hearing submissions, legitimizing some facts against others in order to make a series of recommendations which would ultimately give rise to state policy – in the case of *Book I*, the Official Languages Act. This attempt to systematize and explain the principles underlying the proposed policy required both a careful definition of key words in the terms of reference and a shrewd treatment of the inquiry's findings. Not only would the Official Languages Act emerge out of this report, but it would also set the terms within which other ethnic groups and their claims could be considered.

The publication of *Book I* also meant that the inquiry had once again entered a persuasive phase. Responses to *Book I* can be tracked in the *House of Commons Debates*, first as the report was tabled on 5 December 1967 and then again as Bill C-120, regarding the official languages of Canada, was discussed on 17 October 1968. There was also a substantive response from the Ukrainian community, which points out the complexities in how other ethnic groups took up the report's recommendations.

Towards the end of his diary, written during the commission years of 1964 to 1967, Laurendeau describes the official handing over of *Book I* to Prime Minister Pearson on 29 November 1967 as 'a rapid and almost furtive ceremony' (Smart, 1991, 169). Pearson unwrapped and examined the English version of the report and congratulated the cochairmen of the commission, but, as Laurendeau stated, 'except when I speak, and that is rare, Pearson addresses all his remarks to Dunton; I think he feels ill at ease with me, I am not of his race' (ibid., 69). Given the content of the report and the fact that Laurendeau was the main author of the blue pages (Jenson, 1994), his use of the word 'race' to distinguish between him and Pearson seems curiously out of place.

Almost a week later, on 5 December 1967, Pearson tabled *Book I* in the House of Commons. Praising the report, Pearson described its findings and recommendations as 'solutions, based on unity in diversity, of equal partnership' (Canada, *House of Commons Debates*, 1967, 5066). As other members of Parliament discussed the report, the broad themes of the terms of reference were echoed, primarily with the invocation of equality between the two founding races; for example, T.C. Douglas, leader of the New Democratic Party, stated, 'We will apply ourselves to the task of strengthening confederation and at the same time bringing about happy and friendly relations between the two great founding races that make up Canada' (ibid., 5068).

The sentiment of 'unity in diversity' was repeated, although turned around and applied to other ethnic groups, by the Social Credit leader, Réal Caouette: 'Mr. Speaker, this is not putting aside those who speak a language other than French and English, specifically the Ukrainians, the Poles, the Italians, the Germans, who are in Canada in large numbers ... We consider them as true and good Canadians and ... They also have the advantage of keeping their own culture, whether it is German, Italian, French, Yugoslavian, it is immaterial. "Diversity in unity"' (Canada, *House of Commons Debates*, 1967, 5069). Caouette's framing that being able to retain one's original culture was an 'advantage' suggested that this was a generous allowance being extended to other ethnic groups by some unspecified central group. His statement also rested on the assumption that these other ethnic groups could not be bilingual in both English and French, a fact that, combined with their speaking another language, highlighted their peripheral placement in the linguistic hierarchy. However, Caouette's definition of other ethnic groups through language – understanding them as 'those who speak a language other than English or French' – and his emphasis on the retention of 'their own culture' both echoed the report's foregrounding of language and culture instead of 'race' and 'ethnicity.'

The 'Blue Pages'

Book I stands apart from the rest of the B and B Commission's volumes not only because it was the first, but also because it contained what are now known as 'the famous blue pages' (Smart, 1991, 4). These blue pages, written by Laurendeau and forming a General Introduction, emerged out of the commission's desire to clarify the terms of reference before embarking on the full report (McRoberts, 1997, 118). Given the strong objections that were mounted and maintained throughout the investigative phase of the inquiry to key terms in the terms of reference – chief among these were the usage of the word 'race' and the implied hierarchy between race and ethnicity – the commissioners had to clarify these terms before they could even begin to report on their findings.

Although they waited until the publication of the report to issue such clarifications, their concerns about the meanings of terms dated back to the start of the inquiry. A confidential commission memo dated 25 August 1964 notes that the first meeting of the commission took place on 4 and 5 September 1963. However, it would take several months of such meetings to discuss the implications of the terms of reference, indicating the complexity of these terms right from the start of the commission ('Confidential,' 1964). The memo then outlines the array of public concerns about the terms of reference that emerged during the preliminary hearings: 'The words "two founding races" in the English version of the terms of reference caused concern in some quarters.' However, the commission insisted that, as far as it was concerned, the word 'races' had not the connotation often given to it in recent years; rather, they were concerned with the partnership between English- and French-speaking Canadians, but would also give special attention to the cultural interests and contributions of people of other origins (ibid., 41). This part of the memo recapitulates some of the most significant objections expressed by other ethnic groups during the preliminary hearings, including the biological connotations that the word race invoked as well as the hierarchy that was established by the particular use of that word in the terms of reference.

These concerns were acknowledged – as the commissioners probably felt they had to be, given the extensive attention focused on the term race – by Co-chairman Dunton at the close of the preliminary hearings, when, as noted in chapter 3, he indicated that certainty about definitions and terms and meanings in the order-in-council would likely not be reached until the commission turned to the preparation of its final report (Canada, *Preliminary Hearing*, 1963, 547). True to his word, it would be another three-and-a-half years before concerns about the commission's terminology were addressed in the opening sentence of the blue pages. In fact, the entire blue-pages section is devoted to 'The Key Words of the Terms of Reference.'

Explaining the delay in providing definitions for the terms of reference, the report opened with a nod to Dunton's remarks at the closing of the preliminary hearings: 'At such times our answer was that these definitions "often imply the adoption of a point of view of lengthy research on related topics" [cited from the *Preliminary Report*] which had yet to be undertaken. Moreover ... we wished to avoid giving the appearance of imposing a definition; furthermore we had no wish to start lengthy discussions on meanings of words rather than on the realities behind them' (Canada, *Book I*, 1967, xxi). The commissioners, now that they were about to unveil their findings, were finally prepared to end their silence on the issue of terminology and clarify the meanings they would use for significant terms:

> After a long period of listening, we believe it is now necessary to indicate the meaning we shall give in particular to the words 'bilingualism' and 'biculturalism,' and to the expression 'an equal partnership between two founding races.' Since these terms are understood in different ways it is important at the outset to be clear about which meaning or meanings we shall use. Not that other usages are incorrect; we simply wish to advise the reader of those we have adopted for our purposes ... The words 'bilingualism' and 'biculturalism' are given prominence, but there are other terms of equal importance, especially the terms 'race' (in the French text 'peuple'), 'ethnic group,' and 'the contribution made by the other ethnic groups to the cultural enrichment of Canada.' (Canada, *Book I*, 1967, xxi–xxii)

Having identified the key terms to be discussed, the authors were also careful to recognize the possibility of multiple interpretations of these terms; however, they clarified that these were to be the commission's set definitions, no matter what others may exist, and would be the ones that the commission would be using from now on. A more important implication was that the commission's definitions would henceforth become paradigmatic for all discussions of these matters at the federal level.

'Race' and 'People'

Arriving at definitions for these key words was not an easy matter for the commission, as the archival records attest. Two of the first words that the blue pages set out to define were 'race' and 'people.' Efforts to define race can be traced back to a memo submitted in October 1963 by Michael Oliver, director of research, to the members of the commission. The memo was in response to a letter sent by Commissioner Paul

Lacoste to Oliver, 'outlining the Commissioners' desire for a discussion of definitions' (Oliver, 1963, 1). Although there was an extensive discussion in this long memo about words such as 'culture,' 'nation,' and 'nationality,' the remarks on 'race' and 'people' were substantially shorter. For 'people,' Oliver just listed a paragraph of definitions from the *Oxford English Dictionary (OED)*. In the next section, Oliver began by citing scientific studies on race and, after acknowledging the various meanings of the word, began: 'In everyday language the term "race" has a number of different meanings. It is applied to groups of people, animals, plants, and things where the numbers of the groups have some characteristics in common' (ibid., 13–14). Following a few *OED* definitions, he stated: 'It may be said that to the scientist the term race ... is essentially a biological concept and implies that the physical characteristics which the members of the group have in common are genetically determined. It completely excludes from consideration any characteristics which are entirely the result of external environmental influences and not the consequence of heredity' (ibid., 14). Another scientific perspective on race that Oliver drew upon came from anthropology: 'An exhaustive treatise on physical anthropology which appeared in 1962 divides the species into "five basically geographical groups: The Caucasoid, Mongoloid, Australoid, Congoid, and Capoid" [Coon, 1962, 3] ... There is a debate about this and other classifications which have been proposed, but no modern physical anthropologist would use "race" as a synonym for either "nation" or "culture"' (ibid., 14).

In all the above definitions of race, the biological and genetic model was dominant; however, Oliver also alluded to race as a synonym for nation, referring to Lord Durham's famous phrase: 'Two nations warring in the bosom of a single state ... a struggle, not of principles but of races' [Lucas, 1970, 16]. He ended his discussion on race by noting the term's current popularity with politicians: 'It is perhaps interesting that members of the federal cabinet in Canada have recently taken to using the term "race" to describe the French and English in this country' (Oliver, 1963, 14). In sum, Oliver did not offer a single prescriptive definition of race; rather, he outlined an array of definitions for the commissioners' consideration.

In the blue pages of *Book I*, definitions for 'race' and 'people' were discussed in tandem. Although the term 'people' was not used consistently in the English version of the terms of reference, in the French version it was; there, 'les deux peuples qui ont fondé la Confédération' took the place of 'two founding races' (Canada, *Book I*, 1967, xxii). This may have been the rationale behind discussing the definitions of both people and race together in the blue pages, but in any event, the discussion was short – indeed, it was the shortest discussion of any of the key terms – consisting of only two paragraphs. The authors began by admitting that 'this wording, particularly the use in the English text of the word "race," has been a source of misunderstanding' (ibid.). Referring to the submissions made by groups during the preliminary and public hearings, the misunderstanding was outlined as: 'Should it be taken to mean that two "races" or two "peoples" will receive special treatment at the expense of the "other ethnic groups"?' The authors were clear on this point: in no way did they understand the terms of reference to indicate a 'special birthright of the two founding peoples ... perpetuating itself from father to son,' or any suggestion of a 'lower order of other ethnic groups, forever excluded from spheres of influence' (ibid.). Rather, the report explained, 'in our view, the reference to the two "founding races" or "peoples who founded Confederation" was an allusion to the undisputed role played by Canadians of French and British origin in 1867, and long before Confederation' (ibid., xxii). More important was the further explanation that 'the word "race" is used in an older meaning as referring to a national group, and carries no biological significance' (ibid.). The report found additional proof of this in the fact that, in the subsequent paragraphs of the terms of reference, there was 'no mention of race, people, or ethnic group'; rather, it focused on just the 'bicultural character' of the country and the issues of teaching English and French (ibid.).

This usage of race hearkened back to Oliver's memorandum, which noted Durham's use of race as a synonym for nation. The authors of the report were in a difficult position here; they had at all costs to divorce the notion of race from any biological significance, not only because the idea of biological races had become anathema in the aftermath of the Second World War, but also because the division of the French and English people into two races would not survive scrutiny under any scientific definitions of race. However, by invoking the older meaning of race as nation, the commissioners conceptualized the country as being composed of two nations – an idea that had difficulties of its own. As Oliver stated at the end of his eleven-page discussion on the various meanings of nation: 'Evidence that new usages are being essayed come also from the *Montreal Star* which, it its editorial columns on the 5th September 1963, stated: "Bi-national, therefore, we must be, and ungrudgingly recognizing it too. But let there be recognition of the fact that there will be trouble in selling this bill of goods across the country as a whole"' (Oliver, 1963, 13). The *Star*'s editors were prescient in their anticipation of the anxiety about national unity that the concept of two nations would provoke, particularly in anglophone Canada.

Perhaps foreseeing this, Oliver devoted the bulk of his memorandum to a review of the evolution and current definitions of the words 'nation' and 'nationality.' His extensive discussion covered the range of meanings of these words, from nation as race, to groups of people linked through a common language, to current thinking on the word nation from the New Democratic Party (NDP). As Oliver stated, 'the New Democratic Party's use of the word "nation" has, indeed, been central to much of the discussion of the term in English Canada,' and accordingly, he felt, its definition deserved special consideration (ibid., 12). At their 1963 convention, the NDP had agreed on this statement about the concept of nation in Canada, which was cited by Oliver: 'By the English Canadian nation we mean all Canadian citizens whose mother tongue or adopted language in Canada is English. By French Canadian nation we mean all Canadian citizens whose mother tongue or adopted language in Canada is French' (ibid.). Oliver commented that the NDP's emphasis on a linguistic criterion for identifying membership in a nation was probably unique in that it intended to exclude not only a political, but also an ethnic basis for definition and was based on the assumption by the NDP that – in the Canadian context, at least – 'language was the chief vehicle of the culture' for the two major national groups (ibid.).

Although Oliver delivered his extensive research on the term 'nation' to the commissioners, there was no substantive discussion on the words nation or nationality in the blue pages. However, the NDP's idea that 'language is the chief vehicle of culture' retained its importance for the commission, and the final paragraph in the blue pages' section on the terms 'race' and 'people' concluded: 'Consequently, we feel that language and culture are truly central concepts in the terms of reference.' For this reason, we shall give them more emphasis than the notions "race," "people," or even "ethnic groups"' (Canada, *Book I*, 1967, xxii). Therefore, at this point in the blue pages, language and culture had been catapulted into prominence over race, people, and ethnicity, even before a discussion of the key term 'ethnic group' has taken place. This quick and early dismissal of the term 'race' was driven not just by the fact that its meaning was hard to pin down, but also by larger contextual factors, including the word's increasingly poor reputation – as was underlined by the consistent condemnation of it during the hearings.

'Ethnic Groups'

The commission, aware of the strong objections mounted against the key terms of 'race' and 'other ethnic groups,' had to address these two terms directly in its definitions of terminology. At this point in the blue pages, race – with its outmoded biological connotations – had been redefined as really a question of language and culture. However, the term 'other ethnic groups' posed its own challenges and therefore required a different strategy. Understanding that the objections to the phrase 'other ethnic groups' lay mainly in it being 'other' to 'two founding races,' and having already jettisoned the term race, the commissioners stated that '"ethnic" seemed to be given a sense something like "foreigner" ... We object in the strongest terms to this practice' (Canada, *Book I*, 1967, xxiv). While conceding that 'ethnicity was a "natural" but often complex phenomenon,' the commission had decided that it was 'on the whole unrelated' to the inquiry's objectives (ibid., xxv). In this way, 'ethnic groups,' which was a key term in the original terms of reference, was also discounted.

The report further rejected the term 'ethnic groups' by discussing its various definitions. It began by highlighting the biological and linguistic elements of ethnic 'origins': 'Thus, quite apart from heredity, much of the culture of one's forbears can be preserved even when one no longer speaks their language' (Canada, *Book I*, 1967, xxii). Expanding on a sociological definition of ethnic groups, the report stated: 'The important phenomenon is not ethnic origin itself, or even mother tongue, but the feeling of belonging to a group and the desire of the group to exist as such ... because the people in it and the people out of it ... feel and act as if it were a separate group' (xxiii). On the basis of this exclusionary definition of an ethnic group, the commissioners, echoing Oliver's caution against an ethnic definition of the nation, built their argument against using ethnicity as a basic principle for shaping society: 'This would tend to create closed-membership groups with newcomers condemned to remain outsiders; accidents of ancestry would be emphasized and rigid barriers would divide people. Legislation based on ethnic origin or ethnic group would be a direct denial of the principle that all men are equal before the law' (ibid.). The report explained how ethnicity would also be hard to track 'in a multi-ethnic country' where the frequency of intermarriage was increasing and the difficulties of measuring ethnic influence were considerable (ibid., xxiv). As a result of these intangible qualities of ethnicity, the report reprised its earlier conclusion, namely, that 'since it [the commission] must make recommendations based on easily discernable realities ... it must give much more importance to language than to ethnic origin' (ibid.).

Offering additional reflections on the issue of language, the report drew on census data to indicate that, although ethnic groups and mother tongues often coincided, a sizable number of non-British Canadians – amounting to 26 per cent of the population – identified English as their mother tongue. Even the French-speaking group, which 'has assimilated others to a much lesser extent,' also included people of non-French origin who spoke French as their mother tongue, representing about 3 per cent of the population. The implications were clear:

> In Canada, membership in linguistic group is a matter of personal choice, provided that the conditions and consequences are accepted. There is nothing at least in law, to bind Canadians to the prevailing language of their ethnic group. Since their choice is free, it would be grossly unfair not to accept the results of this freedom, and to make two classes of citizens, one consisting of Anglophones of British origin and Francophones of French origin and the other of Anglophones and Francophones of other origins. (Canada, *Book I*, 1967, xxiv)

This statement was paradigmatic, for, besides introducing the terms anglophone and francophone, it laid the foundation for future understandings of how non-French and non-English groups could fit into the nation (Jenson, 1994, 316). By describing language as a personal choice, the commissioners implied that language shifts were also a matter of personal choosing, discounting the larger structural constraints that channelled language choices in society and across generations. Even more important, this matter of personal choice suggested to the commissioners that 'free choice' resulted in 'two classes of citizens'; classes that replicated the divisions set out in the original terms of reference between the 'two founding races.' On the one hand, the founding races were now termed 'Anglophones of British origin and Francophones of French origin,' while, on the other, 'other ethnic groups' were designated 'Anglophones and Francophones of other origins.' Therefore, although the commission had so far handily discounted the key terms of 'race' and 'ethnicity' by foregrounding language in the blue pages, it had duplicated the original divisions of the groups, albeit now in linguistic terms. In fact, by retaining the division of the two groups in this way, the report had not eliminated the hierarchy of race and ethnicity but rather transformed it into a linguistic hierarchy.

This bifurcation into two groups, originally based on race and ethnicity and now defined through language, was repeated in the description of how the inquiry intended to consider the case of other ethnic groups:

> Canadians who are of neither British nor French origin are covered by our inquiry in two ways: a) to the extent that they are integrated into English- or French-speaking society, all that is said of Anglophones or Francophones applies to them; and b) to the extent that they remain attached to their original language and culture, they belong to other ethnic groups, whose existence is definitely beneficial to the country. (Canada, *Book I*, 1967, xxv)

Two points need to be made here. First, the commission was implying that the integration of other ethnic groups was a linguistic process, since the two 'founding' societies were now defined no longer as 'races' but rather through the language they spoke. Second, the elements of 'ethnic' difference were clearly delineated as a linguistic or cultural difference. Therefore, although ostensibly not defined through race and/ or ethnicity anymore, the elements of 'ethnic' difference actually remained; they were now just specified as differences of language and culture. Again, although race and ethnic groups had been relegated to the background as language moved to the foreground, it was clear that this still had not shifted the distinction between founding groups and Others.

'The Contribution of Other Ethnic Groups'

The next key theme to be considered in the report was 'the contribution made by other ethnic groups to the cultural enrichment of Canada.' In a mere half-page, the report outlined all the claims that other ethnic groups brought to the hearings about their contributions to the building of the nation. Since the terms of reference had designated all contributions from other ethnic groups as 'cultural,' the report had to follow suit. It began by outlining a 'broad' sense of culture: 'In the broadest sense of the term "culture," the sheer fact that men came from elsewhere to take part in building the country has contributed to our cultural enrichment ... By settling the country they helped to lay the basis for Canada's cultural growth' (Canada, *Book I,* 1967, xxv). Thus, although the report acknowledged all the claims made by other ethnic groups during the hearings that their contributions, such as settlement, were as vital to nation-building as those of the 'two founding races,' these efforts were labelled as cultural contributions. Furthermore, these contributions were couched as a work joined in progress, where men arrived 'from elsewhere' to 'continue the work of carrying civilization into thinly populated areas' (ibid.).

A 'narrower' sense of cultural contribution was also specified: the 'knowledge, skills, and tradition which all the immigrant groups brought with them' (Canada, *Book I,* 1967, xxv). This understood the contributions of other ethnic groups as something from another place, or exotic – not modern but 'traditional' – a notion that fit these contributions neatly into the Canadian milieu as part of a cultural-diversity model; 'cultural diversity has widened our horizons' (ibid.). The final sense of cultural contribution from other ethnic groups was artistic in nature: 'The coming together of diverse peoples in Canada has also benefited our culture in the humanistic sense of the term' (ibid.). The report explained that, although 'for a long time the frontier was not a rich soil for the arts and letters,' as time went on and 'as it matured ... Canadian society turned to the search for grace and leisure' (ibid.). Under this formulation, all contributions by other ethnic groups, ranging from land settlement to 'traditional' knowledge and skills as well as artistic achievements, were lumped together as 'cultural.' Moreover, not only was the specificity of the contributions by other ethnic groups elided under the rubric of culture, they were also made peripheral to some unnamed central culture through the commissioners' description of settlement as a civilizing mission joined . in progress; other, narrower cultural contributions were marked as traditional and exotic, and artistic contributions constituted mere additions to an established canon. Organizing other-ethnic-group contributions to the nation as 'cultural' defined these groups on the basis of culture and fit them into the nation through a strict cultural-diversity formulation. Furthermore, this narrow definition of culture separated it from any substantive political or economic concerns, again minimizing the basis of any other ethnic group claims and reinscribing the racialized hierarchy of the terms of reference. As well, it was not specified where and how languages other than English and French fit as cultural contributions.

'Indigenous Cultures'

In the next section, the 'Indigenous cultures,' which until now had been referred to in the inquiry in terms of the 'Indians and Eskimos,' were discussed. This was a very short section that began: 'We should point out here that the Commission will not examine the question of the Indians and the Eskimos' (Canada, *Book I*, 1967, xxvi). The commission then justified its decision by citing the terms of reference:

> Our terms of reference contain no allusion to Canada's native populations. They speak of 'two founding races,' namely Canadians of British and French origin, and 'other ethnic groups,' but mention neither the Indians nor the Eskimos. Since it is obvious that these two groups do not form part of the 'founding races,' as the phrase is used in the terms of reference, it would logically be necessary to include them under the heading 'other ethnic groups.' Yet is it clear that the term 'other ethnic groups' means those peoples of diverse origins who came to Canada during or after the founding of the Canadian state and that it does not include the first inhabitants of this country. (Canada, *Book I*, 1967, xxvi)

Although it was true that there was no allusion to Indigenous groups in the terms of reference, this did not originally prevent the commission from stating that it would consider Indigenous issues both within its internal deliberations and in public – nor did it stop them from encouraging submissions from Indigenous groups during the hearings. Additionally, it did not prevent the commission from collecting information from conferences and through private meetings, or by commissioning research reports on Indigenous communities during the research phase of the inquiry, as outlined in the previous chapter. The justification for disregarding all the information on Indigenous issues as they emerged during the inquiry was nothing more than a dismissal of the idea of Indigenous communities as 'founding races' or as any of the 'other ethnic groups.'

Given the complexity of the findings on Indigenous concerns as they emerged throughout the inquiry, and the complications these introduced for the claims of both founding races and other ethnic groups, the elimination of Indigenous matters from the final report was not surprising: the commissioners increasingly felt that they could not be dealt with within the terms of the inquiry. But it was disingenuous to claim that this omission was due to the terms of reference when, instead, it represented a complete reversal of the commission's original position on the matter. As the range of research and submissions in the public hearings attested; Indigenous issues greatly complicated the notion of founding races in the commission's reformulation of Canadian nation-building.

The section on Indigenous cultures in the blue pages ended with a reminder that the 'integration of native populations into Canadian society raises very complex problems' (Canada, *Book I*,1967, xxvi), and that the proper authorities should be reminded that everything possible must be done to help native populations preserve 'their cultural heritage' (ibid., xxvii). The only elaboration on what this cultural heritage might be came in the last sentence of the section, which urged that 'the Canadian government, in close co-operation with the provinces concerned, should take the necessary steps to assist the survival of the Eskimo language and the most common Indian dialects' (ibid.). In this way the commission could acknowledge Indigenous groups' claims that their cultural survival revolved around the preservation of their languages while simultaneously absolving itself of the responsibility of preserving them. As well, the linguistic hierarchy that subordinated Indigenous languages was maintained, with 'Indian' languages reduced to dialects and multiple 'Eskimo' languages collapsed into one.

Bilingualism

The next section of the blue pages was on bilingualism. Upon the start of the inquiry, Commissioner Rudnyckyj had provided a short research report to his colleagues entitled 'Bilingualism and Biculturalism in Canada: Preliminary Review of Concepts and Definitions,' dated 14 September 1963. For his definitions, Rudnyckyj drew on the academic expertise of linguist and language-planning expert Einar Haugen:

> In this connection, the following specification of bilingualism in Canada is suggested for the Royal Commission:
>
> 1. official bilingualism – the knowledge and use of English and French in certain spheres of individual community life in Canada.
> 2. inofficial [*sic*] bilingualism – the knowledge and use of either English or French, or both in addition to mother tongue of other ethnic groups in Canada.

The term 'inofficial bilingualism' might be substituted by 'national bilingualism' (similarly to the distinction 'official' and 'national' languages in Switzerland), 'extensive bilingualism,' or even 'multiple bilingualism' (to use Haugen's term). (Rudnyckyj, 1963, 2)

This model, with its two types of bilingualism, was sensitive to the various arguments made – particularly by other ethnic groups – that bilingualism might be about more than just facility in English and French. This would be the foundation of Rudnyckyj's own argument for a broader notion of bi/multilingualism in his separate *Statement* at the end of *Book I*. Along the same vein, the commission's final report acknowledged the concerns which were raised during the hearings about the definition of bilingualism: 'In everyday language "bilingualism" involves the use of any two languages. In Canada there are many persons considered unilingual in terms of the two official languages, but who are actually bilingual' (Canada, *Book I*, 1967, xxvii). The designation here of members of any other ethnic group as being 'unilingual' in relation to the two official languages meant that Rudnyckyj's model of bilingualism, which was one way to officially include the bilingualism of 'other ethnic groups,' was not at all considered in the final report; rather, the report stated categorically that 'our attention is directed to the two languages mentioned in section 133 of the B.N.A. Act, namely English and French,' and, therefore, that the bilingualism of concern 'applies only to Canada's two official languages, English and French' (ibid.).

During the inquiry, John A. Woodsworth had submitted a report to the commission entitled 'On Bilingualism: As Applied to Canada.' This report, dated 20 November 1963 but submitted in 1964, was a mélange of historical, comparative, and other sources of information on bilingualism. As it turned out, it was one of Woodsworth's first definitions of the term 'bilingual' that would be taken up in the final report. Drawing on a dictionary definition, Woodsworth divided 'bilingual' into 'the inanimate or collectivity of animates' and the 'individual person,' (Woodsworth, 1964, 2), a classification that informed the structure of the final report's discussion on bilingualism into individual and then institutional bilingualism. Individual bilingualism, where people 'know, *more or less*, two languages' – at this time, the number of such people in Canada was only about 2,230,000 – was not as important for the report as the idea of institutional bilingualism (Canada, *Book I*, 1967, xxviii). In this case, institutional bilingualism could be expanded to include the bilingual nature of 'the province, or a country' (ibid.). Following Woodsworth, the commission's final report clarified that this was quite different from individual bilingualism: 'A bilingual country is not one where all the inhabitants necessarily have to speak two languages; rather it is a country where the principal public and private institutions must provide services in two languages to citizens . . . the vast majority of whom may very well be unilingual' (ibid.). By highlighting the importance of institutional bilingualism over individual bilingualism, the commission made its priority clear – 'the life and vigour' of either the French or English language.

In order to emphasize the importance of institutional bilingualism, the report drew on one of the inquiry's larger, and later to be published, commissioned reports, written by R.L. Watts and entitled 'Multicultural Societies and Federalism.' In his report, Watts stated that language was 'fundamental to activities which are distinctively human,' since it is through language that community and social organization came into being (Watts, 1970, 16). Therefore, according to Watts, questions of institutional bilingualism required larger consideration of the viability of communities within which these languages were used. He continued: 'Any community which is governed through the medium of language other than its own has usually felt itself to some extent disenfranchised' (ibid.). This statement framed the inquiry findings, as stated in the final report, about those who were functioning in a second-language milieu and were faced with 'dramatic' difficulties leading to a 'sense of being diminished,' irritation, and loss of efficiency (Canada, *Book I*, 1967, xxix–xxx). Significantly, it was the English/French bilingual whose disenfranchisement was being discussed, not the 'other ethnic' bilingual who may have been bilingual in English or French and another language. This was a critical distinction, since for the report to acknowledge that other ethnic bilinguals could experience a 'sense of being diminished' would be to open the door to claims for linguistically viable communities in languages other than English or French.

Watts also admitted the political potential for language, as a symbol of identification, to be as volatile a sign of exclusion as race, stating: 'Moreover, like skin colour, language is an easily identifiable badge for those who wish to take issue with a different group, and thus it provides them with a rallying sign for contests which are basically not those of language or race' (Watts, 1970, 16). The final report acknowledged the political potential of language in its reference to the 'language problem and the explosive character it often acquires,' but it then challenged the idea because it saw its main task as tackling the political demands of French Canadians, who denied that these demands were only linguistic; 'there are many French Canadians ... especially in the last few years, [who] approach the problem not at the linguistic but at the political and economic level, refusing to admit that new language arrangements could really improve the situation' (Canada, *Book I*, 1967, xxx). The report also had to refute the French Canadians' de-emphasis of language and their concomitant emphasis on the political and economic because the inquiry had shifted the terrain upon which it would reconfigure national unity – particularly equality between the French and English – onto the terrain of language and linguistic equality. Hence, the report stated: 'It is necessary to emphasize the importance of the language question ... because of ... the strong bond between a language and culture' (ibid.). The discussion concluded by repeating the NDP's statement that language was the chief vehicle of culture: 'Language is the most evident expression of culture, the one which most readily distinguishes cultural groups even for the most superficial observer' (ibid.).

In this section of the blue pages, the importance of language for addressing concrete inequities between the two founding communities was maintained by arguing that there was a close connection between language and culture. However, despite Watts's arguments, the commission could only reach this conclusion by eliding language into race as identification, thus foreclosing the openness of language. There was a slippage between language and race here which foreshadowed how language, in the commission's thinking, would function as a technology of exclusion to limit the boundaries of culture. This elision highlighted the disjuncture between earlier assertions in the first part of the blue pages, where race was jettisoned in favour of the more porous notions of language and culture, and the argument here, where the limits of race – although refuted – were smuggled back in through the acknowledgment of the limits of language. Also, the emphasis on the strong link between language and culture for maintaining the viability of official-language communities – 'language is the most evident expression of culture' – was in direct contrast to the earlier discussion of ethnic groups, where the report had asserted that 'quite apart from heredity, much of the culture of one's forbears could be preserved even when one no longer spoke their language' (Canada, *Book I*, 1967, xxiii). The emergence of this differentiation between the importance of language for cultural expression and preservation reinforced the hierarchy between founding and other ethnic groups. The distinction between language necessary for the cultural preservation of 'founding' groups and language insignificant to the cultural welfare of the Other, as it was laid out in the blue pages, set the mode of differential inclusion for these two groups. And this differentiation turned on language.

In the report, bilingualism was clearly defined as something that pertained only to English and French, despite the suggested model of official and unofficial bilingualisms by Commissioner Rudnyckyj. Also, institutional bilingualism was given precedence over individual bilingualism in the commission's concerns, thus according priority to the maintenance of viable official-language communities, particularly French ones. The report argued that tackling language arrangements could address the concrete inequities between the French and English because of the strong bond between language and culture; that is, since language was the strongest expression of culture, it could be the key to developing and maintaining viable communities. However, only by eliding language into the limits of race as a strong badge of identification and a surrogate for other contests could this argument be developed, thereby reintroducing previously discounted ideas of race as the shadow of linguistic exclusion. As well, the described strong bond between language and culture vis-à-vis the two founding groups differentiated them from the other ethnic groups, for whom language was deemed unnecessary for cultural preservation. And so language, as it operated through culture, was the technology of hierarchicalization between the two different groups, providing the template for future modes of differential inclusion. Having outlined the links between language and culture, the section concluded: 'The problems of bilingualism and biculturalism are inseparably linked' (Canada, *Book I*, 1967, xxx).

Biculturalism

The next section of the blue pages was on biculturalism, but before this discussion could begin, the report stated that the sense of culture that underpinned biculturalism first had to be explained. On 4 April 1966 the commission's Press Section presented a working paper that set out definitions of 'culture' and 'biculturalism' in order to 'give the Commission a picture of the range of definitions proposed in the briefs' (Canada, *Press Section*, 1966, 1). This working paper found a variety of ideas about culture in the briefs, ranging from culture as the 'total matrix' of society, or a 'universal' part of life, to culture as nation (ibid., 4). In the blue pages of the final report, and particularly in this section where the discussion was about the biculturalism of the two founding races, the very broad sense of the term 'culture' was rejected: 'It suggests that all North Americans, if not most of the people of the Western world, live in highly industrialized societies within the Judeo-Christian tradition, and consequently possess a common culture. This conclusion is true, but it is too broad to help us much' (Canada, *Book I*, 1967, xxxi). Yet the commission did accept one broad aspect of culture – the idea of a 'Judeo-Christian' culture for the people of the Western World – since it clearly delineated the boundaries of the larger culture and therefore also signalled who was outside it. This broad sense of culture in relation to English-French biculturalism was clearly different in scope from the broad sense of culture previously discussed in relation to other ethnic groups, where it was characterized mainly as settlement activity. The difference underlined the assumptions about whose culture was understood to set the parameters of the nation, and whose culture was more closely linked to the labour required for nation-building.

The next idea to be raised was the 'humanistic' sense of culture as a pursuit of the arts and letters. In the final report, this was also rejected as inapplicable to the culture of biculturalism: 'The same can be said of the traditional humanistic sense of the word "culture," but for the opposite reason: it is too restricted. We will have occasion to use the word in this sense, for instance, when we examine "the contribution made by other ethnic groups to the cultural enrichment of Canada," and in the Book on the arts and letters in certain federal institutions' (Canada, *Book I*, 1967, xxxi). The implication was that, whereas the humanistic definition of culture was too narrow with respect to the cultures of the two founding races, when it came to the other ethnic groups, this restricted sense of culture – that is, of the arts and letters – would be of sufficient interest to merit further consideration, again underscoring the limited notion of the culture of other ethnic groups.

Finally, the commissioners presented their definition of culture that they saw as underpinning the word biculturalism:

The reality covered by the neologisms 'biculturalism' and 'bicultural' appears to us to be broader, including more than intellectual and artistic activity ... In this sense, which we ourselves shall use, culture is a way of being, thinking, and feeling. It is a driving force animating a significant group of individuals united by a common tongue, and sharing the same customs, habits, and experiences. Clearly the two cultures designated in our terms of reference are those associated with the English and the French languages in Canada. But as there are the two dominant languages, there are two principal cultures, and their influence extends, in greatly varying degrees, to the whole country. (Canada, *Book I*, 1967, xxxi)

In this statement, the already established predominance of the two official languages assured an equally dominant place for the related cultures. As in the case of language, then, the precise definition of culture through which a group was defined could reinscribe the hierarchy between founding and other ethnic groups. This definition of culture, which underlay biculturalism, also made it clear that any further discussion of biculturalism pertained to that of the English and French culture alone.

Despite the commission's exclusive focus on the culture of the founding groups, it is instructive to consider certain elements of its examination in greater detail, particularly in order to compare the commission's thinking on this subject to its discussion on the cultural contribution of other ethnic groups. In the working paper on definitions of bilingualism and biculturalism, definitions of biculturalism as they were culled from the various submissions were reduced to one particular model in the final report that the commissioners were interested in advocating: 'We use the words "bilingualism" and "biculturalism" to indicate two styles of living which are distinct, even though they obviously have much in common. Just as bilingualism should not lead to a *blend* of two languages, so Canada's cultural duality cannot be taken to mean a *mixture* of the two cultures; each has its own existence' (Canada, *Book I*, 1967, xxxi). In other words, the model of two 'distinct' societies emerged from this formulation of bilingualism and biculturalism, clearly eliminating the bicultural individuals in the one-society model suggested in many submissions and briefs. This notion of distinct societies echoed the idea of institutional bilingualism, where the importance given to the 'life and vigour of each language' meant that the viability of each separate founding community was the primary concern.

In reiterating that there were two dominant and therefore distinct societies, the report revisited its formulation of a society in the *Preliminary Report*: 'We have already said the two dominant cultures in Canada are embodied in distinct societies, and that the word "society" designates "the types of organization and the institutions that a rather large population, *inspired by a common culture*, has created for itself or has received"' (Canada, *Book I*, 1967, xxxiii, emphasis in original). In light of the different models of biculturalism suggested in the briefs and submissions, *Book I*'s blue pages needed to outline the complexities of the distinct-societies formulation while acknowledging, on the French side, that not only was there a distinct society in Quebec, but also the development of 'autonomous society' emerging as in the example of New Brunswick (ibid.). Thus, even in the relatively homogeneous French group, the existence of viable French-speaking communities outside the territorial boundary of Quebec was acknowledged; however, it was the heterogeneity of the English-speaking society that was the commission's main preoccupation:

> It is the English-speaking society which displays the greatest complexity, because of its provincial divisions, and because of the more diversified origins of its members. In some areas the English-speaking society incorporates partial societies which the bearers of cultures other than the English and French have set up in parts of the country where they are numerous enough to support organization and institutions of their own. Although in the nature of things these cannot be complete – since they operate within a framework of institutions shaped by the British tradition and employ for some purpose the English language – they are vital and significant for those who participate in them. Nevertheless, despite these centrifugal influences, the fundamental unity of the English-speaking society appears to us beyond question. (Canada, *Book I*, 1967, xxxiii–iv)

Identifying these societies as 'partial' because they had to operate within the framework of unspecified, traditionally British institutions ignored the hegemony of British culture and the English language as well as the impossibility of operating outside this framework anywhere in anglophone Canada. Furthermore, these partial societies were understood as centrifugal or peripheral elements, again pointing to the radial positioning and heterogeneity of 'other' cultures in relation to the centrality and unity of an 'English-speaking society.' In short, when the presence of other cultures or societies was to be accounted for, they were deemed partial, incomplete, and marginal, although the very elements of their partiality remained elusive and ambiguous.

To sum up, the definition of biculturalism in the blue pages began with an effort to find a foundational definition of culture. A Judeo-Christian norm was accepted as an already encompassing characteristic of Western society, regardless of the unstated exclusions that this acceptance built into the broad definitions of society and culture. Yet a narrow humanistic definition of culture was also not considered for English and French groups, although it was deemed appropriate for future discussions of the culture of other ethnic groups. The sense of culture that was finally accepted was one seen to be a 'driving force animating' a 'significant' group united through, among other things, a 'common tongue.' The conclusion was clear: culture in this sense could be only that of the principal English and French groups. This led to the definition of biculturalism as that of two distinct groups, particularly in order to ensure the life and vigour of each of the groups' languages. Although the heterogeneity of each of the two principal cultures was acknowledged, the separate positioning of 'partial societies' in relation to the principal societies – especially English society – once again reflected the hierarchical positioning of other ethnic groups in relation to the two founding races.

Relations between Language and Culture

In the next section of the blue pages, the commissioners, having repeatedly invoked language and culture, reached the point where they had to delineate clearly the relationship between the two. They began by restating their position that language was 'an essential expression of culture in the full sense of the word' (Canada, *Book I*, 1967, xxxiv). However, the final report was also clear that a culture had to be able to function through its own language in its contemporary daily life if it was to thrive, 'for nobody will maintain that a group still has a living culture, in the full sense of the term, when it is forced to use another language in order to express to itself the realities which make up a large part of its daily life'; it made this point even as it cautioned that 'the vitality of a language is a necessary condition for the complete preservation of a culture, but it is not at all the *sole* condition' (ibid.).

So far, the report had made a range of statements about the relation between language and culture with respect to the two founding races, including that language was the primary expression and chief vehicle of culture. On the other hand, the discussion in the report on the link between language and culture for other ethnic groups was outlined as a much looser relation, with cultural preservation deemed relatively unhampered by language loss. This meant refuting the argument made by many other ethnic groups that loss of language would lead to loss of culture:

Many seem to believe that the members of a group who have adopted another language have completely lost their original culture. This is yet another illusion which has given rise to many misunderstandings. In

Canada we can observe the indisputable survival of some cultural traits among native groups and among a number of groups of other ethnic origins. In fact, some of these groups attach the greatest importance to these elements of their ancestral culture. Such is the case, for example, among Jewish people, for whom the question of language hardly arises in everyday life. Similar phenomena are found among people of British and French origin themselves . . . (Canada, *Book I*, 1967, xxxvii)

The report had refuted the strong link between language and culture by advancing examples of unspecified native groups and those with other ethnic origins whose ancestral and cultural traits had apparently survived despite their adoption of another language. This logic was put forward despite the overwhelming arguments made by other ethnic and Indigenous groups during the hearings in favour of language preservation as a central element of cultural retention and survival. As well, there was no indication of whether the original languages were retained through bilingualism; rather, culture was emphasized as ancestral in order to diminish its link to language preservation in the present.

The one other ethnic group that the report specified in order to make the argument that language was not necessarily a central element of cultural preservation was the Jewish community. But this did not mean that the question of language was not important for Canadian Jews. As stated by Garber of the Jewish Canadian Congress during the preliminary hearings, language, although considered a 'private reserve,' was nevertheless something that the community was willing to ask for – to the extent that they were willing to ask the government to recognize Hebrew as a third language (Canada, *Preliminary Hearing*, 1963, 261), even as the community itself was willing to pay for it. Therefore, the Jewish community was as concerned about language preservation as many of the other ethnic groups; they even ran their own community Hebrew schools.

The contrary position put forward by many of the anglophone communities had to be countered. 'During our hearings we often heard Anglophones overstating, with understandable complacency, the possibilities of survival for a culture even after the language has been lost' (Canada, *Book I*, 1967, xxxviii). This view was refuted explicitly and emphatically in the report: 'Original cultural traits survive only partially after the adoption of the English language, especially when several generations have passed' (ibid.). Rather, the report argued that without language maintenance, culture became increasingly narrow in meaning and became reduced to a few family customs. For the commission, this narrow sense of the word 'culture' was untenable for official language groups: 'We feel that it is unacceptable to consider the French language in Canada, or the English language in Quebec, as a mere personal or family trait, encountered in church, in some associations, or at best in elementary school, but not elsewhere' (ibid., xxxviii). In fact, the commission embraced a broader definition of culture which laid the foundation for what would come to be enshrined in the Canadian Charter of Rights as official language minority rights. As this section of the blue pages concluded, 'The life of the two cultures implies in principle the life of the two languages ... every possible provision for cultural equality is primarily an attempt to make every possible provision for linguistic equality' (ibid., xxxviii).

'Equal Partnership'

This concluding section of the blue pages addressed the issue of an 'equal partnership.' The terms of reference specified that the inquiry would seek to determine the 'basis of an equal partnership between the two founding races.' Yet, by this point in the report, the notion of 'races' had been discarded in favour of language and culture, leading the report to conclude: 'As we understand our mandate, this equality should be the equal partnership not only of the two peoples which founded Confederation but also of each of their respective languages and cultures. What we are aiming for, then, is the equal partnership of all who speak either language and participate in either culture, whatever their ethnic origin' (Canada, *Book I*, 1967, xxxix).

The reluctance to use the word 'race' was highlighted in this statement, with what were once 'founding races' now becoming 'two peoples which founded Confederation,' a phrase taken directly from the French terms of reference. The shift away from the restrictive category of race to the purportedly more porous groupings of language and culture made it possible to include individuals 'whatever their ethnic origin.' The report had thereby twice reconfigured its central concern from the original terms of reference: first, from the equal partnership between the 'two founding races' to one between 'two peoples which founded Confederation'; and second, to the equal partnership of their (English and French) 'respective languages and cultures.' In so doing, it could solve the problem of equality for all others who were not part of the 'two peoples which founded Confederation' as long as they were linguistically and culturally part of either dominant group. Nowhere in this organization of equality was there any concession for those who were not culturally or linguistically homogenized into one of the two 'founding groups.'

This formulation of equality emerged directly from the terms of reference, which couched the examination of equality in terms of a bicultural and bilingual partnership between the two dominant groups. As well, the blue pages had thus far argued that language and cultural rights were a group phenomenon and not just individual rights, at least for the founding groups. That is, extrapolating from the model of institutional bilingualism, the commission saw the life and vigour of each language as depending on the provision of linguistically viable, distinct cultural communities. It did acknowledge that 'there is a more basic equality antecedent to that postulated in our mandate,' which was that of the 'inalienable rights' that all human beings possess from birth (Canada, *Book I*, 1967, xxxix), and it went on to state that 'these individual human rights are unquestionable, and are already in place for all Canadians without exception,' since the federal Parliament had already adopted the Canadian Bill of Rights in 1960 (ibid.). The inquiry's concern, therefore, was not the individual, fundamental rights that were already enshrined, but rather the collective linguistic and cultural rights of 'English-speaking and French-speaking Canadians as such, whatever their ethnic origin may happen to be.' With the focus on collective rights, the importance of two distinct societies could be maintained, 'Hence the great importance of the concept of two distinct societies as developed in our Preliminary Report. Individual equality can fully exist only if each community has, throughout the country, the means to progress within its culture and to express that culture' (ibid., xliv).

Therefore, with individual rights subsumed within collective language and cultural rights and able to flourish only within distinct societies, this particular formulation of collective rights could be seen as viable only for the distinct English and French groups in Canada. Furthermore, by deeming these distinct groups to be porous through language and culture, and confirming that other ethnic groups already had the guaranteed individual right to integrate into either of the two founding groups, the commission saw to it that other ethnic groups could not mount their own claims for any form of group rights.

The Main Chapters of *Book I*

The main body of *Book I* consisted of seven chapters. However, I will focus on chapter 1, which addresses the 'Bilingualism of Individuals and States'; chapter 2, 'Composition of the Population: The Two Main Language Groups,' which develops the demographic argument for English and French as official languages; chapter 4, 'The Territorial Principle and the Personality Principle,' which argues for the proposed form of official bilingualism; and conclude with a brief discussion of the recommendations laid out in chapter 7, 'The Necessary Legislation,' for an Official Languages Act. These chapters, particularly chapters 1, 2, and 4, outline the rationales and philosophical underpinnings of the formulation for national belonging which would eventually emerge as multiculturalism within a bilingual framework.

Chapter 1: Bilingualism

Chapter 1 of the report began with the complex task of highlighting language and culture over 'race,' yet at the same time emphasizing the distinctiveness of an English and French community in order to bolster the rationale for English and French bilingualism:

> People of all sorts of ethnic origins speak English and French as mother tongues; there is no such thing as an English or a French 'race.' Indeed the racial stocks from which the English- and French-speaking peoples who settled in Canada have sprung are largely identical, even in the aspects of the Celtic and Nordic mixtures which each represented . . . Still, as we have pointed out earlier, there is such a thing as a French culture and a British culture. Of course, the differences between them are not as great as they would be if either were compared to one of the many Asian or African cultures. In Canada, the Anglophones and Francophones wear the same sort of clothing, live in the same sort of houses, and use the same tools. They are very similar in their social behaviours, belong to religions which are not exclusive, and share the same general knowledge. To a greater or lesser extent, they share a North American way of living. But at the same time the cultures of the two are clearly different in many important aspects, including modes of thought and even styles of life. Perhaps it is chiefly because they do not share the same language that they do not belong to the same cultural group. For language is the main instrument of social consciousness. Language defines group boundaries and excludes outsiders. (Canada, *Book I*, 1967, 9)

Even as the preceding blue pages rejected the idea of two founding races, the idea of a similar Celtic- and Nordic-based 'racial stock' for the English and French reintroduced the idea of race in the 'two founding races.' Thus, this was not the rejection of the concept of race per se; rather, race was to be disregarded because the racial difference between the two groups was deemed negligible. Moreover, the concept of race was actually reinscribed by the very fact that, if these racial stocks were a similar admixture, then there must be others that were completely different. Even religion, which until a short time ago was a distinctive marker of French identity, was now considered a commonality, since each group belonged to religions that were not exclusive. These were all elements of a cultural and geographical commonality between the English and French that differed markedly from 'Asian and African cultures.'

At the same time as the report had to argue that there were cultural similarities between the two groups, it had also to make the case that each group was culturally distinct, since this was the basis for English-French bilingualism. As the report considered the basis of difference between the two groups, language emerged as the chief arbiter, serving as 'the main instrument of social consciousness,' defining 'groups' boundaries,' and excluding 'outsiders.' By holding out language as the key element of cultural distinctiveness, the commission recapitulated the conclusions of the blue pages while also setting out the framework for discussion on English and French bilingualism in the rest of the report. The report had to strike the difficult balance between maintaining that the two main groups were culturally similar enough that they could be joined in nationhood, on the one hand, and making a compelling case of cultural distinctiveness in order to argue for an English and French bilingual nation, on the other. This balance was upheld both through language and through the Other. Specifically, language was the key element that marked the boundaries of cultural difference between the two groups. And, as defined here through geography, race, and culture, it was through the reinscription of a common Other that the two main groups *were made the same,* laying a foundation of their common nationhood.

Chapter 2: Demography

As in the case of the *Preliminary Report,* demographic analysis was an important basis for building arguments. Having made the case for official English and French bilingualism in Canada, the report's next chapter, 'Composition of the Population: The Two Main Language Groups,' began by underscoring the centrality of other ethnic groups to this argument. The opening paragraph laid out the importance of determining who the people of 'different origin' were in relation to the overall population, as well as their linguistic relation to official languages: 'What are the ethnic origins of the various components of the country's population? To what extent do they keep their original languages, and what choices do they make about the two official languages?' (Canada, *Book I*, 1967, 17). These questions on the linguistic make-up of the nation built on the discussion of census data in the *Preliminary Report*. There, data from the 1961 census on ethnic origin and mother tongue was used to challenge the collective bases for claims made by other ethnic groups during the preliminary hearings, and also to confirm that the crisis facing the nation was between the two 'founding races.' Specifically, the *Preliminary Report* argued that *mother-tongue data*, which identified 13.5 per cent of the population as having a non-English or non-French mother tongue, was more relevant for determining the size of the other ethnic group than *ethnic-origin data*, which identified a 'third force' representing about 28.5 per cent of the total population. This argument rested on the principle that, for other ethnic groups, mother-tongue data was more germane since language and culture were more relevant than ethnic origin as the bases of 'other ethnic group' definition – despite the definitional, paternal connection to language for ethnic origin.

In *The Politics of Population*, Bruce Curtis argues that census making is a set of disciplinary procedures that attempts to govern populations within a sovereign territory by isolating social relations, then grouping social relations and practices in order to turn them into objects of administration (Curtis, 2002, 43). As he puts it: 'Census making ... involves applying a grid to social relations, and tying human beings and their social relations and activities to particular identities' (ibid., 311). For the B and B Commission, the particular 'grids of intelligibility' through which the census data organized the population were ethnic origin, mother tongue, and official languages. In the report, reflecting Foucault's idea of dividing practices, the census categories partitioned the population into three main identities which echoed the divisions of the terms of reference: an English group; a French group; and those of all other ethnic origins, lumped together as either as a single non-English and non-French group or as an immigrant group. Social relations between these groups were determined through the aggregate quantities obtained in each respective census category.

In *Census and Identity*, David Kretzer and Dominique Arel trace the historical reasons for the collection of 'ethnic origin' data in Canada as the need to register the changing proportions of the descendants of French and English settlers in relation to themselves and other groups (Kretzer and Arel, 2002). The 1961 census was the first census where the actual term 'ethnic origin' was used – previous censuses had referred to 'racial origin' – but the purpose was the same: to allow for the continuous monitoring of the proportions of the two main groups in order to ensure that the society's fundamental duality remained stable.

The ethnic-origin data was also used to show that Canada's duality was being diluted through the substantial increase in the proportion of 'other groups.' The analysis began by outlining the increase in ethnic-origin numbers for non-British and non-French groups (from 11 per cent in 1881 to 26 per cent in 1961), the relative stability of the French-origin population numbers (30 per cent in 1881 and 1961), and the sharp decrease in the British-origin numbers (from 59 per cent in 1991 to 44 per cent in 1961) (Kretzer and Arel, 2002, 19). These shifts were attributed to a variety of causes, including immigration from continental Europe, but also emigration from Canada to the United States and the unequal birth rate of Canada's various ethnic groups (ibid.). Extrapolation of these trends had clear implications since, in both absolute figures and percentages, the part of the population that was neither British nor French in origin has continued to increase. The report stated their concern clearly: 'if immigration and emigration continue in the patterns that have prevailed in Canada since World War I, it is possible that the total number of people of other ethnic origins could in the not distant future surpass both the number of those of French origin and those of British origin' (ibid., 22). In this discussion, the report aggregated all the non-French and non-English groups together to emphasize their diluting effect on the British-origin category. Yet, at the same time, the report had to be careful not to bolster the case made by many other ethnic groups that they constituted a significant third force. Thus, as in the *Preliminary Report*, the commission invoked the mother-tongue category, here using the census results to determine language choice:

We shall try to measure the phenomenon of language choice in this country – and consequently the degree of linguistic assimilation of Canadians of different ethnic origins – through the mother tongue criterion. The first thing to note is the increasing homogeneity of the Canadian population according to mother tongue in spite of increasing heterogeneity according to ethnic origin . . . In fact, about one out of six Canadians no longer speaks the language of his forbears. Of those who changed languages, 93 percent are English speaking today. The tendency towards English is so strong that 25 percent of those who now claim it as their mother tongue – 2,775,000 people – can be considered 'immigrants to English' or, as it is popularly called, 'Anglicized.' (Kretzer and Arel, 2002, 22–3)

Even though the census data showed that the linguistic composition of the nation remained overwhelmingly a duality as a result of the choices made by immigrants, what these grids of intelligibility could not capture and show were the various reasons, as had been revealed during the hearings, why the shift into the dominant language of English had occurred. That is, the use of a census category that focused on the aftermath of the language shift meant that the push/pull factors that caused it in the first place – either for the individual or for the community – were left out of the overall calculation, and thus anglicization was normalized.

The commission highlighted the tendency of immigrants to 'choose' English, as well as the increasing rate of transfer: 'There is one notable feature of the Canadian situation as a whole: the steadily increasing transfer to English through the years' (Kretzer and Arel, 2002, 24). It also underlined the sharp accentuation of this trend in the past decade: 'During the decade from 1951 to 1961, the proportion of those of English mother tongue increased despite the relatively heavy immigration of at least 11 groups of various ethnic origins' (ibid., 26). Thus, for the commission, the census data showed that immigrants were increasingly choosing language transfer into English. This argument, as it was constructed in the report through the use of census data, had two important consequences. First, claims made by other ethnic groups on the basis of their growing numbers were undercut by arguing that immigrant groups were increasingly choosing to shift their mother tongues to English. The report acknowledged that this shift was not uniform for all groups and was determined by a large number of factors, 'of which numbers, place and time of settlement in Canada' were critical (ibid., 23). However, the report maintained that ultimately there could not be a single collectivity within the 'immigrant' group, since immigrants eventually chose to transfer into the English language.

The second consequence of the argument that immigrants were increasingly choosing English was that it allowed the report to maintain that there was a fundamental linguistic duality in the nation: 'It follows from all this that, despite the constant increase in numbers of Canadians of other ethnic origins, as a result of immigration, linguistic duality remains the basic characteristic and foundation of the Canadian community' (Kretzer and Arel, 2002, 39). Kretzer and Arel claim that census numbers are crucial to making the case for political entitlements: 'Since census politics is expressed numbers, the pursuit of entitlement translates into a contest for achieving the "right" numbers' (ibid., 30). For their part, the commissioners were building the case for a model of bilingualism that was predicated on there being two main languages in Canada. Earlier, they had based this case on the idea of prior history and claims of cultural distinctiveness; now, however, they were using the 'right' numbers to maintain the 'majority' status of the two languages. Since the French ethnic-origin numbers had remained stable to date – that is, the 1961 census – but the British ethnic-origin majority numbers had decreased as a result of the growth in other ethnic group numbers, the report had to defend the idea that there still was a majority. This was accomplished by turning to the mother-tongue data and showing that, although British ethnic-origin numbers were decreasing, in fact English-language numbers still represented the majority. Furthermore, the report contended that immigrant groups would maintain the English-language majority numbers through their continued transfer into English. In this way, the present and future majority of the two languages were assured, as was the English and French linguistic duality that had long been 'the foundation of the Canadian community' (Canada, *Book I*, 1967, 39).

Chapter 4: Minority Rights

In its simplest form, the personality principle of bilingualism means that citizens of a nation are able to use either language in any part of the nation. Jean-Pierre Beaud and Jean-Guy Prévost explain the centrality of numbers for this model of bilingualism: 'A political linguistic regime based on the principle of personality must deal with the problem of regularly assessing the necessarily fluctuating linguistic distribution of population. A political-linguistic regime based on the principle of personality will thus be characterized by statistical activism' (Beaud and Prévost, 2002, 92). The statistical activism of the final report had been designed to make the compelling case that, in fact, dual linguistic majorities existed at the 'foundation of the Canadian nation.' This was to ensure that the concept of 'equal partnership between the two founding races' from the terms of reference, which now had been recast as the complete 'linguistic equality of the two official languages' (Canada, *Book I*, 1967, 74), could be assured even for official-language minorities – that is, English and French speakers who lived in areas of the country where they were not part of a majority official-language community. Accordingly, despite the relatively homogeneous territorialization of English and French in Canada (comparatively speaking), the commission decided that true linguistic equality could not be established without including elements of the personality principle of bilingualism.

Having established that English and French were the 'majority languages' between which there should be 'linguistic equality,' chapter 4 considered what model of bilingualism would ensure this. The report deduced its 'guiding principles for a truly viable Canadian bilingualism' by looking at four countries that had 'accorded full equality to their linguistic minorities' (Canada, *Book I*, 1967, 75). The countries, whose linguistic situation was dissected at length, were Finland, Switzerland, Belgium, and South Africa. The report outlined the models of bilingualism in all four countries, with Finland, Belgium, and Switzerland being described principally as examples of territorial bilingualism, although it was careful to state that all of these countries also 'more or less admit some considerations of personality' (ibid., 82). South Africa's model of bilingualism was seen to be different:

> South Africa differs linguistically from the countries so far considered mainly in three respects. First, bilingualism in English and Afrikaans is widespread: approximately two-thirds of the white population claimed a knowledge of the two official languages in 1960. Second, as in Canada, neither language is Indigenous to the area; both have been introduced or developed by settlers from Europe. Third, while the regimes in the preceding three bilingual states were based on the natural or fostered existence of unilingual areas, in South Africa the two linguistic groups are relatively mixed. Each of the four provinces has a linguistic minority of 23 to 39 per cent of its white population. (Canada, *Book I*, 1967, 81)

South Africa differed significantly from the Canadian situation in that the interpenetration of both languages throughout the country and levels of bilingualism were relatively high, which made this an ideal setting for the personality principle of bilingualism. However, what South Africa and Canada had in common, and what Canada did not have in common with the other three European examples, was that both were white-settler societies and in both cases the languages in consideration were colonial languages. Since the report reviewed the situation of South Africa in order to deduce 'guiding principles for a truly Canadian bilingualism,' it was interested only in the linguistic situation of white South Africans, which meant that the erasure of Canadian Indigenous groups from the commission was paralleled by the erasure of South African Indigenous groups and the institution of Apartheid. In both cases, the focus was on maintaining not only the dominance of the two colonial languages but also the centrality of the particular European colonial identity: in the case of South Africa, English and Afrikaans; and in the case of Canada, English and French. The result was the entrenchment of white-settler identity and dominance.

The 'Canadian reality' included the fact that territorial concentrations of each majority-language group existed; however, there were significant official-language minorities located within specific regions as well. Although the territorial principle of bilingualism could be applied, it would 'lead to the recognition of only the majority's rights and to oppression of the official-language minorities,' effectively denying 'minority groups *en bloc* (the English-speaking in Quebec and the French-speaking in the rest of the country) of essential language rights' (Canada, *Book I*, 1967, 86). This meant that elements of the personality principle of bilingualism had also to be applied, but this model of bilingualism required the determination of a quantitative threshold, hence the importance of statistical data for determining at which point services would be offered in both official languages. The principles that would guide language policy for the official languages were stated as follows: 'we take as guiding principle the recognition of both official languages, in law and in practice, wherever the minority is numerous enough to be viable as a group' (ibid.). This was seen to be a positive conception of equality, where official-language minority rights were to be respected and would come into force when a language group was large enough to exercise them (ibid.).

Overall, this was an important explication of the proposed official-language policies. It entrenched the reality of a quantitative threshold, ensuring a future fraught with the statistical reckonings of various linguistic distributions. Also, it erased the 'other languages' and those they represented, although people of other ethnic origins with official-language facility may have been embedded within the porous domain of at least one of the two recognized languages. Finally, the most significant shift that this articulation of language policy inaugurated was the birth of the category of 'language minority' or 'official language minority.' In the Canadian context, the specification of English-speaking people in Quebec, and French-speaking people in the rest of the country, as minorities meant that the category of linguistic minority (official or otherwise), which was always the starting point for claiming linguistic rights, was henceforth discursively unavailable to any group who would demand rights to any other 'minority' language – that is, neither English nor French.

Chapter 7: The Necessary Legislation

The final chapter of *Book I*, 'The Necessary Legislation,' spelled out the proposed principles for an official-language policy. It recommended an extension of Section 93 of the BNA Act, a new section 133 of the same act, a new Federal Official Languages Act, and a Provincial Languages Act. The new section 133 of the BNA Act would include a threshold for official minority-language rights – 10 per cent of the population of any given province.

Although in the end the government did not act on the commission's suggestions for changes to the BNA Act – nor did it bring the Provincial Languages Act into force as proposed – it did pass an Official Languages Act, which would go on to become what is probably the best-known direct outcome of the B and B Commission. The Official Languages Act was first proposed at an internal commission study group[1] meeting in Ottawa on 7 July 1966. The minutes of the meeting showed the germ of a proposal for a language act essentially along the lines of that which was finally proposed in the report: 'It was felt by some that a clear statement of Government policy, possibly in the form of a Language Act, was needed as a base which would set forth specific policy about matters of right and provide a basic document on which to centre decisions' (Study Group C, 1966).

On 17 October 1968, Bill No. C-120, respecting the status of the official languages of Canada (Canada, *House of Commons Debates*, 1968, 1509), was read for the first time by Prime Minister Trudeau in the House of Commons. In his speech, Trudeau began by emphasizing the importance of diversity, particularly as it was manifested in the existence of the 'two major language groups in Canada' (ibid., 1481). He then linked the emergence of this duality to Canada's supposedly nonviolent past: 'In the past, multi-cultural states have often resulted from conquest or colonialism. In the modern world, many are based on a conscious appreciation of the facts of history, geography, and economics. This latter case is the case of Canada, a country blessed with more prosperity and political stability than most countries, and where we are making our choices methodically and democratically' (ibid.). Building on this sanitized version of Canadian history which disavowed any notions of colonial conquest, Trudeau echoed the B and B Commission's terms of reference and foreshadowed his future formulation of multiculturalism, stating: 'We believe in two official languages and in a pluralist society, not merely as a political necessity but as an enrichment' (ibid.). He ended by tying the bill to the cause of national unity, one of the chief spurs to the creation of the B and B Commission: 'I believe that there will be widespread agreement among members and their constituents in all parts of Canada that this bill is of the greatest importance in promoting national unity' (ibid., 1484).

In the house, this theme of national unity was taken up by the Conservative Party's leader of the opposition, Robert Stanfield: 'This resolution, preceding what has been called an official languages bill, is part of the much larger question of national unity and of constitutional agreements that will be devised for the future of the country' (Canada, *House of Commons Debates*, 1968, 1484). Although acknowledging that the issue of official languages was part of the question of national unity, Stanfield was skeptical that this bill was a sufficient response: 'Within the framework of Canada's constitutional evolution and of the problems we still have to resolve, this resolution can hardly be regarded as a very significant or decisive step' (ibid.). A short nine months after the Confederation of Tomorrow Conference in Ottawa,[2] constitutional issues, particularly as they related to federal-provincial relations and powers, were not Stanfield's concern alone. In fact, Commission Co-chairman Laurendeau was also a strong proponent of constitutional reform, believing that without essential changes to the constitution, full and equal partnership between the two founding groups could not be guaranteed.

David Lewis of the NDP was next to respond to Trudeau. Drawing on some of the nascent discourses about multiculturalism, Lewis also showed his support for the bill:

> I say to my fellow Canadians whose mother tongue, like mine, was neither English nor French that this country is a bilingual country, that Canada is a country of mosaic design and is not a melting pot. I say to my fellow Canadians with origins other than English or French that it is precisely because Canada is a bilingual country, and has always been, that

communities in Canada with languages other than English and French have been able to develop within an economic, intellectual and moral concepts much higher than such communities have achieved in any other country in the world. I emphasize to my fellow Canadians whose origins are other than English or French that they would not have these rights, this kind of recognition, or the enthusiastic acceptance of their rights in this democratic country were it not for the basic fact that this country is not unilingual, not unicultural and never has been. The fact is that while this country recognized two languages and two cultures as official there is opportunity for the recognition of other languages and other cultures as well. (Canada, *House of Commons Debates*, 1968, 1487)

Lewis's argument – which was a common one – that the 'founding' duality of the country had facilitated the advance and recognition of Canadians from origins other than English or French gave primacy to a de facto English and French dualism, countering the challenges from other ethnic or Indigenous groups that the nation sprung from much more heterogeneous roots. Although Lewis pointed to the alleged opportunities provided by bilingualism to other ethnic groups – that is, 'opportunities for the recognition of other languages and other cultures' – he did not appraise the limited possibility for 'official' recognition, erasing the hierarchical distinction between that which was officially recognized and that which was not.

Lewis also invoked the mosaic metaphor, which was almost always presented in opposition to the model of the American melting pot. In fact, he stated this explicitly: 'I believe that bilingualism is one of the great bulwarks in protecting this country from being completely swallowed by the country to the south of us,' since French was a language and culture that could not be overwhelmed by the 'powerful voice from the south' (Canada, *House of Commons Debates*, 1968, 1487). In this framing, the French language and culture was characterized as something that made and maintained the country as distinctively Canadian; French was the boundary of differentiation between Canada and the United States. However, René Matte, an MP from Quebec and the next person to speak, decried Lewis's championing of French simply as a bulwark against encroaching American cultural hegemony: 'As we know, Quebeckers do not want any longer to be recognized in Canada as ordinary shock absorbers against the invasion of American culture ... and to accept us just because our particular culture is a buffer against the invasion of the American culture is, in 1968, I think, an insult. We want to participate in the progress of the country by giving our best, that is, by staying ourselves' (ibid., 1491). This argument – that Quebecers sought inclusion in the nation on the basis of their own recognizance and agency, and not just as a buffer that made English Canada feel distinctively Canadian vis-à-vis the Americans – was an important counter to the celebratory Anglo discourse on 'biculturalism,' which found its counterpart in the mosaic metaphor and the future discourse on 'multiculturalism.' Matte also placed this discussion on the bill within the context of the concurrent tensions in Saint-Leonard, Montreal. He stated that the Anglicization of Saint Leonard would lead to the loss of French 'characteristics' and prevent the country from 'being culturally stronger and richer' (ibid., 1490), even as this contradicted, to some extent, his repudiation of the use of Quebec as a buffer to American cultural encroachment.

After Matte had spoken, Conservative MP Jack Horner gave one of the most cautious speeches on the bill. Horner argued that the low percentages of francophone populations in the west – at the time, francophones made up only about 5 per cent of the population 'in the whole of Western Canada including British Columbia' – meant that the introduction of bilingualism would make it very difficult for people from Western Canada to acquire jobs in the civil service (Canada, *House of Commons Debates*, 1968, 1491). The cornerstone of Horner's position was the low number of francophones in the west compared to the high number of Ukrainian speakers: 'In the province of Manitoba, which has quite a large French settlement, less that 7 per cent speak French while 14 per cent speak Ukrainian' (ibid.). The construction of other ethnic groups' claims based on demographics had been a common strategy during the commission hearings, but in the final report these claims were muted – particularly those calling for substantive federal support and recognition of other languages. However, one last attempt at this argument was made at the end of *Book I*, where Commissioner J.B. Rudnyckyj appended a 'Separate Statement.' Although Rudnyckyj's statement would not be taken up as policy, it would foreshadow future shifts in the category of other ethnic groups – or, as it would soon be known, the category of 'cultural groups.'

Rudnyckyj's Statement

In his diary, Laurendeau recalled the months leading up to the formation of the B and B Commission; in particular, the offer to him of the co-chairmanship of the commission as well as concerns about the commission's membership. In his discussion with the editorial board members of *Le Devoir* about whether or not he should accept the appointment, one of his colleagues emphasized that he should demand parity between the English and French commissioners:

> The least enthusiastic was François-Albert Angers, but he definitely leaned towards acceptance, with one condition: it was understood that there would be four French Canadians and four English Canadians on this commission, and one 'New Canadian'; and that this 'New Canadian' would necessarily be an anglophone, which according to Angers, would make it five against four. 'You should suggest to make it very clear that there are two cultures, that the commission also include one francophone "New Canadian."' (Smart, 1991, 24)

And so, even before the commissioners were appointed, the tricky balancing act between the 'two cultures' had begun, and already the problem of the 'New Canadian' as a potential upset to this balance was anticipated. From the commission's inception, the New Canadian was a spectre in the discussions regarding the two founding races.

In subsequent conversations with Pearson and Maurice Lamontagne, clerk of the Privy Council, Laurendeau raised Angers's suggestion and 'it was immediately accepted' (Smart, 1991, 27). Laurendeau recalled: 'The two Canadians who were to be neither French nor English were particularly difficult to find,' partly because of the decision to 'insist on bilingualism' (ibid.). Eventually, the government selected J.B. Rudnyckyj to be one of these commissioners; however, his appointment, although supported by the Canadian Linguistic Association and the Ukrainian Canadian Council of Learned Societies (among others), proved contentious within the Ukrainian community. At the time, while Rudnyckyj was a distinguished academic, the Ukrainian Canadian Committee was not unanimous in its support of him, believing that 'his appointment to the Commission was not in accordance with the hierarchy of the Ukrainian Canadian Committee' (Rudnyckyj, n.d.a). Nonetheless, Rudnyckyj became one of the 'New Canadian' commissioners and, as his activism on behalf of the third force would show, was not necessarily the anglophile on the commission that Angers had feared.

Rudnyckyj was the only bona fide linguist of the commissioners, and therefore most of his work for the inquiry and all the arguments he marshalled were grounded in the linguistic theory that was current at the time. Within the first few months of the inauguration of the commission, he drafted an internal memo setting out a preliminary review of concepts and definitions on bilingualism and biculturalism in Canada (Rudnyckyj, 1963). In this memo, as discussed earlier, he outlined his model of official and 'inofficial' bilingualism, and he also specified his interpretation of the terms of reference with regard to the three main groups of concern to the inquiry: 'The specification of the three constituent segments of the contemporary Canadian society – the founding peoples and the third element – indicates clearly that the Canadian authorities issuing the Order in Council had multiple bilingualism and multiple biculturalism in view entrusting the members of the Royal Commission with their task' (ibid., 3). Even at this early stage, Rudnyckyj was laying the groundwork of his arguments for language rights for other ethnic groups. In particular, he first raised the notion of multiple bilingualism and multiple biculturalism, which would become a large part of his future proposals.

Approximately five months later, Rudnyckyj produced an extensive fifteen-page research document for the commission entitled 'Ethnolingual Groups in Canada' (Rudnyckyj, 1964). This document began by reiterating the position set out by many other ethnic groups during the preliminary hearings that, given the wording of the terms of reference, all three groups were ethnic groups: 'It is clear that by using the word "other" the Government of Canada indicates that it considers the French and English element as "ethnic" as the other groups of Canadian population' (ibid., 1). For Rudnyckyj, placing the 'founding races' on par with 'other ethnic groups' in terms of their ethnicity was a crucial first step to claiming language rights for non-French and non-English groups. Rudnyckyj also linguistically historicized the various languages in Canada, giving rise to a taxonomy of language families and groupings that would feature prominently in his future petitions for language rights.

The rest of the report outlined Rudnyckyj's description of the various types of bilingualisms that existed in Canada through language contact, with a special focus on the Ukrainian language. His arguments drew heavily on current linguistic theory, concluding with two pages of proposals for bilingualism in Canada. Much of what he wrote in this report would surface again in another 'Separate Statement' that he would pen four years later in defending the principle of regional languages. Clearly, Rudnyckyj's commitment to representing the 'third force' was constant right from the start of his appointment to the commission. Yet, despite his ongoing attempts to make a linguistically grounded case for ethnic languages throughout the course of the inquiry's work, his arguments would appear nowhere else but in his separate statement appended to *Book I* of the final report. Rudnyckyj's statement is significant in that it is a final – officially acknowledged – effort within the context of the inquiry to have other ethnic groups' claims for some form of substantive recognition for their languages. Given the complexity of such a proposal, Rudnyckyj's strategies include using demographic, historical, and linguistic rationales; strategies which echo those used by the commission itself.

Rudnyckyj's Statement, dated 8 August 1967, began by stating that the supplementary considerations and additional recommendations it was to put forward were 'necessary if our Report has to stand the test of time, and if I personally am to be satisfied and convinced that our work was done well' (Canada, *Book I*, 1967, 155). He went on to stress that the words 'bilingualism and biculturalism' in the terms of reference were not just specific to English and French 'but also of all other forms of bilingualism in Canada' (ibid.). Rudnyckyj also drew on the very arguments made in the blue pages about the relation between language and culture with respect to the English and French groups, and applied them to other ethnic groups: 'Since its language is one of the most important components of any culture, languages other than English and French must be considered in an examination of the cultural contribution and cultural enrichment of Canada by other ethnic groups' (ibid., 156). In this way, he was able to build his argument that 'safeguarding' other ethnic groups' contributions would require additional constitutional consideration for 'the position of regional languages in Canada' (ibid.).

Rudnyckyj also put forward a historical rationale for his support for regional languages, specifying that some languages, which in the present were considered immigrant languages, had actually at some point been colonial languages in North America. His examples were the Russian and Ukrainian languages: 'In the 18th century, the Eastern Slavs had firmly established on the Pacific Coast of North America. The expansion of the Russian and Ukrainian languages in this area was connected with the development of the Russian American Company (1799)' (Canada, *Book I*, 1967, 157). Highlighting this particular history of the Russian and Ukrainian languages on the North American continent gave them a colonial provenance to naturalize their belonging in the present.[3]

In making the case for regional languages in Canada, Rudnyckyj drew not just on historical claims but also on demographic data: 'It is also obvious that among the Indigenous and immigrant languages, some are minor, numerically insignificant, and others are major, stretching through considerable areas of the country. Among the latter are the Eskimo-Indian languages in the Northwest Territories and the Yukon, Slavic (Ukrainian), and German languages in the Prairie Provinces, and Italian in the metropolitan areas of Toronto and Montreal' (Canada, *Book I*, 1967, 157). It was not just that these languages were the largest in demographic numbers after English and French; what was just as important was that 'no other unofficial languages can compare with these in their degree of concentration and contiguousness' (ibid., 158). Thus, the spatial concentration and boundedness of these languages provided a basis for a territorial claim within the nation.

Finally, Rudnyckyj used a taxonomic outline of language families to embed his argument in linguistic theory. He broke down the global spread of Indo-European language families into the Teutonic, Romance, and Slavic languages (Canada, *Book I*, 1967, 157). In his 1964 report, Rudnyckyj had used this classification and broken down the collective numbers for each language family in Canada. Under the Teutonic language family, 10,660,534 of this group were English speakers and 563,713 were German speakers; under the Romance language family, 5,123,151 were French speakers and 339,626 were Italian speakers; and under the Slavic language family, 361,496 were Ukrainian speakers (Rudnyckyj, 1964). This provided the basis for Rudnyckyj's conclusion that, after English and French, 'as far as the regional languages are concerned, the following lead quantitatively: German, Italian and Ukrainian in the Teutonic, Romance and Slavic language groups respectively' (Canada, *Book I*, 1967, 157). Although he had previously stated that the Indigenous languages were a historical-language classification in Canada with a territorially based claim, Rudnyckyj now shifted the focus exclusively to immigrant languages with the rationale that '[t]here are no leading languages in the Eskimo-Indian group, which are spoken by 167,000 people ... Thus German, Italian and Ukrainian should be regarded not only as the main regional languages, but also as the representative of the main immigrant linguistic families in Canada' (ibid.). The argument that there were no 'leading' languages in the Eskimo-Indian group echoed earlier statements in the commission research reports that Indigenous languages were too numerous and fragmented to merit official consideration.

Rudnyckyj's identification of three main regional languages was linked to his recognition of two types of bilingualism – official bilingualism and regional bilingualism – which in turn was related to his advocacy of multiple bilingualisms. Defining regional bilingualism as the 'knowledge and use of one of the official languages (English or French) along with another mother tongue' (Canada, *Book I*, 1967, 161), he elaborated that 'the main types of such bilingualism in Canada are English-German, English-Italian, English-Ukrainian, and French-Italian, French-Ukrainian, French-German' (ibid.). This was the form of bilingualism that Rudnyckyj advocated for the preservation of regional languages.

Rudnyckyj's rationale for the recognition of regional languages and regional bilingualism was closely tied to his concern for the prestige of ethnic languages. In particular, he quoted submissions from Ukrainian communities about discriminatory attitudes towards ethnic languages, linking this to the decline in mother-tongue levels of Ukrainian. Rudnyckyj cited census data which showed that in the last decade, approximately 13 per cent of Canadians of Ukrainian origin had lost command of their language and, in most cases, had switched to English (Canada, *Book I*, 1967, 166). He connected such language loss to the Ukrainian language's lack of formal recognition, which he argued was 'essential for diminishing the discriminatory attitudes of some Canadians towards "non-Canadian" languages (are they are sometimes branded), and for raising their low-prestige status in comparison with languages formally recognized by the Constitution' (ibid., 163).

Besides making explicit the link between mother-tongue language retention and language prestige and legal status, Rudnyckyj, using Ukrainian as an example, also warned of mother-tongue decline and the eventual extinction of immigrant languages. In effect, through his formulation of regional languages and bilingualisms, Rudnyckyj was calling for an action plan for defending what he deemed to be the main immigrant languages. The alternative, as he pointed out, was linguicide: 'Some governments deliberately inflict on ethno-lingual groups conditions of cultural backwardness by refusing to help in their organic linguistic and cultural development. As a result the low-prestige feeling develops within the groups concerned and lingual switches to dominant languages occur' (Canada, *Book I*, 1967, 164). This was the passive form of linguicide that Rudnyckyj identified in the Canadian case – that is, the neglect and the failure to accord status to non-official languages. He made a connection between the lack of government aid for ethno-lingual groups and the need for recognition of regional languages if the decline and eventual linguicide of immigrant mother-tongues were to be halted. His comments foreshadowed *Book IV*'s weak recommendations concerning government 'help' for other ethnic groups' language preservation.

As in chapter 4 of *Book I*, Rudnyckyj compared the constitutional protection of minority-language rights in various countries in order to extrapolate a set of guiding principles for regional and minority-language rights. Although chapter 4 looked mainly to Western Europe – Finland, Switzerland, Belgium – and to the white-settler society of South Africa as countries that had accorded full equality to their linguistic minorities (Canada, *Book I*,1967, 75), Rudnyckyj looked to other multilingual societies in Eastern Europe – Romania, Byelorussia, and the Ukraine – as well as to Austria in Western Europe and to India and Burma in Asia for his comparisons. In his examples, the protection of minority, regional, or unofficial languages was constitutionally specified, a fact that helped him to bolster his case for the constitutional recognition of regional languages in Canada.

Rudnyckyj claimed that, for the commission, constitutional provisions for unofficial languages were not completely out of the question, given public demand for recognition of languages other than English and French, and that these provisions could be modelled on the Swiss example which distinguished between 'official' and 'national' languages (Canada, *Book I*, 1967, 165). Citing specific studies and statements supporting the recognition of 'unofficial' languages in Canada, Rudnyckyj proposed a new subsection 5 of section 133 of the BNA Act, which was to read as follows: 'Notwithstanding anything in this section, any language other than English and French used by 10 per cent or more of the population of an appropriate administrative district of a province or territory shall have the status of a regional language; the legislation of the provisions for regional languages shall be vested in the governments concerned' (ibid., 168).

Anticipating one of the major criticisms of this model, Rudnyckyj stated that 'the new recommended subsection on regional languages provided the necessary checks against any "Balkanization" of the linguistic scene in Canada, since to be recognized as a regional language required the existence of a group of adherents comprising 10 per cent or more of the population in the given region' (Canada, *Book I*, 1967, 168); here drawing on the commission's recommendation that a language be used by 10 per cent or more of the population in order to qualify for recognition of official-language minority rights. Rudnyckyj ended his statement with the assertion that constitutional provisions for the recognition of regional languages would not only provide the 'indisputable legal means to safeguard the cultural contribution of major ethnic groups,' as outlined in the terms of reference, but would be an open-ended provision offering opportunities to retain and develop the language and culture of any viable ethno-lingual group in Canada (ibid., 169).

Although Rudnyckyj's recommendations regarding regional languages ultimately were never reflected in the Official Languages Act, his statement did surface as part of the debate on official languages in Parliament. In the House of Commons, Edward Schreyer of the NDP supported the idea of multiple official languages by citing Trudeau's address in Winnipeg to six hundred Liberals – which had included representatives from Winnipeg's Ukrainian population and other large ethnic minorities (Canada, *House of Commons Debates*, 1968, 1500) – a half-year earlier, while Trudeau was still justice minister. Quoting a Winnipeg *Free Press* article, Schreyer referred to Trudeau's rejection of the common notion that French deserved official recognition because the French were one of the 'two founding groups'; rather, Trudeau had claimed that after French, he would even be prepared to say that 'if in the immediate future or far future a third important group speaking a third language ... wanted to use their language to communicate with the state, this third language will have to be recognized,' and even that 'a fourth official language was also conceivable' (ibid.). Schreyer then turned to Rudnyckyj's recommendations: 'I sincerely believe that although it may not be practical to extend an official status to other languages, nevertheless it is desirable ... to aid through the instrumentality of the state, federal or provincial, the sustenance of the other languages' (ibid.).

Although Schreyer professed not to concur entirely with Rudnyckyj's recommendation that all the regional languages be given 'official status,' his views were congruent with Rudnyckyj's insofar as he also believed that cultural preservation for other ethnic groups required the preservation of their language. Schreyer concluded that the Prime Minister should at least 'give consideration to ways and means in which these other languages could be materially supported by assistance through the schools' (Canada, *House of Commons Debates*, 1968, 1500). His suggestions for ethnic-language preservation, although more modest than those of Rudnyckyj, still advocated and specified concrete support for this objective, 'to provide the teachers, to provide the audio-visual aids and books which would make it possible to teach the various ethnic languages, and to amend the law in the several provinces so that it will be possible to use those languages as languages of instruction in the schools for at least part of the day' (ibid., 1501).

Schreyer's suggestions, though muted in comparison to Rudnyckyj's, provoked a swift response in the House. Bernard Dumont, a member of the Social Credit Party, which he described as 'the official opposition of Quebec,' declared: 'I cannot imagine myself in a Canada, where in addition to French and English, we would have to learn Chinese, Russian, Spanish and maybe ten more languages. We are instead a country where bilingualism [French, English] should be recognized' (Canada, *House of Commons Debates*, 1968, 1501). Given the lack of demand for non-official language support from the Chinese community, placing Chinese as the first language of the 'ten more' that might have to be learned was meant to underscore the absurdity of ethnic-language preservation, but the tactic also emphasized the racist underpinnings of a point of view that designated Chinese-language preservation as the essence of the absurd. Nevertheless, despite Shreyer's detailed intervention and muted support for the spirit of Rudnyckyj's statement, it would be Dumont's formulation of language recognition that would become official.

Concluding Summary

Book I of the final report was the first official, published statement of the inquiry's findings since the publication of the *Preliminary Report* in 1965. It was primarily concerned with engineering the 'equal partnership' between the two official language groups as a response to the crisis outlined in the *Preliminary Report*. *Book I* was also the place where some facts were legitimized against others in order to justify certain features and forms of recommendations for policy. In particular, the definition of key words in the terms of reference, and a set organization of inquiry findings into textually reified form, developed the recommendations for an equal partnership between the two founding groups.

This task began through rearticulation of the precise operation for language and culture as the new terrain for organizing inclusion. The blue pages were paradigmatic in the sense of demonstrating that federal definitions and discourses about key terms and relations between the two founding groups, Indigenous groups, and other ethnic groups were being established. The blue pages began by quickly dismissing 'race' as a term that had any salience within the inquiry, preferring instead to use 'language' and 'culture,' and thereby inaugurating the terms 'anglophone' and 'francophone.' The report also defined biculturalism, as it pertained to the English and French groups, as a driving force which animated a significant group of individuals who were united through a common tongue. This was different from how culture was signified for other ethnic groups, where a narrower definition of culture as a cultural production, and without the requirement of language maintenance, was deemed unproblematic and possible. With this contradictory differentiation in the definition of culture, the report saw the recognition of collective language rights as a necessity, but only for English and French. Although the heterogeneity of the two collective and distinct English and French cultures was acknowledged, other ethnic groups were regarded as partial societies, as centrifugal elements always moving away from the centre and located on the periphery of the central, founding cultures. In this way, the federal definition of culture – already embedded in an exclusionary Judeo-Christian matrix – had a built-in contradiction that turned on the collective right to language in order to differentiate between other ethnic and founding groups.

This contradiction, which became visible as the report mapped out its model for bilingualism and biculturalism for the two founding groups, was based on a particular, inconsistent definition of culture. This definition advanced collective language rights only to English and French on the rationale that these language groups were porous and open enough to assimilate everyone, even as it relegated these other groups to the periphery of the English and French collectivities. The notion that these collective language groups could be infiltrated by other ethnic groups also structured the latter's language shift as a personal and free choice or an exercise of their already guaranteed individual rights, allowing the commission to maintain that its main purpose was to entrench the collective language rights of the two founding groups. Not only did this fail to address the question of those who were left unassimilated and unassimilable into either of the two founding groups but it also prevented any claims by other ethnic groups for collective linguistic rights. Hence, the openness of language as it was advanced in the report was foreclosed through this contradictory definition of culture – or biculturalism, to use the report's word – and language became a technology for differential inclusion which recapitulated the original racial hierarchy of the terms of reference, even as these original terms of inclusion were disavowed.

Indigenous groups, although expediently removed from the purview of the inquiry, were, along with other ethnic groups, essential for the establishment of the equal partnership between the two founding races – even if it was as a foil to the establishment of a white-settler commonality between the English and French in Canada. The commission also drew upon the example of South Africa, a white-settler society with the greatest congruence to the Canadian linguistic situation, in order to inform the new personality principle of bilingualism it was advancing, thereby also emphasizing the colonial foundations of the new *bi*-nation it envisaged. All these discussions were distilled into recommendations at the end of *Book I* for an equal partnership based on English-French bilingualism and biculturalism – recommendations that found fruition almost a year later as a bill on the official languages. As parliamentarians debated that bill, a concern with national unity emerged from different political perspectives. Overall, it was clear that the equal partnership between the two founding groups could not occur without recognition of the rights of Indigenous and other ethnic groups, even as these groups found themselves marginalized in the commission's recommendations.

Rudnyckyj's separate statement represented a final official attempt to resist this marginalization. Rudnyckyj drew on demographic, historical, and linguistic rationales to develop a taxonomy of Canadian languages and set out his model for the constitutional recognition of regional languages. However, his strategy was to push for the inclusion of other ethnic groups into the white-settler template of the two founding peoples, thereby reinscribing some of the fundamental exclusions that were built into the final report. Specifically, he rested his linguistically based claims on the erasure of Indigenous languages, proposing a linguistic taxonomy that entrenched the recognition of European languages only. Such a strategy for inclusion assured that it would offer recognition only to those who could 'pass' as part of the white-settler population, reinforcing the exclusion of all who could not be 'white.' Even though Rudnyckyj's proposals did not become policy, they did reassert the demands for inclusion by other ethnic groups – just as they foreshadowed the future shifts that concurrent changes in immigration policy would bring about in the category of other ethnic groups, with some of the people belonging to this category eventually managing to pass into the white-settler majority. As *Book I* decisively demonstrated, the establishment of an equal partnership between the two founding groups, based on white settler bi-nationalism, required a consideration of the place of other ethnic groups within the nation; this was a question that would be taken up in detail in *Book IV* of the final report.

6 Book IV: The Cultural Contribution of the Other Ethnic Groups

The publication of *Book I* on *The Official Languages* was followed by *Book II* on *Education*, which focused on education particularly as it pertained to the two official languages; and *Book III* on the *Work World*, which focused on the place of the two official languages in the work world of the federal public service. On 23 October 1969 – by which point the Official Languages Act (1969) had already been adopted in Parliament – *Book IV*, entitled *The Cultural Contribution of the Other Ethnic Groups*, was published.

While *Book I* addressed the need to develop an 'equal partnership between the two founding races' in its attempt to engineer a new white-settler *bi-*nation through a contradictory definition of culture, *Book IV* focused on the 'contribution made by the other ethnic groups to the cultural enrichment of Canada and the measures that should be taken to safeguard that contribution' (Canada, *Book IV*, 1969, 3). Specifically, the contradictory operation of language and culture that emerged in *Book I* to organize the relationship between other ethnic and founding groups was reified into a particular set of recommendations in *Book IV*, ostensibly to safeguard other ethnic groups' 'cultural contributions,' which would then ultimately be turned into policy. This chapter first traces the development of the idea of cultural contribution and then turns its attention to the commission's narrow definition of integration as the mode by which cultural contribution would be safeguarded. Next, the focus shifts to community and government responses to the recommendations of *Book IV* and the evolution of these recommendations into policy.

During the course of the inquiry, integration emerged as a 'social theory of Canadian official policy' (Wyczynski, 1966) which could organize the inclusion of other ethnic groups; it came to be narrowly defined in *Book IV* as the progressive, unidirectional contribution of linguistic diversity to the two dominant groups. As well, official-language competency became the concrete measure of integration and, through the commission's definition of language transfer, a continuum of racialized difference was embedded into integration. Language became a central element in the commission's definition of integration, culminating in the acculturation model of integration proposed in *Book IV*, which advocated the adjustment of immigrant behaviour to the norms of the two official-language communities.

The paucity of substantive legislative support for the preservation of the culture of other ethnic groups and the atomization of any notion of a 'third force' entrenched the contradiction of collective rights solely for founding groups against the individual 'freedom' to integrate for other ethnic or 'cultural' groups. Trudeau's announcement of a policy of 'multiculturalism within a bilingual framework' as a response to the recommendations of *Book IV* grew out of the government's need to balance competing forces and tensions in the overriding interest of national unity. However, by adopting the recommendations of the final report almost wholesale, this policy did little to disrupt the original bilingual and bicultural formulation of the white-settler nation advanced by the commission.

Internal Commission Documents

As internal commission documents show, the issue of 'other ethnic groups' had been on the research agenda of the inquiry since its inception. In addition to the collected research documents and submissions regarding other ethnic groups, there were the reports and memoranda from the commission's Study Group D, which was concerned with 'other cultures' and which began to compile and organize the material and ideas that would pertain to the other ethnic groups in the final report. As early as December 1963, the group had produced a working paper with respect to the issue of the other cultures (Study Group D, 1963). This working paper attempted to specify the exact location of the other cultures in the inquiry:

There is no specific allusion to the 'other' cultures in the two paragraphs [of the terms of reference] which deal with the federal administration (1) and education (3). This is rather revealing. It seems that in these two areas it is assumed that Canadians of other backgrounds have opted for one of the two official languages and cultures. Certain people draw from this fact the conclusion that Canada is actually two melting pots. But the opening paragraph strictly forbids, or in any case limits, this interpretation ... In summary we can say that the mainspring (l'idée force) of the terms of reference is the question of bilingualism and biculturalism (i.e. English and French) adding immediately that this mainspring is working in a situation where there is the fact of multiculturalism – multiculturalism that must not be suppressed as quickly as possible (the proverbial melting pot), but on the contrary, respected and safeguarded despite not being given official recognition. (Study Group D, 1963, 1)

Study Group D's working paper laid the groundwork, even before the hearings had been held and the submissions had been considered, for the model of language and culture with respect to founding races and other ethnic groups that would eventually emerge in the final report; that is, a 'safeguarding' of multiculturalism even as it was to have no official recognition.

On 28 May 1966, almost three years after Study Group D's working paper, Commissioner Paul Wyczynski presented a memorandum to the other commission members and staff titled 'Les autres groupes ethniques – Rapport Préliminaire' (Wyczynski, 1966). A preliminary report regarding the volume on other ethnic groups (to become *Book IV*), Wyczynski's memorandum began by lamenting the lack of research on the topic of other ethnic groups: 'Regrettably, most chapters of a well-elaborated plan for the Other Ethnic Groups' section of the Commission's Report still remain in the realm of planning' (ibid., 3). At this point in the inquiry, although the hearings had come to an end, the research portion was still underway. In the end, the commission did complete some research on other ethnic groups, including an extensive overview of immigration history[1] and several ethno-specific histories of groups in Canada.[2] However, it was not clear whether this was sufficient to address Wyczynski's concerns as expressed in his memorandum, which also outlined the basic order of topics that would be covered in the final report, beginning with a historical introduction on the immigration of other ethnic groups to Canada.

Wyczynski made two important points about this immigration history, both of which were about the effects of the immigration of other ethnic groups on the overall composition of the population: 'The most striking characteristic of the Other Ethnic Group immigration is its increased strength at the expense of the British element' and 'the fairly drastic change in its ethnic composition. The Germans retained the top place, but the Scandinavians were displaced by the Ukrainians and Dutch. Equally telling is the upward movement of the Italian group which within one decade, 1951–1961, moved from tenth to fifth place ...' (Wyczynski, 1966, 4–5). These points reflected the concerns of many – which would be expressed in the discussion of census data in *Book I* – that the increase in immigration of other ethnic groups was diluting the population numbers of the 'core societies.' The composition of the other ethnic groups was shifting, becoming less northern European and more southern European. The immigration of other ethnic groups was also affecting the regional distribution of the core societies. All these issues were taken up at length in *Book I*, as described in the previous chapter, presumably because of the importance of demographic shifts for the founding groups.

The next section of Wyczynski's memorandum, titled 'The Social Pattern,' sought an overarching social theory to account for the place of other ethnic groups. Although this quest for a social theory to account for the place of other ethnic groups in official Canadian policy could probably be considered the first step that would eventually lead to an official multiculturalism policy, there was a long way to go before such a policy could be implemented. Wyczynski made no mention of the word *multiculturalism*, even though it had figured in the 1963 working paper, and wrote, 'Anglo-Saxon Conformity, the Melting Pot and Cultural Pluralism ... Each one of these has had its heyday ...' (Wyczynski, 1966, 7). In their place, another model had emerged: 'The Canadian social theorists and pseudo-theorists came up first with the so-called Canadian Mosaic which lately has taken on a more "scientific" name – Integration' (ibid.). The memorandum then discussed the main elements of integration, noting that '[t]he current social pattern may, indeed, not correspond to a classical Anglo-Saxon Conformity concept ... in Canada, under the umbrella of the socio-political patterns and basic cultural values of the two core societies, there exists a myriad of the sub-societies and sub-cultures roughly corresponding to the number of the cultural groups' (ibid.).

Wyczynski's integration model included a reinscription of the hierarchy between the 'sub-societies and sub-cultures,' or other ethnic groups, and the bicultural character of the two core societies, with Anglo-Saxon conformity seen as an overarching socio-political pattern. The idea of other ethnic groups as sub-cultures and sub-societies was also naturalized, 'the degree of their intensity in maintaining a separate identity is the outcome of the multiplicity of factors emanating from the two societies in contact: the receiving and immigrant one. Sociologists suggest that among the most determining forces and factors are ... the cultural distance separating a minority group from the core society; here the racial and religious elements play a crucial role' (Wyczynski, 1966, 8). This bifurcation between 'receiving' and 'immigrant' societies reinforced the hierarchy between 'core' and 'other' groups (ibid).[3]

The memorandum also expanded on integration as a problem of cultural distance, stating that other ethnic groups from the 'Protestant wing of Christianity' showed the lowest intensity of self-identification and highest degree of integration and assimilation, whereas '[a]t the other extreme of the scale we find the groups most removed from the Anglo-Saxon cultural values, i.e. Slavs, Romance and more "exotic" groups' (ibid., 9). By locating the 'more "exotic" groups' at the extreme end of cultural distance, Wyczynski thereby established a continuum that measured difference by a degree of variance from the core Anglo-Saxon cultural values. The characterization of 'more "exotic"' cultures as being the farthest away from Anglo-Saxon once again reinscribed their racialization.

Although Wyczynski's memorandum put integration forward as a 'social theory of Canadian official policy' that could account for other ethnic groups, the distinctions between integration and assimilation were still not clearly and fully formulated. Wyczynski stated categorically that 'most certainly, integration is a euphemism for assimilation, [and] will remain the core of the dominant societies' policies' (Wyczynski, 1966, 11), and then further discussed the different tensions and balances that needed to be considered to achieve a workable Canadian social theory, maintaining all the hierarchies between core and other ethnic groups along a continuum of increasingly racialized difference. It was this narrow definition of integration, authored by one of the 'New Canadian' commissioners, that would eventually be used in relation to other ethnic groups in the final report.

'Cultural Contributions': Ilona M. Varjassy's Report

As the title indicated, the main focus of *Book IV* was supposed to be 'the cultural contribution of the other ethnic groups.' The need to specify exactly what 'cultural contribution' was could be traced back to an internal commission report entitled 'Cultural Contribution' authored by Ilona M. Varjassy on 7 June 1966. This document began by designating the '4 segments' of population that emerged from the terms of reference, which were the English, the French, the official-language minorities, and 'Canadians from other than French or English cultural background' who 'live and express values in one of the two founding societies' (Varjassy, 1966a, 4). Varjassy's main focus, however, was the nature of cultural contribution; this was broken down further into two 'necessary elements' for individuals 'from other than English or French cultural background[s]': a 'positive or progressive integration' and 'progressively active participation' (ibid.6–7). Positive or progressive integration was particular only to the other ethnic groups and implied 'the organization of the various cultural values of the individual and also of the society into one compatibly arranged entity' (ibid.). From this discussion, Varjassy embraced the central point that integration was a key condition for cultural contributions.

Varjassy's (1966a) report also endorsed state support for ethnic mother-tongue retention, which was broken down into a *permissive* acknowledgement of the 'values expressed in "ethnic schools"' as well as a *supportive* attitude towards the values of 'ethnic languages' in society through the offering of 'modern languages of regional interest' in public school on an optional basis (12). Varjassy's proposal for two types of state support for ethnic languages fell considerably short of recommending official-language status, but it resembled the regional recognition for ethnic languages advanced by Rudnyckyj. Support for ethnic languages was also based on the rationale that these were 'modern' languages, a point that Varjassy developed further in a chart that traced the evolution of Canadian society. In the section entitled 'Second Half of the XX Century,' this chart first stated that 'for national and international reasons the societies realized the need to understand cultures, and are realizing the importance of languages' (ibid., 16). It further elaborated: 'Ethnic language is "becoming" a modern language' (ibid., 17). This characterization of ethnic languages as modern languages that were useful for national and international reasons was discernibly different from the usual commission discourse that cast other-ethnic-group languages as mainly traditional and ancestral.

Varjassy added a supplement to this report on 8 July 1966 which she sent to the members of Study Group D. In it, she made this comment on the terms of reference: 'The Terms of Reference refer to a "basically bicultural character" of Canada and to the "contributions made by other cultures." This presentation undoubtedly implies a multicultural reality of our country' (Varjassy, 1966b). Varjassy's acknowledgment that there could be an interpretation of the terms of reference that implied a 'multicultural reality' – as well as the various submissions to the commission that described Canada as a multicultural nation – would be refuted in the final report.

In *Book IV*'s introduction, the discussion on cultural contribution began by revisiting the definition of culture that had been advanced in *Book I*: 'It is a driving force animating a significant group of individuals, united by a common tongue, and sharing the same customs, habits and experiences' (Canada, *Book IV*, 1969, 11). This definition of culture had been applied to the founding groups in *Book I*, and in *Book IV* it was applied to the other ethnic groups as well. However, here it was applied to other ethnic groups in terms of the enrichment they brought as they integrated to the two dominant cultures: 'Thus, streams empty into a river and their waters mix and swell the river's flow ... culture cannot be measured by the pound' (ibid.). The metaphor of streams emptying into a river located the smaller, other ethnic groups (streams) in relation to the larger river (the two founding societies), with the river's flow along its predetermined course being augmented, or in this case enriched, by the waters of the streams. The direction of the contribution, from stream to river, was clear, and the benefits could accrue only to the river – streams 'swell the river's flow' – because rivers were not meant to reverse course and empty into and augment the flow of streams. If culture could not be measured here by the pound, as the report suggested, perhaps it could by the gallon?

Ultimately, whether cast in metaphor, typologies, or plain bureaucratic prose, the cultural contribution of other ethnic groups always came back to integration, and no matter how much was said about mutual accommodation between the founding 'host' society and the 'immigrant' group, this was a model of integration based on what the cultural group could provide as enrichment to the founding society. The Introduction of *Book IV* offered a historical view of cultural contribution that revisited Varjassy's typologies, and, although it did not explicitly name it as such, it did formulate cultural contribution as progressive integration (Canada, *Book IV*, 1969, 12). This discussion came to the conclusion that, as a result of the various individual and group influences in the process of integration, it was 'nearly impossible to officialize culture' (ibid., 11). However, in the next section, official culture was affirmed:

Among those of non-British, non-French origin, some accept official bilingualism without hesitation but categorically reject biculturalism.

They consider Canada to be a country that is officially bilingual but fundamentally multi-cultural. In reply to this objection we wish to repeat that 'in our view the term "biculturalism" covers two main realities. The first is the state of each of the two cultures, and the opportunity of each to exist and flourish. The second is the co-existence and collaborations of these two cultures . . . ' On the other hand, our terms of reference mention the 'basically bicultural nature of our country and the subsequent contribution made by other cultures.' It is thus clear that we must not overlook Canada's cultural diversity, keeping in mind that there are two dominant cultures, the French and the English. (Canada, *Book IV*, 1969, 13)

In this way, a conventional interpretation of the terms of reference that foregrounded the 'basically bicultural nature' of the country served once and for all to dismiss all claims made during the hearings that Canada was a bilingual and multicultural country, and characterized the contributions made by other cultures as 'subsequent' to the primary fact of biculturalism, or the two dominant cultures. This interpretation of the terms of reference (dating back to the *Preliminary Report*) ignored all competing views, even if they were in the commission's own documents – such as the one by Varjassy, discussed above – which suggested that the same passage of the terms of reference implied the 'multicultural reality of our country.' As a result, the racial hierarchy of the terms of reference was reinforced and the white-settler basis of Canadian nationhood could be confirmed. In any event, the term *multiculturalism* did not appear again in the rest of *Book IV* (Momryk, 1988). Instead, cultural contribution was linked to integration and, with the final refutation of multiculturalism in the report, there began to emerge a notion of cultural contribution as a progressive, 'modern' linguistic resource for the founding dualities.

Book IV: Content and Recommendations

Culture and Language

Book IV effectively took important steps towards locating other ethnic groups in the commission's model of a white settle bi-nation, steps that would resonate in federal policies and discourses long after it was published. In some ways, the introduction to this volume of the report was the most significant part, since it consolidated in one place much of the previous thinking about other ethnic groups that had arisen in past reports and commission documents; it was in this introduction that the positioning of other ethnic groups – until now scattered throughout myriad discussions about official languages, cultures, and communities – was explained and summarized. Despite some repetition of previous commission discussions about other ethnic groups, the introduction provided the animating force behind *Book IV*'s recommendations. Key among these was the redefinition of other ethnic groups as cultural groups, emphasizing culture over language – and thus recapitulating the contradictory operation of language and culture in the positioning of other ethnic groups in relation to the two founding groups. As well, the relationship between language and culture, which was a topic of in-depth consideration in the blue pages of *Book I*, was revisited again in *Book IV*'s Introduction with reference to the other ethnic groups: 'We will look at . . . the enrichment that results from the meeting of a number of languages and cultures. This contribution is seen, within the Canadian reality, in the active participation of those whose mother tongue is neither French nor English in various facets of community life' (Canada, *Book IV*, 1969, 3–4).

Other ethnic groups were also now being defined as linguistic groups, albeit still distinctive to the English and French. The groundwork was being laid for defining cultural contribution as substantively about language; other ethnic groups' enrichment of Canadian life was said to result from a kind of cultural and linguistic 'meeting' as opposed to a clash between other ethnic groups and founding races (ibid.). The report explained the relation between ethnic languages and other cultural groups as follows: 'Culture and language which serves as its vehicle cannot be dissociated . . . The vitality of the different languages spoken in Canada, other than French or English, varies from one cultural group to another, and even within these groups, where many people speak their ancestral language poorly or not at all' (ibid., 13). In *Book I*, the argument that language was the vehicle of culture meant that the two could not be dissociated, which was one of the fundamental reasons why the commission recommended a full range of English and French official-language legislation and constitutional changes. By comparison, in *Book IV*, other ethnic groups were characterized as having varying levels of competence in their 'different languages,' and these languages were characterized as 'ancestral languages' in direct distinction from the earlier characterization of ethnic languages as modern and cosmopolitan in Varjassy's report in June 1966. This qualitative differentiation between ethnic languages as represented in Varjassy's report and in *Book IV* translated into concrete differences in the types of recommended state support:

> We have already stressed the ties between language and culture. In Book I of our Report, on the official languages, we proposed a new version of section 133 of the British North America Act, whose subsection 5 would read:
>
> Nothing in this section shall be taken to diminish or restrict the use, as established by present or future law or practice, of any other language in Canada. (Canada, *Book IV*, 1969, 13)

In Varjassy's report, a 'permissive' and 'supportive' approach to state support was recommended, while *Book IV* offered 'ancestral' ethnic languages only 'permissive' or, effectively, passive constitutional protection. The report provided the rationale that, 'with the exception of our colleague, Commissioner J.B. Rudnyckyj, we interpret our terms of reference as limiting constitutional change to the country's two official languages' (ibid., 13–14). Furthermore, the commissioners were convinced that the new subsection 5 in section 133, as well as measures taken at the provincial levels, would suffice for the preservation of the languages of other cultural groups (ibid.). Rudnyckyj referred to the proposed subsection 5 as a 'preventative anti-lingual clause' (Rudnyckyj, n.d.b), and the Ukrainian Canadian Committee stated that at best it 'provides for a toleration' and called for a more 'positive formulation' (Ukrainian Canadian Committee, 1971).

The Introduction to *Book IV* ended with an assessment of the cultural contribution of other ethnic groups or, as they were known at this point, cultural groups (Canada, *Book IV*, 1969, 14). Cultural groups were set apart by their language and culture, either by birth or ancestry, and were seen to provide enrichment to Canadian society. But it was clear that, as in the metaphor of the river and the streams, the enrichment was accrued by the 'dominant cultures' and that the substance of these benefits was 'linguistic variety.' Thus, even when language had been stripped from other ethnic groups to give rise to the moniker *cultural groups*, ethnic languages still constituted the limit of their cultural contribution.

Moreover, the report stated that the purportedly valuable enrichment of linguistic variety had to be maintained through the efforts of the cultural groups themselves: 'Their [cultural groups in Canada] members must always enjoy the right – a basic one – to safeguard their languages and cultures. The exercise of this right requires an extra effort on their part, for which their fellow Canadians owe them a debt of gratitude' (Canada, *Book IV*, 1969, 14). This extra effort stemmed from the paucity of legislation and constitutional protection for the other ethnic languages, which relegated linguistic and cultural preservation to the private sphere. However, this debt would be acknowledged – if not with concrete state support, then at least with gratitude.

By the end of the introduction, the cultural contributions of cultural groups were said to transcend 'ethnic differences,' and instead it was proposed that these contributions were assets for the country as a whole. This recalled the narrow and humanistic definition of culture that was outlined in *Book IV* as opposed to the more expansive definition of culture that was applied to the two founding groups. The commodification of the cultural contribution of other ethnic groups foreshadowed the focus and recommendations to come in the rest of *Book IV*.

The Redefinition of Ethnic Groups

If the introduction was significantly concerned with the 'contribution made by other ethnic groups to the cultural enrichment of Canada' (Canada, *Book IV*, 1969, 3), then subsequently – as was customary by now in commission publications – the concerns of other ethnic groups were located in relation to the two founding groups in the terms of reference:

> It will be noted immediately that while the terms of reference deal with the questions of those of ethnic origin other than British or French, they do so in relation to the basic problem of bilingualism and biculturalism, from which they are inseparable, and the context of the coexistence of the Francophone and Anglophone communities. Also the terms of reference do not call for an exhaustive study of the position of those of non-British, non-French origin, but rather an examination of the way they have taken their place within the two societies that have provided Canada's social structures and institutions. (Canada, *Book IV*, 1969, 3)

The shift from 'founding races' to 'official linguistic communities' or 'Anglophones and Francophones' was meant to suggest that these core communities were supposedly open to any member of any other ethnic group, although this was countered by the contradictory relation between culture and language developed in *Book I*. Nevertheless, the commission's sole concern regarding other ethnic groups was still articulated in terms of 'their place within the two societies' or their integration into the 'two official linguistic communities.'

Book IV also had an extensive discussion of integration. This began with the responsibilities of citizenship on the part of the newcomer – recognition of the 'fundamental principles' of two official languages and two distinct and predominant cultures (ibid). The commission made it clear that the maintenance of the hegemony of biculturalism and bilingualism was an essential function of integration. It did note that a linguistically defined duality was open to the integration of the newcomer. Yet immigrants, although at liberty to integrate into either of the 'two societies,' were still differentiated from those of French or British origin through history – that is, a history of colonization, couched here as the 'definite advantage of having colonized Canada.' As well, equality of rights and obligations for all Canadians was mounted on the bedrock of a fundamental duality. In short, in order to have the same rights as all Canadians, a newcomer had to integrate into one of the founding communities.

Integration

Integration had been discussed, in some depth, in the commission reports and research documents that preceded *Book IV*. In a report on a private meeting with the director of the Citizenship Branch (and in contrast with the memorandum by Commissioner Wyczynski), Jean Lagasse stated that his definition of integration was 'language assimilation' although not cultural assimilation (Stinson, 1966). However, a few years later, *Book IV* completely severed integration from any notion of assimilation. 'Integration is not synonymous with assimilation,' the Introduction said, because 'assimilation implies almost total absorption into another linguistic and cultural group' (Canada, *Book IV*, 1969, 5). Instead, the report advanced a definition of integration that was tied to acculturation, which it defined as follows:

> Acculturation is the process of adaptation to the environment in which an individual is compelled to live as he adjusts his behaviour to that of the community ... in adopting fully the Canadian way of life, sharing its advantages and disadvantages, those whose origin is neither French nor British do not have to cast off or hide their own culture ... Canadian

society, open and modern, should be able to integrate heterogeneous elements into a harmonious system, to achieve 'unity in diversity.' (Ibid., 6–7).

This definition made it plain that the responsibility for behavioural adjustment to 'Canadian' community norms lay with the integrating newcomers, who did not necessarily have to cast off or hide their culture; it could remain a 'heterogeneous' element in the homogeneity of the two founding cultures as 'unity within diversity.' In effect, integration as acculturation was the social theory that would account for the location of other ethnic groups within what was now a modern anglophone and francophone society. Therefore, other ethnic groups occupied a paradoxical position. On the one hand, they were at 'liberty' to enjoy their full rights if they integrated into the linguistically defined anglophone and francophone societies. On the other, as members of non-British and non-French ethnic groups, they were also distinct and apart from each founding society.

Given the importance of integration as the social theory of choice, the report was next concerned with how to gauge the integration of other ethnic groups (Canada, *Book IV*, 1969, 8). The need to integrate these groups arose from their status as people in between their ancestral language and culture, which served to set them apart from the open and modern founding Canadian societies. The commission also mentioned ethnic groups' determination to maintain their ancestral languages and cultures through, for example, 'associations, clubs, parishes, and religious organizations' (ibid., 9). Although the commission acknowledged the existence of a private network committed to preserving the languages and cultures of other ethnic groups, it in no way considered this to be a public issue; rather, such matters were a private concern beyond the purview of the commission's mandate. Nor was the maintenance of ancestral linguistic and cultural ties in the private realm seen as a 'balkanizing' threat to national unity, since, in the commission's estimation, 'only 1 per cent of the Canadian population speaks neither English nor French' (ibid.). The number of people who spoke an official language was a measure of the success of immigrant integration, which meant that integration could now be quantified through the official-language competency of immigrant groups.

In *Book IV*, the commission decisively separated integration from assimilation by linking it to acculturation, a process that required the adjustment of immigrant behaviour to the norms of the two official-language communities. In this way, integration gave rise to the rhetoric of diversity or unity in diversity, where cultural groups were at liberty to integrate into anglophone and francophone societies – something they had to do in order to enjoy full citizenship rights, while paradoxically they remained heterogeneous, diverse, and centrifugal elements within these fundamental dualities. Ease of integration was also defined along a cultural and racial continuum of difference, which measured the cultural and racial proximity of other ethnic groups to the 'normal' pole of the 'North American cultural base.' Thus, the increasingly narrowed and specified definition of integration, as it was elaborated in *Book IV*, served to maintain the white-settler, bilingual, and bicultural hegemony.

'The Historical Background'

The main section of *Book IV* began with a chapter, entitled 'The Historical Background,' that traced the history of immigration to Canada through the census records. As the commissioners stated, however, this account gave 'less than the full story' because the questions asked on ethnic origin differed over the years, making the data difficult to compare. Other problems included difficulties people had in accurately identifying, or wishing to identify, their ethnic backgrounds; as well as the fact that no figures were available regarding the ethnic origin of immigrants, other than the three categories of 'British,' 'others,' and 'from the United States,' for the years 1896–1900 (Canada, *Book IV*, 1969, 17–18). Nevertheless, despite its shortcomings, the evidence was sufficient to allow the commission to conclude that 'although the French and British have been predominant both in their number and cultural influence, the population of what is now Canada has always been ethnically diverse' (ibid., 18).

Book IV introduced a narrative of migration to the land mass that was to become Canada in order to justify the legitimacy and order of claims by different groups: 'Canada, a vast territory inhabited in the beginning by Indians and Eskimos⁴ was first colonized by the French, beginning early in the 17th century, and then by the British. Late in this century, immigrants of different ethnic origins began to arrive' (Canada, *Book IV*, 1969, 4). Chapter 1 built on this narrative of migration to provide a detailed accounting of the different groups and their arrival patterns throughout the various phases of Canadian immigration. This account drew heavily on the research reports of the commission, as well as census data, to outline the immigration history and settlement patterns of

Germans, Ukrainians, Japanese, the 'Negro population,' and 'Asians,' among other groups (ibid.). Immigration restrictions, European refugee influxes, and the internment of the Japanese were also mentioned. Significantly, though, the data on which the chapter was based ended with the census of 1961, and therefore the analysis could not trace the gradually shifting immigration patterns that were emerging because of the substantive changes to Canadian immigration policy that occurred after the tabling of the White Paper on immigration in 1966.

The chapter had other weaknesses as well. First, the exact moment of arrival for different groups was obscured by the shifting ethnic-origin categories in the census, which helped to affirm the numerical and cultural hegemony of the English and French. More importantly, with the excision of Indigenous groups from the purview of the commission, the first arrivals were said to be the English and the French, which allowed the report to assert that the English and French had always enjoyed numerical and cultural ascendancy over other ethnic groups. As well, in detailing the specific immigration histories of the various cultural groups, the chapter located each as separate entities; not a third force but separate from the homogeneous British or French groups all the same. In fact, the report did not give any details on the different waves of British or French immigration, nor did it break down either of these homogeneous categories into their regional specificities – Scottish, Irish, and so on. Immigration as a history of other ethnic groups framed and limited the possible claims that could be made by these various groups. That is, claims based on the historical order of arrival on 'land which would eventually become' Canada, tracked through ambiguous census data, were constructed to favour British and French dominance.

The Repudiation of the Existence of a 'Third Force'

Book IV also repudiated the historical and demographic claims to collectivity that had been made by other ethnic groups during the hearings. In the report, the history of immigration in Canada, as it was tracked through ambiguous census data and bolstered through the excision of Indigenous groups, relegated other ethnic groups to the status of 'immigrants' – thereby undercutting their claim to being a cohesive third force – while characterizing the arrival of the homogenized British and French colonizers as the originary moment from which Canadian nation-building commenced, thus reinscribing their numerical and cultural dominance.

The report's introduction also considered the 'semantic problems' associated with the term 'other ethnic groups.' This was an important point because, to date in the report, there had been only a qualified semantic shift from 'founding races' to 'Anglophones and Francophones' and that had still left the awkward terms 'other ethnic groups' and 'non-British and non-French communities' to refer to all 'immigrant' groups. If the foregrounding of language and culture over 'race,' 'people,' and 'ethnic group' was to encompass the French and English, then the next step in *Book IV* was to apply this logic to other ethnic groups as well. The commission explained why it was jettisoning three of the most common terms used to refer to other ethnic groups:

> The whole topic of the non-British, non-French cultural groups raises great difficulties of semantics. Terms such as, 'other ethnic groups,' 'New Canadians,' and 'the Canadian mosaic' are often used in reference to the 'ethnic' question in Canada. The adjective 'ethnic' is ambiguous at best, and often appears to be more or less synonymous with 'foreign' ... Any term which implies 'foreignness' such as 'New Canadian,' is not only misleading but incorrect when it applies to a person whose forebears arrived in Canada 50 or 100 years ago. The idea of the 'Canadian mosaic' is a picturesque and appealing metaphor and may describe the ethnic diversity of a country stretching from the Atlantic to the Pacific, but it does not really provide a satisfactory designation for the sociological of cultural phenomenon in question. (Canada, *Book IV*, 1969, 9–10)

That left one other term, which had been used by other ethnic groups themselves to mount claims for recognition based on demographic strength, and which even Commissioner Rudnyckyj had drawn upon in his reports and separate statement: 'the third force.' The commission had earlier voiced criticisms of the term 'third force,' but here the concept was laid to rest once and for all. Drawing on and reinforcing the now-common argument that the groups comprising the third force were too heterogeneous to be considered a unified collective, the commission juxtaposed the 'aspirations of those of Chinese origin in Vancouver' with the 'aspirations of those of Ukrainian origin in Winnipeg' (Canada, *Book IV*, 1969, 10). In this argument, the Chinese group represented the extreme limit of difference – in this case, racial difference – against the more established and vocal Ukrainian community, with both groups being located in Western Canada. The passage also directly addressed and refuted the arguments that Rudnyckyj had presented in his separate statement. By pronouncing the concentration of other ethnic groups to be inadequate, the report directly attacked the basis of Rudnyckyj's claims for official recognition of other languages based on population concentration in specific regional areas. In this way, not only was Rudnyckyj's argument countered, but also the claims for the existence of a third force were undermined. The report could therefore conclude that the notion of a third force, given the disparate heterogeneity of the other ethnic populations, did 'not exist in any political sense' but was instead a statistical artifact. Having dismissed the terms 'third force' and 'the third element' as well, the commission was left with only one recourse: 'Consequently, we would rather regard the "other ethnic groups" as *cultural groups*' (ibid., 11, emphasis added).

The decision to turn away from the terms 'other ethnic group,' 'third force,' 'new Canadian,' and 'Canadian mosaic' was more than just a semantic slide. There was a conceptual shift as well. This shift, based on the foregrounding of 'language' and 'culture' over 'race' and 'ethnicity,' was akin to that which modified the closed boundaries of founding races (based on physical signification) to the more porous and linguistically defined 'anglophone' and 'francophone.' In the case of other ethnic groups, the closed idea of ethnicity became the more amorphous 'cultural groups'; here, however, the critical difference was that although culture was foregrounded, language was not. The transformation of other ethnic groups into cultural groups was therefore a critical step in the reconceptualization and rearticulation of the place of other ethnic groups; although the terms of reference had indicated other ethnic groups as playing a secondary role to the founding races, the change in terminology now specified a consistency in the differentiation between the 'anglophones and francophones' and the 'cultural groups' on the terrain of language and culture for both groups. In this way, the bicultural and bilingual model could prevail.

Discrimination

Only two recommendations in the report addressed issues of discrimination, equal citizenship, and political rights. Furthermore, although the report linked immigration and the resulting shifts in population composition to different forms of discrimination in Canadian society, it purported to detect in history a gradual waning of racism and prejudice; and, by placing discrimination along a historical continuum as something that was experienced and practised, at some point, by every group, it downplayed the reality of British dominance.

In chapter 2, 'The Economic Structure,' the analysis of discrimination in Canada attributed the difficulty of tracking discrimination to the paucity of legislation as well as to the problems involved in identifying discrimination and proving it. As well, the lack of discriminatory legislation was related to the discriminatory nature of immigration policy with its racial and geographical preferences. However, the report clarified that these policies were increasingly hard to defend as Canadians became more sensitive to human rights, and that there were many indications and recent declarations that 'discrimination on racial or ethnic lines will be eradicated through, for example the White Paper in Immigration which was tabled in the House of Commons by the Minister of Manpower and Immigration in October 1966' (Canada, *Book IV*, 1969, 59).

In addition to immigration policy discrimination, the report dealt with the various types of historical discrimination faced by different ethnic groups in Canada, including employment discrimination faced by the Asians, quotas imposed on Jewish communities for various training and educational programs, and the restrictions on the expansion of Hutterite colonies through provincial legislation (Canada, *Book IV*, 1969, 59). The report stated: 'As members of virtually every group have experienced discrimination, so members of almost every group have practiced it, even upon those of the same ethnic background'[5] (ibid., 60). However, the report's statement minimized the hegemony of the British, who, as the commission had repeatedly documented elsewhere, maintained economic dominance and a preponderance of institutional control over every other ethnic group, including the French.

What was most notable was the discussion about the Japanese community in Canada. The deprivations and discrimination suffered by the Japanese were acknowledged several times in this volume. Describing the prejudice the Japanese experienced both before the war and during internment, the report stated that 'after the war they dispersed to cities in central Canada, where less discrimination was directed against them and they were able to escape their dependence on the group' (Canada, *Book IV*, 1969, 63). The fact that the Japanese had, after their internment, been legally obligated to move away from the west coast – which was what drove most of them into central Canada – was neatly side-stepped. The focus here was rather on the improved employment situation that the Japanese enjoyed at the time of the report as a result of their increasing integration (ibid., 64).

The forced dispersion of close-knit Japanese communities as a result of internment was recast as an opportunity for integration, which had had positive employment consequences for the group. Although the report acknowledged the existence of discrimination, particularly in light of the extensive range of submissions from other ethnic groups, it was placed on a continuum of discrimination suffered by 'members of virtually every group.' As well, discrimination was couched in terms that ignored British domination and privilege. Finally, the historical emphasis on past discrimination suggested a gradual amelioration of prejudice and discrimination in Canada.

Despite these mitigating strategies, and the fact that the commission 'was not asked by the terms of reference to deal with fundamental human rights,' the report's first recommendation did address discrimination:

> We recommend that all provinces that have not yet enacted fair employment practices, fair accommodation practices, or housing legislation prohibiting discrimination because of race, creed, colour, nationality, ancestry, or place of origin, do so; and that this legislation be made binding upon the Crown and its agencies. We further recommend that all provinces make provision for full-time administrators of their human rights legislation. (Canada, Book IV, 1969, 64–5, emphasis in original)

Yet these recommendations would be the only two out of sixteen that responded to the myriad concerns with discrimination and equal rights that had been raised by many ethnic groups over the course of the hearings.

The Safeguarding of Ethnic Languages

The report's recommendations regarding the safeguarding of other ethnic languages focused mainly on institutional education. The commission had to balance their support for non-official languages against the risk of weakening the federal government's material and symbolic support for both official languages and cultures. What support it did advocate required ethnic languages to subscribe to a Eurocentric notion of 'modern' languages as linguistic commodities. In any event, the disparity in support between official and non-official languages, as envisaged in the report, thrust the main task of non-official-language preservation back into the private realm of other ethnic groups and reasserted the dominance of official bilingualism. Also, the commission had to weigh support for non-official-language preservation against the need for increasing official-language competence on the part of immigrants and their children, since such competence was deemed to be a measure of integration.

The last four chapters of *Book IV*, chapters 5–8, were part of a section entitled 'The Maintenance of Language and Culture.' In this section, the commission assessed the factors that affected the retention rate of other ethnic group languages (Canada, *Book IV*, 1969, 117). The commission used the terms 'linguistic integration' and 'linguistic and cultural assimilation' interchangeably, highlighting the fact that loss of 'ancestral language' also indicated the degree of integration and assimilation (ibid). Further, in noting that a 'greater cultural difference' between an immigrant group and 'receiving society' could slow that group's rate of integration, the commission's analysis recalled Rudnyckyj's taxonomy of language families. Its view that immigrants with Germanic or Romance mother-tongue languages might find the adoption of English and French easier, and might also receive a warmer welcome than those whose cultures were 'more alien to Canadian society,' placed the emphasis on the degree of separation between the immigrant's language and the 'cultural base' of North America—that is, the United States and Canada—as a central factor in language transfer or integration. This, too, was similar to the idea of a continuum of racialized difference in relation to the pole of core cultures established in Commissioner Wyczynski's preliminary memorandum.

This section also drew upon census data in order to trace the main trends in language-transfer patterns among other ethnic groups in Canada. Studying four of the larger ethnic groups – Germans, Ukrainians, Italians, and Dutch – the report found that multiple factors were relevant to language transfer: 'Three of the most important [factors] are the degree of cultural distinctiveness of a cultural group, percentages of foreign born and Canadian born, and rural-urban settlement patterns' (Canada, *Book IV*, 1969, 117). Yet the degree of 'cultural distinctiveness' was an amorphous concept that could not be measured through the analysis of census data. In fact, there was no clear study of the measure of cultural distinctiveness beyond the descriptions of language transfer and retention patterns in the four larger ethnic groups. Cultural distinctiveness in this context recalled the preceding discussion about the cultural difference of ethnic groups from the cultural base of North America.

Moreover, the commission's findings on the Italian community contradicted its thesis of cultural distinctiveness: 'It is worth noting that, although Italian like French is a Romance language, its affinity with the French language does not seem to mean that retention of the Italian tongue is less likely in Quebec. Indeed the native born of Italian origin in Quebec give slightly greater support to their ancestral language than do those living in Ontario' (Canada, *Book IV*, 1969, 134). Census data revealed that immigrants belonging to the same language family (for example, Italian) did not necessarily 'find it easier to adopt ... French.' Indeed, belonging to the same language family seemed to have the opposite effect; that is, mother-tongue retention was stronger within the context of the other Romance language. This example pointed to the inadequacy of a solely census-based analysis of the language-transfer patterns of other ethnic groups. Although the factors that emerged from this quantitative analysis were relevant, other factors that were external to the ethnic group and specific to the core societies had not been considered. For instance, in the case of language-transfer patterns of Italians in Quebec, social isolation, discrimination, and the economic pull of English were all significant factors in language shift, and none of these were part of the commission's calculations. Instead, the commission took the easy route of relying on the notion of cultural distinctiveness, which located these external factors as unidentifiable and immeasurable idiosyncrasies within the community itself. In the end, despite the commission's identification of a close relationship between language and culture, this relationship did not translate in *Book IV* into substantive, concrete legislative support and protection for other ethnic groups' ancestral languages. Although commission documents show that more supportive forms of state support for ethnic languages had been considered and even advocated by commission staff, by the time the final report was prepared these suggestions had been scaled back in favour of maintaining the dominance of the two founding societies – and a French- and English-language hegemony.

Education

At all levels of education, the inquiry marginalized non-official-language preservation by suggesting little in the way of legislative support, an approach that derived from the commissioners' conviction that the maintenance of non-official languages must not compromise the hegemony of bilingualism and biculturalism: 'Canada's public school systems are primarily concerned with the transmission of knowledge that is essential to all citizens, including knowledge about Canadian institutions, the traditions and circumstances that have shaped them, and the two official languages'(Canada, *Book IV*, 1969, 137). The given rationale that the British and French were the main ethnic groups in Canada made it appropriate that 'the British and French cultures dominate in the public schools' (ibid.), and clearly laid out the two-founding-races context within which public schooling was embedded. Within this hegemonic framework, space was made for the languages of other ethnic groups as an 'additional benefit of increasing the country's linguistic resources – resources important to any modern country and especially to one that wishes to play a role in the international community' (ibid., 138).

Providing an opportunity for the preservation of other languages and cultures within the English- and French-dominated school system had long been an objective of other ethnic groups, as was attested during the inquiry hearings. Here, the commission's reasoning recast non-English and non-French languages into commodities that benefited 'the country's linguistic resources.' Furthermore, these languages, classified as linguistic resources, were useful only so far as they were important to a 'modern' country and served to expand Canada's international role. In other words, non-official-language preservation could be justified only if these languages could be useful in the building of the larger society. This view was similar to the one expressed in Varjassy's 1966 submission, where state support for the preservation of ethnic languages was based on redefining them as modern and internationally productive languages. Characterizing non-official languages as modern, cosmopolitan, and socially useful resources had implications for exactly which languages would be able to garner support for their preservation.

Before the report could outline what language-preservation strategies could be implemented within the school system, it had to define the place of non-official languages within its recommendations for official languages. The commissioners had already recommended in *Book II: Education* that there be a systematic development of full educational opportunities in both the official languages, and opportunities for teaching the second official language to members of both the major linguistic communities. However, here in *Book IV*, the commissioners were clear: 'We do not recommend the same degree of development for the teaching of other languages in Canada; rather we recommend that there be opportunities to study many languages within the context of the public education system' (Canada, *Book IV*, 1969, 138). The report established the hierarchy between official languages and non-official languages, emphasizing that the bilingual and bicultural context had to be considered at all times: 'Where public support is concerned, the question of language and cultural maintenance must be seen within the broader context of the question of bilingualism and biculturalism in Canada as a whole; for example, the learning of third languages should not be carried on at the expense of public support for learning the second official language' (ibid., 138–9). Given the extremely low rates of official-language bilingualism at this time, particularly among other ethnic groups, the commission's stance meant that the possibility of acquiring a third non-official language was remote. But the commission was explicit: 'It is not feasible for Canada's public education systems to employ languages other than English and French extensively as languages of instruction . . . the aim of improving educational opportunities in the official languages must be maintained as the primary objective' (ibid., 139). Support for non-official languages, accordingly, must not compromise the bilingual and bicultural hegemony.

Almost everywhere that the topic of support for non-official languages was raised, the report reiterated that the founding groups' dominance over language and culture in schooling must not be jeopardized. In chapter 6 of *Book IV*, the commissioners took special care to make sure that their suggested support for non-official languages did not in any way detract from their previous three volumes of recommendations about the official languages and cultures. Yet they did make a series of recommendations for the support of non-official languages in this chapter, beginning with Recommendation 3 on public elementary schooling: '*We recommend that the teaching of languages other than English and French, and cultural subjects related to them, be incorporated as options in the public elementary school programme, where there is sufficient demand for such classes*' (Canada, *Book IV*, 1969, 141, emphasis in original). The fact that non-official languages and related cultural subjects could only be 'options' in the school system was key – as was the commission's failure to define 'sufficient' demand.

The next recommendation dealt with the teaching of official languages to immigrant children. As the report stated, this was a federal responsibility and a necessary part of the integration process, as 'part of their education for citizenship is language education' (Canada, *Book IV*, 1969, 143). Identifying official-language knowledge with the process of integration emphasized the role of official-language learning in integrating ethnic groups into one of the founding communities. In addition, the statement that official-language knowledge was part of these children's 'education for citizenship' echoed the idea set out in the introduction to *Book IV* that the full exercise of citizenship rights implied integration – that is, official-language knowledge – into either of the two official-language communities. This was deemed to be a federal responsibility because the benefits of immigration and 'linguistic diversity' accrued to the country as a whole.

Recommendation 5 was specific to the teaching of languages other than English and French in secondary schools. There was a vacillation in the report between characterizing other ethnic languages as ancestral and as modern. In the discussion about language instruction at the secondary school level, the latter idea was stressed: 'A total of five modern languages other than French and English are authorized and taught in public high schools in Canada: German, Spanish, Italian, Russian, and Ukrainian' (Canada, *Book IV*, 1969, 144). As the report explained, Spanish, Italian, and Russian had their place in high school curricula as world languages, while German owed its position in the curriculum in part to the size and long history of the German cultural group in Canada and in part to its status as a world language (ibid.). However, the teaching of Ukrainian in the Prairie Provinces was clearly due to their sizeable population of Ukrainian ethnic origin – people with a strong interest in maintaining their ancestral language. Spanish, Italian, and Russian were all seen to have some place in high school curricula as world languages (ibid.).

Characterizing the non-official languages taught in high school as 'modern' restricted the languages that could be taught to those which were deemed to be 'world languages' – save for Ukrainian. The report did make mention of 'widening the range of modern languages offered in the high schools' (Canada, *Book IV*, 1969, 144), but it remained to be seen how this could be squared with its Eurocentric emphasis on 'modern' languages.

There was also an extensive discussion about private ethnic schools. Understanding the mandate of most of these schools to be ethnic language and cultural preservation, the commission researchers had conducted a survey of language schools from twenty different cultural groups (Canada, *Book IV*, 1969, 149), with both part-time and full-time schools being considered. The report detailed the persistence of these schools and the variety of their programs, as well as the numerous requests for the support of such schools made during the inquiry by other ethnic groups, which saw private ethnic schools – both part-time and full-time – as crucial for their linguistic and cultural futures. The report made no recommendations regarding such schools, how-ever, and rejected the provision of any public financial support because it would place 'heavy demands on educational resources,' and because 'the public school system would suffer in many communities if several cultural groups were to set up their own schools supported by taxes' (ibid., 159). As a result, with the view that local arrangements seemed the most appropriate form of support, the report recommended that private ethnic schools should receive the same treatment from provin-cial educational authorities as other private schools (ibid.). The report concluded, 'We have no recommendations to make concerning these schools although we feel it important to record the part they play in the maintenance of the languages and cultures of those of other than British or French ethnic origin' (ibid.). The conclusion that these schools should rely instead on local arrangements placed them on par with other private schools and in effect ignored the special role they played in 'maintaining the languages and cultures' of ethnic groups.

The next section on education considered the teaching of modern lan-guages at colleges and universities. Commission research showed that, in 1965–6, twenty-seven different languages other than English and French were taught in Canadian universities (Canada, *Book IV*, 1969, 159). Yet not all ethnic languages were taught, and 'no university or college taught any of the Eskimo tongues, and of the native Indian lan-guages only Cree was offered as a subject for linguistic analysis, at the University of Alberta' (ibid., 160). The commission couched its support for the teaching of non-official languages at the post-secondary level as something advantageous for the country, echoing the earlier portrayal of non-official languages as useful resources. Clearly, native languages, aside from being objects of linguistic analysis, did not fit this criterion.

Two concrete recommendations emerged from this discussion. The first was that universities accept a broader range of modern languages for standing of credit (Canada, *Book IV*, 1969, 161); the second was related to the development of area-studies programs at the post-secondary level. The post-secondary area-studies programs included non-official language instruction; however, these programs were com-prehensive studies of particular regions or countries of the world within the larger context of the social sciences and humanities, rather than programs concerned with the maintenance of Canada's non-official linguistic and cultural heritage. In fact, there was little correspondence between the various areas of study and the ethnic composition of the Canadian population. In the report, the two main area-studies programs discussed were Soviet and Eastern European studies and 'Far and Other Eastern' studies. The more exotic languages – those farthest from the core Germanic and Romance languages – were thus folded into the objectivizing gaze of area studies, where the linguistic and cultural preservation of other ethnic groups was not a concern. In effect, two distinct groups of language instruction at the post-secondary level were evident. The first group contained modern languages, whose justification for instruction lay in their characterization as modern and therefore useful linguistic resources. The second group consisted of those languages embedded within area-studies programs, where they were considered interesting mainly as objects of scientific inquiry. A possible third category would be Indigenous languages, significant as a group by virtue of their pointed absence at the post-secondary level, whether as part of a broader agenda of Indigenous linguistic or cultural preservation, or (except for Cree) as objects of scientific interest and inquiry. This discussion gave rise to the final recommendation of this chapter, Recommendation 7, which suggested the expansion of the scope of area studies.

The chapter ended with a brief overview of adult education, with the focus on programs run by ethnic organizations for their adult community members in order to maintain 'the cultural heritage of these groups' (Canada, *Book IV*, 1969, 168). Since the commission did not undertake any survey of these programs, it provided little beyond a cursory description of some programs and groups and offered no recommendations. The brevity and superficiality of the chapter perhaps stemmed from the fact that language barriers for adult immigrants had already been addressed in chapter 2, the chapter on economic structure, which highlighted the importance of official-language competency for participation in Canadian life. There, the commission stated:

> Lack of fluency in at least one of the official languages of Canada is obviously a barrier to participation in Canadian life, and one which is first felt in the economic sphere. Since Canada receives immigrants from many countries where neither English nor French is the language of daily life, they are inevitably handicapped by this lack and it is essential that we attempt to minimize this handicap by making available facilities for learning the official languages of the country. Such facilities should be available both to young people in conjunction with their education and to adults in conjunction with their work. (Canada, *Book IV*, 1969, 65)

The idea that official-language competency was required for full participation in Canadian life and citizenship resembled earlier statements that full citizenship rights were confined to native-born members of official-language communities and those who had been integrated into them.

The commission described the role of the provincial and municipal levels of government, as well as private agencies, in providing official-language training to immigrants. As for the federal contribution, the report declared: 'The federal government enters into agreements with the provinces to reimburse them for the expense of language textbooks used by adult immigrants in programmes of language instruction, and for half the teaching costs of citizenship instruction (including English and French) for adult immigrants' (Canada, *Book IV*, 1969, 65). Thus, in the case of official-language instruction for adult immigrants, the federal government would provide some concrete support. In the same vein, *Book II* of the commission's report had recommended the creation of a Language Research Council, whose activities related to second-language teaching in Canada would be a resource for the instruction of adult immigrants in the official languages. Clearly, then, there was a marked difference in the support provided for official-language instruction, both for children and for immigrants who did not speak the official languages, and for adult ethnic languages. In the case of the former, financial help was provided and structural assistance was recommended, but for the latter, the commission offered nothing.

Other Recommendations

The rest of *Book IV*'s recommendations – the majority – were about increasing other ethnic groups' representation within, and access to, narrowly defined, humanistic cultural arenas, such as media and the arts and letters. Here, too, competing pressures and perspectives gave rise to a set of recommendations that were well-meaning but anemic. The discussion dealt mainly with ethnic-group access to and representation within different forms of media, and it gave rise to recommendations on expanding broadcast regulations to accommodate other ethnic groups and their languages. In total, there were six recommendations regarding the Canadian Radio-television Telecommunications Commission (CRTC), the Canadian Broadcasting Corporation (CBC), and the National Film Board (NFB), and all of them sought to expand the role and participation of other ethnic groups. No recommendations were made specifically in relation to the ethnic press.

The report proceeded in a descriptive fashion, outlining the myriad 'humanistic' cultural contributions of various major ethnic groups and ending with three recommendations. The first recommendation suggested an expansion in funding to federal, provincial, and municipal agencies so they could foster the arts and letters of ethnic cultural groups (Canada, *Book IV*, 1969, 220). The second recommendation suggested direct federal funding for the Folk Arts Council, and the last recommendation advocated the provision of adequate space, funding, and facilities to the Museum of Man that would enable it to 'carry out its projects regarding the history, social organizations, and folk arts of cultural groups other than the British and French' (ibid., 222).

The last two chapters of *Book IV* gave rise to nine of the sixteen final recommendations in the volume. These nine recommendations focused on expanding ethnic groups' access to and involvement in the media and the arts and letters. Of the other recommendations, five pertained to education; one explicitly targeted official-language education for children, two suggested supporting non-official-language education as 'options' only, and the remaining two addressed post-secondary language institutions wherein language instruction was not geared to the preservation of other-ethnic-group languages or cultures. Only the first two recommendations directly addressed the fundamental rights of the members of other ethnic groups, suggesting that legislation against different forms of discrimination be enacted and that there be equality in the conditions of citizenship and full political participation.

In conclusion, the main focus of the recommendations was not on recognizing the fundamental rights of other ethnic groups – only two recommendations did this – but rather on expanding access to a narrowly defined version of cultural support and providing some limited assistance to non-official languages. *Book IV* ended with a full listing of all these recommendations (Canada, *Book IV*, 1969, 228–30). Nothing that the commission recommended in the way of government support to ethnic cultural organizations and programs could conceal the basic fact that the commission's priorities lay elsewhere.

Ethnic Groups' Responses

As noted in the previous chapter in connection with *Book I*, the publication of each volume of the B and B Commission's final report symbolized an invitation to a discussion or dialogue between state and society. *Book IV* was no exception. The public response to this volume helped to construct, symbolically speaking, the neutrality of the state, giving persuasive force to the emerging policy of multiculturalism within a bilingual framework.

The publication of *Book IV* provoked great interest from other ethnic groups. Ironically enough, their series of varied responses – conferences, newspaper articles, and so on – revived the very issue of multiculturalism that the volume had taken such pains to downplay. The myriad reactions from other ethnic groups to the recommendations of *Book IV*, although not uniform in content, did mean that some response from the federal government was required.

The groundwork for the responses by other ethnic groups was laid long before the publication of *Book IV*. On 3 March 1964 Senator Paul Yuzyk, today known as 'the father of multiculturalism,' made the 'multicultural fact' of Canada the focus of his maiden speech in the Senate. As articles from the ethnic press attest, Yuzyk was considered to be 'an eloquent speaker for the '"third force"' (Kirschbaum, 1965) and a 'Defender of Multiculturalism' (Kirschbaum, 1964). The fact that he delivered his speech at a time when the inquiry's public hearings were still underway drew added attention to the issues he raised. Among them was the issue of the third element, which was then the subject of much discussion both in government circles and in society at large.

Using strategies that had become familiar through the inquiry submissions from other ethnic groups, Yuzyk began his speech by citing population statistics that pointed, in particular, to the historical, proportional decline in the population of Canadians of British descent and the rapid increase in that of other ethnic groups: 'The third element ethnic groups, now numbering approximately five million persons, are co-builders of the West and other parts of Canada, along with the British and French Canadians, and are just as permanent a part of the Canadian scene' (*Ukrainian Voice*, 1964, 8). Demographic force and the historical claims of settlement and sacrifice in the cause of nation-building were common themes in strategies to build claims for recognition. Yuzyk's own strategies were transparent; he aimed to expand the white-settler category to gain inclusion for others, since even as he invoked equality for the third element through the Canadian Bill of Rights, he restricted its purview in his quest for common ground with the founding groups: 'Fundamentally, we are a Christian and a democratic nation' (ibid., 16). His assertions that 'Canada has become multicultural in fact,' and that there is a 'principle of "unity in diversity,"' were framed within this exclusionary and colonial white-settler model (ibid., 21).

At this early point in the inquiry, in light of the reference to the 'fact of multiculturalism' in the commission's own working paper, Yuzyk's speech contained an optimistic reference to the commission's work: 'I would like to state it is gratifying to learn that the Royal Commission on Bilingualism and Biculturalism has recognized the potentiality and vitality of multiculturalism' (*Ukrainian Voice*, 1964, 21). For his part, Yuzyk suggested a formulation for the multicultural inclusion of other ethnic groups which acknowledged that, '[a]s the founding peoples of our country, the British and the French should be regarded as the senior partners whose special rights include the recognition of English and French as the official languages in accordance with the British North America Act' (ibid., 17). However, he proposed a co-partner status for the third-element or other cultural groups, who starting in grade one would be guaranteed the right to maintain their mother tongues and cultures as 'optional subjects in the public and high school systems and the separate schools of the provinces, and the universities, wherever there would be sufficient number of students to warrant the maintenance of such classes' (ibid., 17). Yuzyk's suggestions installed a modified hierarchy of founding and other ethnic groups, foreshadowing the final recommendations of *Book IV*. The key difference was his desire for the recognition of co-partnership for third-element groups, no matter how exclusionary the terrain of partnership was for those who did not and could not pass into his expanded definition of white-settler 'co-partner.'

As coverage in the ethnic press showed, Yuzyk's advocacy on behalf of the third element, through talks and presentations in various informal community and official government contexts, continued throughout the duration of the inquiry. There was a variety of conferences dealing with the various issues of other ethnic groups, and one of Yuzyk's major initiatives on behalf of multiculturalism during this time was his organization of the 'Thinkers' Conference' in the winter of 1968. As demonstrated by a memorandum of 7 May 1968, sent from Peter C. Findley to all the commissioners, this conference was of interest to the inquiry. The memo, which came with Yuzyk's press release about the conference attached, stated that the gathering would address the 'relevance and the relationship of this country's distinctive minority cultures to Canadian society as a whole and in part to Canada's multicultural heritage and its development of a new Constitution' (Findley, 1968). As the press release stated, the motto of the meeting may have well been: 'We too, have contributed – to every aspect of Canadian life'

(Yuzyk, 1968, 1). The press release went on to state that the purpose of the conference was to provide a place where the third element could be heard on 'social and cultural issues of national concern,' and to offer recommendations on the 'ethnic groups of Canada' (ibid., 1–2).

At the Multiculturalism for Canada Conference held two years later in Edmonton, Yuzyk indicated that the exclusion of other ethnic groups from the federal-provincial conference on constitutional reform in February 1968 – as well as the 'indefinite postponement' of the tabling of Book IV – 'had caused considerable concern' among the third element. This had led to Yuzyk's call for the Thinkers' Conference of ethnic and cultural groups in Canadian society, in order 'to make it possible for these groups to make their views known to the Government, the Parliament and the Canadian people' (Multiculturalism for Canada Conference, 1970, 12). Sponsorship for this conference had been sought from private and public sources, and the royal commission endorsed the idea of the conference and offered their cooperation with it (ibid., 3).

On 13–15 December 1968, the 'Thinkers' Conference on Cultural Rights: A Conference to Study Canada's Multicultural Patterns in the Sixties' was held in Toronto. Presentations and panels featured a range of people, including journalists, such as Claude Ryan; university professors; politicians such as Bill Davis, the Minister of Education of Ontario; representatives from various cultural institutions such as the Royal Ontario Museum and the Indian-Eskimo Association; and Commissioner Royce Frith. The topics covered included 'Striking a Balance in the Canadian Cultural Pattern' and 'Public Policy and the Preservation of Multicultural Traditions.' The conference was sponsored by a range of institutions, among them the Canadian Citizenship Branch of the Department of Secretary of State, the Canadian Folk Arts Council, the Canadian Council of Christians and Jews, and the Canada Ethnic Press Federation. As Leon Kossar, conference chairman and executive chairman of the Canadian Folk Arts Council, wrote in the preface to the conference summary: 'Some 150 delegates and 50 observers, representing 20 linguistic backgrounds, gathered to discuss papers by prominent Canadians' (Canadian Cultural Rights Committee, 1968, iii–iv). In the summary itself, Kossar evoked the spirit of the era within which the conference took place, a time between the publication of Book I and Book IV:

> In the final months of the sixties, Canadians have been studying their national make-up, – the linguistic and cultural foundations of their land – further

dramatized by official implementations of reports of the Royal Commission on Bilingualism and Biculturalism, and the current desperate search for a made-in-Canada constitution. And John Q. Man-In-The-Middle is the Canadian of Non- French, Non-Anglo-Saxon origin who nevertheless feels the same concerns as his Francophone or Anglophone neighbour about the current cultural stance Canada assumes at home and abroad. (Canadian Cultural Rights Committee, 1968, iii)

Here, Kossar captured the overwhelming sense that this was a period when the cultural landscape of the country was being redrawn through the royal commission. The desperate search for a 'made-in-Canada constitution' – which, as it turned out, would not end until repatriation in 1982 – seemed close to a conclusion. But it was Kossar's evocation of the 'Non-French, Non-Anglo-Saxon' 'John Q. Man-In-the-Middle' that best revealed the mood of the conference-goers; members of other ethnic groups, they thought, were the same as their Anglo-Saxon and French neighbours in that they had the same concerns about cultural recognition. These concerns were well expressed in the resolutions that came out of the conference; resolutions that demonstrated the existence of 'a third mainstream of thought in current Canadian affairs, a stream representing nearly one-third of Canadians whose backgrounds are neither English nor French' (Canadian Cultural Rights Committee, 1968, iv).

Yet the identification of this third element or third force was a controversial issue during the conference; in his preface, Kossar pointed out that it was significant that the various societies and individuals at the conference were hyper-careful to state that the conference 'should in no way be considered a formation of a third political force – but rather the expressions of a serious concern by those citizens making up the third element of Canada's population in the cultural development of Canada' (Canadian Cultural Rights Committee, 1968, iv). This concern with not just the name but also the political significance of a discretely identifiable third element was contentious on many fronts. For the commission, the third element posed a threat to the dominance of the two official groups, and so the inquiry's published volumes had repeatedly repudiated it. For the other ethnic groups, there was also some discomfort with the idea of themselves as a third 'political' force as opposed to a non-British and non-French element concerned with 'cultural' issues.

The conference ended with six resolutions specific to other ethnic groups, as well as four resolutions regarding 'Indians and Eskimos.' The six resolutions on ethnic groups covered a wide range of issues, including the continuation of the work of the Canadian Cultural Rights Committee with a view to establishing a representative and advisory body to the federal government in 'the interests of Canada's ethnic groups to ensure their full participation in the cultural development of Canada' (Canadian Cultural Rights Committee, 1968, xiv). The conference also called for increased support to the Canadian Folk Arts Council; the expansion of ethnic representation within the national media, such as the CBC and NFB; and national grants 'to support the research and development of standardized history texts for the schools' (ibid.). The conference further urged the expansion of language courses and teaching for all cultural groups and their recognition as credit subjects 'to the matriculation level,' as well as passing a strong resolution affirming multiculturalism and rejecting biculturalism: 'Whereas the Conference supports the efforts of the Federal and Provincial governments in formulating a viable Canadian constitution, the Conference unequivocally rejects the concept of biculturalism and seeks official recognition of the multicultural character of Canada' (ibid.). This last declaration implied some type of official, presumably constitutional, recognition of multiculturalism.

In contrast to the conference's statements on other ethnic groups, the four resolutions with respect to 'Indians and Eskimos' moved clearly beyond just the 'cultural' realm to cover economic, political, and social issues. The first resolutions began with firm criticism of past and present-day treatment of Indigenous groups by the Federal and Provincial governments, which had led to the problem that 'Indigenous peoples are seriously lagging behind in social, cultural, economic and political attainments' (Canadian Cultural Rights Committee, 1968, xv). The subsequent three resolutions had a wider focus, calling for governments to institute programs that dealt with the socio-economic gaps between Indigenous and non-Indigenous groups, amended exclusionary school curricula, censored discriminatory film portrayals of 'Indians and Eskimos as savage and inferior people,' and involved Indigenous communities in 'all stages of planning and policy formulation' (ibid.). These resolutions were all the more striking in that the B and B Commission's *Book I* had already categorically stated that issues related to Indigenous groups were beyond the scope of the inquiry.

Yuzyk sent the conference resolutions to various provincial ministers as well as the Prime Minister's Office, and the mainstream media also gave the conference extensive coverage. Headlines in newspapers across the country included 'Ethnics Attack Biculturalism' (Toronto *Telegram*) and 'Third Canadian Force Just Can't Be Ignored' (Welland-Port Colborne *Tribune*) (Canadian Cultural Rights Committee, 1968, 144–7). Except for the rejection of biculturalism and the adoption of multiculturalism, the resolutions specific to other ethnic groups were to a large extent addressed by the recommendations of *Book IV*, but the four resolutions regarding Indigenous groups were never mentioned by the commission.

After the publication of *Book IV* and its tabling in the House of Commons on 15 April 1970, two conferences were held to provide a forum for public opinions and analysis regarding the volume. The first of these, called 'Canada: Multicultural,' was held on 7 and 8 August 1970 at Hart House, University of Toronto ('Canada: Multicultural,' 1970); and the second was the aforementioned 'Multiculturalism for Canada' conference, held in Edmonton at the University of Alberta on 28 and 29 August 1970 (Multiculturalism for Canada Conference, 1970). The proceedings of both conferences were quite similar, except that the second conference included an extensive opening speech from Yuzyk. Sponsored by the Citizenship Branch of the Department of the Secretary of State, the University of Alberta Students' Union, and the Ukrainian Students' Club at the University of Alberta, the conference was billed as a community-university conference 'designed to provide a forum for a statement of opinions and analysis of Book IV of the report' (ibid.).

In his speech to this conference, Yuzyk responded to the content of *Book IV*. He discussed the commission's rejection of the idea of the third force, which had been echoed by some ethnic groups: 'There are many sceptics not only in the British and French groups but also in the other ethnic groups who believe that a united voice and action of the Third element is impossible and even undesirable' (Multiculturalism for Canada Conference, 1970, 4). Repudiating this position, Yuzyk spoke of the idea's long history in the publications of the Canada Ethnic Press Federation and the Canadian Folk Arts Council, among other groups and institutions. He also mentioned that the notion of a third element had even been suggested as 'a sort of cement that can serve to bind the two founding peoples' (ibid.). But it was his strongly critical view of biculturalism, as it was promulgated in *Book IV*, that attracted the most attention. Commenting on the report's advocacy of the integration of other ethnic groups into one of the bi-cultures, Yuzyk pinpointed the contradiction inherent in this project:

> The Commission does not reject the 'melting pot theory,' and in adhering to biculturalism actually advocates the 'two melting-pots' or the 'double

melting pot' theory, advising other ethnic groups to 'integrate,' but they really mean to assimilate them into one of the two pots. Obviously, the commission has totally disregarded the numerous briefs that were submitted by the organizations of the ethnic groups. In my opinion, and I am sure it is the opinion of a large segment of the Canadian population, the premise and basic concept of the Canadian nation that is adhered to by the Bilingual and Bicultural Commission is wrong, as bicultural policies contradict the principles of equality and justice. Nevertheless, the recommendations regarding the preservation and safeguarding of ethnic cultures are practical and satisfactory, as far as they go, providing positive proof that multiculturalism is a fact of Canadian life, the very basis of 'unity in continuing diversity.' (Multiculturalism for Canada Conference, 1970, 14)

Yuzyk's negative view of biculturalism was consistently reflected in the presentations and comments of most other participants in both conferences. For example, Sab Roncucci, founder of the Dante Alighieri Cultural Society, stated, 'I like to compare the fourth volume of the B. & B. Commission to a watermelon: – a lot of water and seeds, but very poor nourishment' (Multiculturalism for Canada Conference, 1970, 18). Similarly, the Ukrainian Canadian University Students' Union gave a detailed analysis of *Book IV* and found it sorely lacking. A central concern which emerged from its analysis was the Federal government's allocation of funding; fifty million dollars for French language and culture development outside the province of Quebec and forty thousand dollars for all other minorities combined. As the Students' Union stated, 'There are eight hundred fifty thousand French speaking Canadians outside Quebec. In comparison there are two and one half million Canadians who have native language fluency in languages other than French and English and who are capable of developing culture in those languages' (ibid., 30). The union was also quick to add that they did not believe that French minorities were receiving too much funding, but rather that 'ethnic groups have been short changed' (ibid.). The gross disparity in funding was a common concern of many members of the cultural groups and, as it turned out, for politicians too. Comparing spending for French-language minorities to that for other ethnic groups demonstrated the government's skewed funding priorities up to that date.

In its analysis, the Ukrainian Canadian University Students' Union compared *Book IV* to the previous three volumes and concluded: 'Books One, Two and Three of the Report, when dealing with French-English relations, were highly specific in nature, their recommendations numerous and factual. Book Four is mainly a study of the past history of ethnic groups. Very rarely is the future mentioned' (Multiculturalism for Canada Conference, 1970, 32). The rooting of other ethnic groups in the past was consistent with the volume's framing of other ethnic languages and cultures as ancestral and traditional. Yuzyk, although displeased with the notion of biculturalism, was satisfied overall with the recommendations of *Book IV*; the union, recognizing that these recommendations were the very backbone of biculturalism, was not. The union began its analysis by identifying Recommendations 1 and 2, dealing with human rights and equal citizenship rights, as the most important and also long overdue: 'We are not about to congratulate the Commission for suggesting something that is rightfully ours to begin with ... Let us however, not confuse common decency for enlightenment' (ibid.).

With respect to *Book IV*'s other recommendations, the union regarded the ones dealing with education for other ethnic groups as inadequate when compared to those for official-language groups. It linked language back to cultural preservation and survival for other ethnic groups, citing the commission's own principle that the French language was the key to the development of the French culture in Canada: 'This statement of principle for the Commission is a truism which must also apply to the development of multiculturalism. Every ethnic group in Canada which wishes to develop its culture must also develop its own language. Without language development in all facets, no minority culture can exist' (Multiculturalism for Canada Conference, 1970, 33). This observation revealed the union's recognition of the contradictory relationship between language and culture for other ethnic and founding groups, and, responding to this reality, it demanded support for non-official languages similar to that provided to the official languages. In addition, it outlined the need for a 'mechanism for implementation' since none had yet been proposed at that time (ibid.). The union also deemed the recommendations for the expansion of access and representation for other ethnic groups within larger media organizations, such as the CBC and NFB, to be inadequate, and called for the establishment of a CBC department to deal with developing programs in minority languages (ibid.). As well as providing a critique of *Book IV*'s recommendations, the union presented a list of its own demands, which included a comprehensive education program, participatory democracy, community development programs, and an expansion of relevant government programs and departments. These demands were all 'political' or substantive in nature, reflecting the criticism that, unlike the other volumes of the final report, 'the Fourth Volume of the B and B Commission deals with questions of culture rather than with politics' (Costa, 1970, 17).

Addressing this point, E. Costa of the Federation of Italian Clubs and Associations, in a presentation to the 'Canada: Multicultural' conference, argued that the tendency to respond to ethnic group demands by emphasizing culture rather than politics helped to explain why 'the ethnic minorities have not been able to rally behind real and concrete issues the way the French in this country have,' since 'the French question in this country, despite attempts to describe it otherwise in terms of language and culture, is basically political' (Multiculturalism for Canada Conference, 1970, 17). In the case of *Book IV*, its cultural focus was similarly the reason why it had not 'caused a debate equal to the healthy controversy that originated from the publication of the first three volumes' and why the 'mass media, too, has been almost completely absent from any kind of debate' (ibid.). This understanding that *Book IV* was more 'cultural' than 'political' was a recurring theme in both conferences, and pointed to the meagerness of its recommendations concerning concrete policies, legislation, and funding for other ethnic groups.

While the other ethnic groups were united in their resistance to biculturalism and their support of multiculturalism, there were divisions among them on certain subjects. While some, such as Yuzyk, were relatively content with the volume's recommendations, others found them limited and too cultural, pushing instead for a more political or substantive set of proposals and funding commitments. Related to this was the controversy over the actual existence of a third force or third element and, if there was such a thing, whether it was 'political' or 'cultural' in nature. Ultimately, all these views would be subsumed into Pierre Trudeau's response to *Book IV*, more than a year hence, when he announced a new policy of multiculturalism within a bilingual framework.

The Federal Government's Response

The federal government did not formally respond to *Book IV* until almost a year and a half after its tabling in the House of Commons. Even though the B and B Commission had come into being under the auspices of Lester Pearson, it would be Trudeau, prime minister since August 1968, who would become associated with the fruits of its work – first by overseeing the institution of the Official Languages Act and then by inaugurating the policy of multiculturalism in response to *Book IV*'s recommendations.

On the morning of 8 October 1971, under the gaze of a visiting dignitary in the Speaker's Gallery, Prime Minister Tun Abdul Razak of Malaysia, Trudeau made his famous and often-cited speech announcing the implementation of a policy of multiculturalism within a bilingual framework. He began by stating that the government had accepted all the recommendations contained in *Book IV* which were 'directed to federal departments and agencies' (Canada, *House of Commons Debates*, 1971a, 8545). The rationale for this acceptance laid the groundwork for multiculturalism:

> It was the view of the royal commission, shared by the government and, I am sure, by all Canadians, that there cannot be one cultural policy for Canadians of British and French origin, another for the original peoples and yet a third for all others. For although there are two official languages, there is no official culture, nor does any ethnic group take precedence over any other. No citizen or group of citizens is other than Canadian, and all should be treated fairly. The royal commission was guided by the belief that adherence to one's ethnic group is influenced not so much by one's origin or mother tongue as by one's sense of belonging to the group, and by what the commission calls the group's 'collective will to exist.' The government shares this belief. (Ibid.)

Trudeau's comments reprised the contradiction of language and culture developed in *Book I*, which maintained the hierarchy of founding races on the terrain of language and culture. Whereas the commission had declared its support of the hegemony of French and English bilingualism and biculturalism, Trudeau took a different tack, homogenizing all groups as 'Canadian.' Here, he was drawing upon the commission's own view that culture was not so much about origin or mother tongue as it was about one's sense of belonging to the group or the 'collective will to exist' (Canada, *Book IV*, 1969, 7). However, in *Book I* of the commission's report, this formulation was applied only to the other ethnic groups, not to the two official linguistic communities, for whom the report stated: 'The life of two cultures implies in principle the life of the two languages' (Canada, *Book I*, 1967, xxxviii). This was the foundation of the commission's bilingual and bicultural vision.

Trudeau seemed to overturn the implicit hierarchy of biculturalism by stating that ethnicity or mother tongue was not a central feature

of cultural identity, since we were all Canadians; yet, by also maintaining that there were two official languages, he revived the cultural
contradiction at the heart of *Book I* in order to sustain the dominance
of the two founding groups. To put this another way, even as Trudeau
disavowed the hierarchy of biculturalism, he smuggled it back in by
declaring that there were two official languages. Moreover, when
Trudeau identified the various groups composing the Canadian population, he used the same demographic divisions as the inquiry: the
British and French, the Aboriginal or 'original peoples,' and 'all others.'
The homogenization of other ethnic groups as 'all others' resurrected
the third element/third force categorization that the commission had
worked so hard to dispel.

   In the next part of his speech, Trudeau outlined his view of the most
suitable framework for national unity:

> The individual's freedom would be hampered if he were locked for life
> within a particular cultural compartment by the accident of birth or lan-
> guage. It is vital, therefore, that every Canadian, whatever his ethnic
> origin, be given a chance to learn at least one of the two languages in
> which his country conducts its official business and its politics. A policy
> of multiculturalism within a bilingual framework commends itself to the
> government as the most suitable means of assuring the cultural freedom
> of Canadians. Such a policy should help to break down discriminatory
> attitudes and cultural jealousies. National unity if it is to mean anything
> in the deeply personal sense, must be founded on the confidence in one's
> own individual identity; out of this can grow respect for that of others and
> a willingness to share ideas, attitudes and assumptions. A vigorous policy
> of multiculturalism will help create this initial confidence. It can form the
> base of a society which is based on fair play for all. (Canada, *House of
> Commons Debates*, 1971a, 8545)

The organization of the sentences in this passage placed the emphasis
on the individual's freedom to learn one of the two official languages,
a freedom that putatively encompassed 'every Canadian, whatever his
ethnic origin' – that is, official-language minorities and other ethnic
groups. Yet, in substance, Trudeau's remarks were mainly addressed
to the other ethnic groups; although he did not mention the word
integration in his speech, the 'cultural freedom' he was espousing was
the freedom of members of other ethnic groups to integrate into one
of the two official-language communities. This echoed *Book IV*'s assertion that other ethnic groups were at 'liberty' to integrate, particularly if

they wanted to enjoy and exercise full citizenship rights. For Trudeau, a policy of multiculturalism within a bilingual framework could ensure this cultural freedom and safeguard national unity.

Where Trudeau seemed to depart significantly from the commission was in his argument that national unity could be founded on 'individual identity.' On the surface, this set him apart from the commission, which saw the collective rights of the two official-languages communities as essential for national unity. Indeed, an emphasis on individual rights and freedoms would come to be an essential part of Trudeau's political legacy, particularly as exemplified through the Charter of Rights and Freedoms. Yet it is also true that Trudeau was very much in support of the notion of two official-language communities, something that would be entrenched and safeguarded as collective rights in the Charter. In effect, individual identity and rights, couched as freedoms, were specific only to the other ethnic groups, in contrast to the collective claims of official bilingualism. The end result was that the individualization of ethnic identity, in contrast to the official-language collectivities, effectively denied any collectively based third-force or third-element claims once and for all.

How then to reconcile these contradictions in Trudeau's declaration of a policy of multiculturalism within a bilingual framework? The picture becomes clearer when we understand that his speech, in fact, only addressed the other ethnic groups. For example, consider that the particular definition of culture that he drew upon, which stated that one's mother tongue or origin did not matter, could be applied only to other ethnic groups – otherwise there would be no policy of bilingualism. As well, Trudeau's emphasis on learning an official language for the cultural freedom of integration, as had been outlined in *Book IV*, could only be relevant to the other ethnic groups. Finally, couching these rights as individual ones could only apply to other ethnic groups, since by now the English- and French-speaking communities had had their collective status as official-language communities recognized through the passage of the Official Languages Act in 1969, a process overseen by Trudeau. Given that Trudeau's speech was a response to *Book IV* and therefore necessarily an engagement with it, all his comments and statements have to be framed and understood within the context of that volume. From this it follows that, although Trudeau was supposedly addressing 'all Canadians,' the substantive elements of his speech were addressed to one party only: other ethnic groups. It should be noted, too, that the 'original peoples' were conspicuous in their absence from Trudeau's speech. Again, this reflected the commission's own approach, and, in Trudeau's case, it undoubtedly spoke to his view that Indigenous peoples were encompassed by his reference to 'all Canadians.' In the wake of the White Paper of 1969, in which the government proposed to repeal the Indian Act, Trudeau's rhetorical flourish fit into the federal assimilative logic which individualized all Indigenous people as 'Canadian' in order to counter their historical collective claims.

There are many theories as to why Trudeau suggested a policy of multiculturalism within a bilingual framework. The main ones suggest that Trudeau, despite his long silence on *Book IV* of the report, eventually had to respond to the ongoing lobbying and submissions from other ethnic groups (Wayland, 1997; Ng, 1995). Some observers see his multiculturalism policy as a perfect way of reconciling anglophone and francophone dualism with increasing ethnocultural pluralism (Lupul, 1982), while others argue that the policy was intended to persuade 'non-English and non-French Canadians to accept official bilingualism' (Knowles, 1997). Kenneth McRoberts (1997) contends that Trudeau viewed the entrenchment of official language rights as the solution to Canada's national unity problems (61). McRoberts also cites Raymond Breton (a *Cité Libre* colleague of Trudeau) and references Bernard Ostry (the senior civil servant in charge of implementation of the policy) to argue that Trudeau saw the importance of multiculturalism as not so much what it offered, but what it excluded; that is, biculturalism – which Trudeau viewed as a position that supported the Quebec independence movement (McRoberts, 1997, 124). Another common political motive given for Trudeau's policy was the need for the Liberals to expand their support base beyond Quebec – especially with the creation of the Parti Québécois – into Western Canada and the ethnic minority populations (Wayland, 1997). Wsevolod Isajiw (1983) offers a larger political context, stating that, in the aftermath of the FLQ crisis of October 1970, multiculturalism within a bilingual framework provided the best hope for 'social integration.' Specifically, and similarly to McRoberts, Isajiw argued that insisting on a policy of bilingualism and biculturalism would have played into the hands of separatists, particularly after the October Crisis, while retaining bilingualism and dropping any reference to culture would have been tantamount to an implicit recognition of Anglo-uniculturalism; thus, 'multiculturalism within a bilingual framework' would be a good way out of the political dilemma the federal government found itself in (Isajiw, 1983). Thus, the pro-federalist political elite that Trudeau represented needed not only to deal firmly with Quebec separatists but also to balance the political agendas of different groups. It was not the pressure from other ethnic – particularly Ukrainian – groups that drove the establishment of multiculturalism policy, but rather the need for a policy of social integration (ibid., 114), which was essential to the overriding goal of both Trudeau and the B and B Commission: national unity.

In the interests of national unity, Trudeau had to tread a fine line in his response to *Book IV*, particularly given that his delay in responding to the report had already been noted and remarked upon by prominent members of the other ethnic communities (Multiculturalism for Canada Conference, 1970). His project of social integration had to balance Quebec's complex demands against the assumptions of dominance held by those of British origin, yet also counter the persistent, centrifugal tug of other ethnic groups. Trudeau outlined the contours of his multiculturalism policy in his speech on 8 October 1971. He made clear that the policy was directed towards what the commission had defined as the narrow humanistic cultural contributions of other ethnic groups. He introduced this policy by first admitting that past public support for the arts, which had been predominantly given to the cultural institutions of English Canada, would now – thanks to the recommendations of *Book I* to *Book III* – be extended to French-language cultural institutions and to the 'cultural educational centres for native people' (Canada, *House of Commons Debates*, 1971a, 8545–6). He continued, 'The policy I am announcing today accepts the contention of the other cultural communities that they, too, are essential elements in Canada and deserve government assistance in order to contribute to regional and national life in ways that derive from their heritage yet are distinctively Canadian' (ibid.). In delineating the spread of government funding in this way, Trudeau glossed over gross inequities in levels of support, both financial and legislative, especially given that English-speaking arts and cultural institutions had long obtained the lion's share of government support. In addition, he did not admit that the commission's recommendations on the funding of culture and education fell far short of equality for English and French groups on the one hand and ethnic and Indigenous ones on the other. The inequities in government funding between official language communities and cultural groups would become crystallized in the federal budgets to come, as in the first year of multiculturalism (1971–2) the secretary of state spent more than $78 million on bilingualism but less than $2 million on multiculturalism (McRoberts, 1997, 128). As McRoberts has noted, despite his announcement of multiculturalism within a bilingual framework Trudeau would go on to treat multiculturalism with indifference, assigning the portfolio to junior ministers and continuing to allocate limited funding, with this disparity in funding for the different groups becoming entrenched in subsequent budgets (ibid.).

Trudeau filled in the details of his multiculturalism policy in a policy paper that he tabled in the House of Commons at the same time as he delivered his speech. Entitled 'Federal Government's Response to Book IV of the Report of the Royal Commission on Bilingualism and Biculturalism,' this document detailed the ways in which the government would provide support to other ethnic groups and included specific responses to each recommendation in *Book IV*. In its opening general remarks, the paper debunked two misconceptions of cultural diversity. The first of these concerned cultural identity and national allegiance, with the paper clearly severing the links between the two: 'The sense of identity developed by each citizen as a unique individual is distinct from his national allegiance' (Canada, *House of Commons Debates*, 1971b, 4). This was the foundation for the statement that Canadian identity would not be undermined by multiculturalism, since '[e]very ethnic group has the right to preserve and develop its own culture and values within the Canadian context. To say we have two official languages is not to say we have two official cultures, and no particular culture is more "official" than another' (ibid.). In this way, it could be claimed that '[a] policy of multiculturalism must be a policy for all Canadians' (ibid.).

By denying that cultural identity was synonymous with national allegiance, the government was advancing an argument that could be made irrespective of the differential levels of public support for members of other cultural communities and official-language communities. That is, in this definition of cultural identity, everyone could have an ethnic background and the right to preserve and develop his or her own culture and values. However, for those whose ethnic background coincided with that of the two official languages communities, there would be an array of institutional and legislative protections completely unlike those for Indigenous and other ethnic groups – even though, as the paper postulated, a policy of multiculturalism must be a policy for 'all Canadians.' National allegiance, separated from this individualized and private cultural identity, was equated with being 'Canadian.' The clear separation of official language from official culture underscored Trudeau's earlier formulation in the House, as well as his unequivocal repudiation of the bilingualism and biculturalism formula advanced by the commission, which he outlined explicitly as the second myth about cultural diversity:

> The distinction between language and culture has never been clearly defined. The very name of the Royal Commission whose recommendations we now seek to implement tends to indicate that bilingualism and biculturalism are indivisible. But, biculturalism does not properly describe our society; multiculturalism is more accurate. The Official Languages Act designated two languages, English and French, as the official languages of Canada for the purposes of all the institutions of the Parliament and Government of Canada; no reference was made to cultures, and this Act does not impinge upon the role of all languages as instruments of the various Canadian cultures. Nor, on the other hand, should the recognition of the cultural values of many languages weaken the position of Canada's two official languages. Their use by all of the citizens of Canada will continue to be promoted and encouraged. (Canada, *House of Commons Debates*, 1971b, 4)

The statement that the distinction between language and culture had never been clearly defined was remarkable, considering the commission's Herculean efforts to provide just such a definition. Nevertheless, it was a necessary argument to justify the government's rejection of the commission's view that bilingualism and biculturalism were indivisible. Once this had been affirmed, Trudeau could assert his policy of multiculturalism within a bilingual framework, where there were cultural rights for all and language rights for some. The Official Languages Act, the scaffolding of legislation that supported English and French language rights, was separated completely from culture since it contained was 'no reference' to cultures. Through this supposed dissociation, it was possible to maintain that the Official Languages Act did not impinge upon the role of languages 'as instruments of the various Canadian cultures,' even if there was a distinction in levels of support and substantive recognition between official languages and other languages. This disparity in support had to be maintained in order to clearly signal that the recognition of only the cultural value of these other languages would in no way weaken the position of Canada's two official languages. Finally, invoking all 'citizens of Canada' elided the differences in support between the various groups of citizens.

In his quest for national unity, therefore, Trudeau had modified the presentation of bilingualism and biculturalism as advanced by the commission. At first, multiculturalism seemed at odds with biculturalism, but the commission itself had provided an opening for Trudeau's formulation by arguing, on the one hand, for the close association between language and culture of official-language groups through collective language rights; and, on the other, by narrowing the definition of culture to the point of dissociating it from language in the case of other ethnic groups, where no collective rights to language were supported. The commission had done the work of identifying language as the concrete element of culture; consequently, Trudeau could now officially repudiate biculturalism, since it was a superfluous signifier, alongside bilingualism, in favour of multiculturalism. Multiculturalism, which in the interests of national unity was ostensibly addressed to 'all Canadians,' was specific to other ethnic groups in its promotion of individual rights and freedoms, but actually guaranteed no collective rights or claims. The safeguards that multiculturalism provided were only for the narrower humanistic cultural contributions of other ethnic groups and were designed to integrate these groups into the two official-language communities, as was the case in the recommendations of *Book IV* – upon which Trudeau based his policy. Nothing much had changed in Trudeau's much-lauded shift from biculturalism and bilingualism to multiculturalism within a bilingual framework, and the differentiation between cultural groups and official-language groups was still embedded in a contradictory notion of culture which operated through language.

The policy paper – in Part B, 'Objectives in the Federal Sphere,' and Part C, 'Programmes of Implementation' – elaborated upon four main policy objectives that Trudeau set out in his speech. The first policy was with respect to 'support for all cultures.' In his speech, Trudeau stated: 'First, resources permitting, the government will seek to assist all Canadian cultural groups that have demonstrated a desire and effort to continue to develop a capacity to grow and contribute to Canada' (Canada, *House of Commons Debates*, 1971a, 8546). In this policy objective, the federal government's support was ostensibly to be directed towards all Canadian cultural groups. However, from the explanatory text in the policy paper, it was clear that this support was in fact directed mainly towards other ethnic groups, since 'the two largest cultures, in areas where they exist in minority situation, are already supported under the aegis of the government's official languages programmes,' and so 'new programmes are proposed to give support to minority cultural groups' (Canada, *House of Commons Debates*, 1971b, 5). This support was not without conditions, since – as was noted in the policy paper – the government could not 'take upon itself the responsibility for the continued viability of all ethnic groups' (ibid.). Rather, the policy's objective was the cultural survival and development of ethnic groups *'to the degree that a given group exhibits a desire for this.* Government aid to cultural groups must proceed on the basis of aid to self-effort' (ibid., emphasis added). Considering the policy objective in tandem with the policy-paper explanation, it becomes clear that federal support was not necessarily meant to assure the continued viability of all ethnic groups but rather only to offer limited and conditional assistance based on the degree of self-effort made by each cultural group – however this effort was to be measured.

The second policy objective was for the government 'to assist members of all cultural groups to overcome cultural barriers to full participation in Canadian society' (Canada, *House of Commons Debates*, 1971a, 8546). The key here was that this assistance was designed to overcome 'cultural barriers' to participation; hence, discrimination was not mentioned under this objective since it was dealt with elsewhere through the law: 'The law can and will protect individuals from overt discrimination' (Canada, *House of Commons Debates*, 1971b, 5). The focus, instead, was on fostering 'confidence in one's individual cultural identity' through 'histories, films and museum exhibits showing the great contributions of Canada's various cultural groups' (ibid.). Again, this was reminiscent of *Book IV's* emphasis on safeguarding the narrowly defined humanistic cultural elements of other ethnic groups.

The third policy objective was the federal government's 'promotion of creative encounters and interchange among all Canadian cultural groups in the interest of national unity' (Canada, *House of Commons Debates*, 1971a, 8546). As detailed in the policy paper, these programs were 'designed to encourage cultural groups to share their heritage with all other Canadians ... to make us all aware of our cultural diversity' (Canada, *House of Commons Debates*, 1971b, 5). This cultural diversity consisted of the narrowly defined cultural realm of the arts and letters and was to be fostered through 'displays of the performing and visual arts,' among other related programs (ibid.). The policy paper stated categorically that '[t]he government has made it very clear that it does not plan on aiding individual groups to cut themselves off from the rest of the society' (ibid.). As a result, government support would be provided to 'ethnic groups' through multiculturalism only to the extent that it contributed to presenting the larger Canadian society as culturally diverse; there was no intention of allowing this support to be used to present individual 'ethnic groups' on their own terms.

The final policy objective reprised the recommendations of *Book IV* in its support for official languages: 'The Government will continue to assist immigrants to acquire at least one of Canada's official languages in order to become full participants in Canadian society' (Canada, *House of Commons Debates*, 1971a, 8546). Significantly, in one of the few instances where the commission favoured government support for language programs, this support was extended only to the official languages and only for the purposes of immigrant integration into 'Canadian society' (ibid., 8546). As the policy paper explained, 'new arrivals in Canada require additional help to adjust to Canadian life, and to participate fully in the economic and social life of Canada'; thus, full economic and social participation, defined and structured as it was through the official languages, could happen only when newcomers were integrated through their mastery of an official language (Canada, *House of Commons Debates*, 1971b, 6).

Part C of the policy paper outlined the specific programs through which the policy objectives of multiculturalism would be implemented, with most of them to be administered through various humanistic, culturally focused programs of the Citizenship Branch of the Department of the Secretary of State (Canada, *House of Commons Debates*, 1971b, 6). In addition to these narrowly defined programs, there was also the usual program for the 'Teaching of Official Languages' as well as one for 'Culture Development.' The latter, as it was described in the policy paper, was the only one directed towards non-official languages. This program was different from the others in that it did address the issue of non-official language retention, acknowledging that the acquisition of what were still termed 'ancestral' languages was crucial for cultural identity. Still, it was as limited in scope as any of the programs recommended in *Book IV*, a fact that again demonstrates Trudeau's desire to balance concrete support for non-official languages against the various forces working against national unity.

In the last part of the policy paper, Trudeau responded to the sixteen recommendations of *Book IV*. In his speech in the House, he had already in principle 'accepted all those recommendations of the Royal Commission ... directed to federal departments and agencies' (Canada, *House of Commons Debates*, 1971a, 8545). However, the federal government's overall response to the recommendations of *Book IV*, already regarded as inadequate by most ethnic groups, did nothing to strengthen the support they provided to those groups. The department responsible for the implementation of these recommendations was the Citizenship Branch of the Department of the Secretary of State, which Trudeau described in his speech as 'the agency now responsible for matters affecting the social integration of immigrants and the cultural activities of all ethnic groups' (Canada, *House of Commons Debates*, 1971a, 8546). By assigning this task to the government branch already dealing with the integration of immigrants and the 'cultural activities of all ethnic groups,' Trudeau made it clear that multiculturalism was an issue pertaining only to the 'social integration' of other ethnic groups in the construction of national unity. As Roxanna Ng states, placing the implementation of multiculturalism under the Citizenship Branch 'is in accordance with separating "culture" from political and economic matters: multiculturalism comes under the jurisdiction of this department rather than the Department of Employment and Immigration, for instance, which deals with immigrants as labour and economic matter' (Ng, 1995, 44–5).

McRoberts notes that for Trudeau, multiculturalism was more about his vision for individual freedoms than it was for the development of cultural groups (McRoberts, 1997, 126). This becomes clear towards the end of Trudeau's speech:

> In conclusion, I wish to emphasize the view of the government that a policy of multiculturalism within a bilingual framework is basically the conscious support of individual freedom of choice. We are free to be ourselves. But this cannot be left to chance. It must be fostered and pursued actively. If freedom of choice is in danger for some ethnic groups, it is in danger for all. It is the policy of this government to eliminate any such danger and to "safeguard" this freedom. (Canada, *House of Commons Debates*, 1971a, 8546)

As Ng notes, in this section of the speech Trudeau 'restates rhetorically the basis for Canadian democracy' (Ng, 1995, 45). Democratic choice as the exercise of individual freedom was the centrepiece of Trudeau's statement, but, as we have shown, the freedom 'to be ourselves' was actually the ongoing pursuit of conscious support – active legislation and funding – for the management of difference in achieving a balance for national unity. The safeguards for these freedoms were provided through a set of policies, legislation, and funding priorities that concretely delineated the hierarchy of difference and belonging in Trudeau's formulation of national unity, regardless of his rhetorical strategy that putatively addressed multiculturalism to 'all Canadians.'

After Trudeau made his speech and tabled the policy paper in the House, other MPs responded. Robert Stanfield, leader of the opposition, began by congratulating the prime minister on his statement and then quickly switched into French to emphasize the importance of the two official groups: 'I wish to state immediately, Mr. Speaker, that the emphasis we have given to multiculturalism in no way constitutes an attack on the basic duality of our country' (Canada, *House of Commons Debates*, 1971a, 8546). He then went on to wax rhapsodic in English about 'the importance of the rights of other cultural groups' and how this recognition was long overdue (ibid.). However, he noted the funding disparities evident in the government's plans: 'I fully agree that a good deal of money must be expended for the encouragement of the development of bilingualism in this country, but I do not think that members of other cultural groups with other cultural traditions are at all happy with the relatively pitiful amounts that have been allocated to this other aspect of the diversity about which the Prime Minister spoke this morning, multiculturalism' (ibid., 8547). David Lewis, leader of the NDP, also stated his support for a policy of multiculturalism but echoed Stanfield's criticism: 'The statement of principles will be a mockery and a betrayal of high ideals and objectives unless collectively we provide the funds to make the principles meaningful in the lives of minorities in Canada' (ibid., 8548). In their statements, both Stanfield and Lewis were also mindful of the need to frame overt statements of support for multiculturalism within the context of their primary support for bilingualism.

The final person to address Trudeau's announcement was Réal Caouette, leader of the Social Credit Party. After expressing his approval of the new policy, Caouette tackled the confusion arising from Trudeau's statement that although 'there are two official languages, there is no official culture,' stating: 'Mr. Speaker, if there is no official culture in Canada, I do not see how we could succeed in really becoming a nation while we would be endowed with only a few cultures unable to get on among themselves or at war with one another. I am positive that we have in Canada a culture peculiar to us ... We have our own Canadian culture' (Canada, *House of Commons Debates*, 1971a, 8548). For Caouette, the lack of an official culture heralded balkanization and fragmentation, and, unable to accept this, he asserted that there *was* in fact an official Canadian culture that was within the reach of everyone, one that offered the 'members of all ethnic groups' the opportunity to become 'good Canadians.' However, this view of culture rested on Caouette's further assertion that 'we have our own history,' which, as the B and B Commission's hearings had demonstrated, was not at all the case. In fact, it was in the context of diverse histories – the histories of Canada's various peoples – that the hierarchy of bilingualism and biculturalism, now recast as multiculturalism, had emerged.

Caouette ended his speech by translating the above statement, made in French, into English, foreshadowing the fear of the balkanization and fragmentation on both sides of the English-French divide (which would increasingly emerge in response to multiculturalism): 'What I said in French was that we do not want to have in Canada a little France, a little England, a little Italy or a little Russia. We want in Canada a great country for all the people of Canada, for all the ethnic groups in our country. Through that channel we will achieve unity and we will reinforce our position in the whole world' (Canada, *House of Commons Debates*, 1971a, 8548). This was a common criticism levelled at multiculturalism, and it had first emerged during the commission's public hearings when multiculturalism was being debated by various groups. However, for Trudeau's specific strategy of national unity, this fear could not be placated with recourse to one official culture, as suggested by Caouette; therefore, claims of fragmentation and balkanization would continue to emerge as a counter-discourse to multiculturalism into the present.

Concluding Summary

Through an integration agenda and a set of recommendations for cultural preservation that were, to put it mildly, limited, *Book IV* advanced white-settler bicultural and bilingual hegemony as the new model for national unity. Not surprisingly, it received poor reviews from many ethnic communities. Other ethnic groups were relatively uniform in their aversion to the bicultural hegemony envisaged in the report, as well as in their desire for multiculturalism. Despite the government's delay in responding officially to *Book IV*, Trudeau's announcement of a policy of multiculturalism within a bilingual framework did address the concerns of other ethnic groups regarding biculturalism. However, the formulation of multiculturalism that emerged in Trudeau's speech, and that was elaborated upon in the policy paper, was a restricted and limited notion of multiculturalism that mainly reprised the exclusions of biculturalism by largely adopting the recommendations of *Book IV*.

Trudeau's version of multiculturalism submerged competing visions of the concept in order to sustain a hegemonic interpretation of the commission's terms of reference and recommendations. Although this policy was putatively addressed to 'all Canadians,' in substance it was directed towards the social integration of other ethnic groups into the official-language communities. Trudeau also couched these rights as individualized freedoms, forever neutralizing the possibility of collective claims made on behalf of a collective third force, even as bilingualism maintained the recognition of collective official-language rights. Moreover, the supposedly universal reach of Trudeau's policy was undermined by the vast disparity in recommended policies, legislation, and funding levels between official-language communities and other ethnic groups. As Evelyn Kallen states, the Trudeau policy of multiculturalism relegated the collective rights of 'minority ethnic Canadians,' such as language, to the 'private sphere,' providing no guarantees of institutional support 'through which a living ethnic-Canadian culture could be constantly revitalized' (Kallen, 1982, 56). Therefore, although Trudeau did finally accept the idea of multiculturalism, it was a highly limited understanding of the concept – quite unlike the fluid and heterogeneous ideas of multiculturalism which were in circulation during the B and B Commission's public hearings.

Trudeau's policy of multiculturalism within a bilingual framework had to balance myriad forces and tensions against the government's overriding interest in national unity. This included facilitating the social integration of other ethnic groups and acknowledging their wishes, while also avoiding being seen as undercutting Quebec's demands and official-language minorities' concerns, all against the backdrop of a historically assumed British dominance. The resulting formulation for national unity was a white-settler bilingual and bicultural hegemony, which entrenched a racialized, hierarchical framework of difference and belonging – articulated on the terrain of language and culture – as multiculturalism within a bilingual framework. This formulation for nation-building, established through the work of the B and B Commission, has come to define the parameters of the contemporary Canadian nation-state, and official state multiculturalism in Canada remains deeply embedded within a bilingual framework. It is a policy that reifies a notion of culture that extends collective language rights only to official-language groups, justified through the purported openness of language and the 'freedom' of other ethnic groups to integrate by way of official-language competence – even as they remain heterogeneous and peripheral elements within Canada's two founding groups.

7   Conclusion: The Impossibility of Multiculturalism?

The opening of this book featured a vignette about Jacques Parizeau's comments on the night of the 1995 referendum in Quebec – comments that ultimately led to his resignation. My ensuing objective was to try and understand how language had become an acceptable site for the articulation of exclusion when race and ethnicity could no longer comfortably do so.

This analysis has demonstrated that the liberal paradox of racial differentiation that Goldberg (1993) identifies as being at the heart of universal identity finds its counterpart in the mobilization of language in contemporary, multicultural nation-building. A racial hierarchy is embedded by way of a contradiction in the use of culture through the proxy of language, thus foreclosing its openness even as racial differentiation is disavowed and the possibility of language as a universal community is declared. In the case of Canada, this is accomplished through, among other means, the policy of multiculturalism within a bilingual framework, which emerged directly out of the work of the Royal Commission on Bilingualism and Biculturalism.

The B and B Commission was struck at a particular historical juncture when a confluence of many factors meant that Canada had to rearticulate its formulation for nation-building and belonging. This commission of inquiry operated as an apparatus to systematize the principles underlying policy – which, in turn, was expressed in language that observed the rules of objective knowledge or facts. Specifically, the heterogeneity of submissions from the 'public' was constructed through the commission's interpretative and organizational practices and included in the textual reality of the final report. One key move during the course of the inquiry included the construction of a singular crisis between the two founding groups to support the embedded hierarchy within the terms of reference, despite myriad petitions from other ethnic groups during the preliminary hearings.

With the publication of the *Preliminary Report*, the public hearings began and 'other ethnic groups,' to use the commission's term, pushed for a shift from *bi-* to *multi-* cultural belonging, albeit with what was as yet an amorphous notion of multiculturalism. Subsequently, as the research program expanded, expertise was rallied to confer legitimacy on the commission's findings, and a rationale began to emerge for excluding Indigenous groups from the inquiry's scope. Also, the basis of the inquiry was starting to shift from race and ethnicity to the terrain of language and culture. With the appearance of *Book I* of the final report, the new perspective became clear: Indigenous groups were decisively removed from the purview of the inquiry, and a contradictory mechanism whereby culture and language would operate to reinscribe the now-disavowed racial and ethnic hierarchy of the original terms of reference was put into place. As well, *Book I* made it obvious that delineating the precise workings of an equal partnership between the two founding groups would require the Other – that is, the Indigenous and ethnic Others. All of this was further underlined in *Book IV*. There, integration emerged as the means through which other ethnic groups, now as cultural groups, would be peripherally located in relation to the two founding groups, and a series of recommendations that embodied this unequal relationship was entrenched as Trudeau adopted them for a new, limited notion of multiculturalism, this time within a bilingual framework.

The commission's goal was to develop a new, unisonant formulation for nation-building; one that could preserve white-settler hegemony at the same time as it disavowed its racialized exclusions. For the commission, the answer lay in the model of a bilingual and bicultural nation and in the entrenchment of asymmetrical collective-language rights through a contradictory operation of language and culture. This disparity was justified by the purported openness of language to the integration of other ethnic groups into the official-language collectives. The workings of this contradictory mechanism were detailed for the first time in the paradigmatic blue pages of *Book I*, which laid out definitions of key terms – among them, language, culture, bilingualism, and ethnicity. Blodgett states that *Book I* can be read as the 'discursive origin for the discussion of ethnicity in Canada' (Blodgett, 1990, 15), and as John Porter notes, determining the limits of the commission's principal terms was a challenging endeavour:

> Book I, The Official Languages, is preceded by a General Introduction printed on blue paper, which discusses the key words of the terms of reference of the Commission. These blue pages contain, in the English language at least, some of the most elegant sophistry about culture, language, society, and other concepts of importance to sociologists and anthropologists ... The blue pages are important because they generate a mythology of culture which goes far beyond any scientific understanding or use of the word. This condition detracts greatly from the convincing case the Commission makes for bilingualism, because their arguments become obscured by ideological, contradictory, and often nonsensical statements about culture, cultural identity, cultural heritage, cultural equality and so forth. (Porter, 1969, 112)

Porter also makes the important point that these blue pages were able, for the first time at the national level, to generate a new mythology about culture in Canada, setting out a story of belonging that could be couched in linguistic and cultural terms while the effects were organized along racial and ethnic lines. It was through the royal commission, therefore, that a new mythology of national belonging appeared – one that could ostensibly claim to envision a pluralist and open nation, multicultural within a bilingual framework.

This national mythology has proven to be durable, becoming naturalized in the understanding of everyday life in a putatively pluralist and open society. In addition, the changes to immigration policy that were taking place concurrently with the emergence of this national mythology provided the basis for contemporary manifestations of the racial ordering of 'immigrant' Others. In the present, Will Kymlicka's (1995) liberal theory of multicultural citizenship and the Charter of Rights and Freedoms can both be seen as examples of the commission's legacy, and yet they both leave unanswered the question of how to think through alternative ways of nation-building and national belonging.

Etienne Balibar discusses the relationship between language, race, and nation in order to unravel the purported openness of linguistic community in the monolingual hegemony of France. As a classic example of modern nation-building, Balibar asserts, the nation-state of France instituted a community that is always a 'fictive ethnicity' against a background of universalistic representation (Balibar, 1991, 96). However, as Balibar says, this invites questions. If national identity is based on a 'fictive ethnicity, "How can ethnicity be produced?" and in particular, "how can it be produced in such a way that it does not appear as fiction, but as the most natural of origins?"' (ibid.). For Balibar, the answer lies in the complementarity between language and race, which roots national character in the people. As he explains, 'they constitute two ways of rooting historical populations in a fact of "nature" (the diversity of languages and the diversity of races appearing predestined), but also two ways of giving a meaning to their continued existence, of transcending its contingency' (ibid., 97). He continues that it is crucial that the national language should 'appear to be the very element of the life of a people,' and that all linguistic practices should feed into a single 'love of the language' which is the 'mother tongue,' since this mother tongue is 'the ideal of a common origin projected back beyond learning processes and specialist forms of usage and which, by that very fact, becomes the metaphor for the love fellow nationals feel for one another' (ibid.).

The complement to this is that the language community is not enough to produce ethnicity, because, by definition, linguistic construction of identity is *open* (Balibar, 1991, 98). That is, although a mother tongue cannot be chosen, it is still possible to 'learn' languages and to 'turn oneself into a different kind of bearer of discourse' (ibid.). With respect to a linguistic community, Balibar concludes that 'ideally, it "assimilates" anyone, but holds no one' (ibid., 99). Thus, for language to be tied down to what he calls 'the frontiers of a particular people,' it needs an extra degree of particularity or principle of closure and exclusion, which is that of being part of a common race (ibid.). This is what Balibar refers to as a second-degree fiction, which, although a fiction, derives a material effectiveness from the everyday practices and relations structuring the lives of individuals. The language community creates equality only by 'naturalizing' the social inequality of linguistic practices, but the race community dissolves social inequalities in an ambivalent 'similarity' by ethnicizing the social difference into a division between the 'genuinely' and 'falsely' national (ibid., 100).

Balibar provides a cogent analysis of how race forecloses the openness of linguistic community in the construction of the modern nation-state. However, in Canada, the nation-building project cannot draw upon a uniform history of origins to organize the demarcation of 'genuine' and 'false' nationals, or 'us' and 'them.' Race necessarily operates differently, in this case through the contradiction of language and culture, in order to foreclose the purportedly open linguistic communities of the nation. Michelle Anne Lee (2003) discusses the tension that multiculturalism, or the politics of diversity, introduces into the inherent dialectic of 'us' and 'them' and embeds in modernist notions of nationalism. She states:

'Nationalism consistently requires some clear demarcation of "us" in distinction from "them." Multiculturalism, on the other hand, purports a discourse that requires "them" continually to become part of "us," *as defined by the dominant culture* tolerating and choosing to accept, or not, other cultures' (Lee, 2003, 111, emphasis in original).

As this book has explored, engineering how 'them' would become a part of 'us' within the dominant framework of bilingualism and biculturalism was a central preoccupation of the B and B Commission, and the project ultimately was realized in the Official Languages Act of 1969 and the Multiculturalism Policy of 1971. Lee does not see multiculturalism as opposed to standard models of nationalism as much as she sees it as an extension of them:

> For newer, more pluralistic societies that do not find their basis for legitimacy in historical continuity, however, challenges also abound. A multicultural society must deal with the realities that recent growth generated by large-scale, economic-driven migration presents. They must also respond to what is now perceived by many members of the imagined community as an *essentially* pluralistic history. (Lee, 2003, 111, emphasis in original)

In the present, this relatively recent construction of multicultural nationalism, dating back now almost forty years, is a naturalized '*essentially* pluralistic history' of Canada. It can incorporate the continuous and contemporary advent of economically driven migration into a similar historical continuity without disrupting the embedded contradiction which maintains the racialized hierarchy of belonging. As Lee explains, in multicultural notions of nation-building, 'direct calls to respect and acknowledge ethnic diversity in a single nation still position a particular group as possessing the power to make such a choice' (ibid., 112). Yet the powerful appeal of this model lies in the fact that, regardless, 'the invention of multicultural tradition is one that diverse members can all and equally commit themselves to' (ibid.). So, today, multicultural nationalism has a powerful, discursive force as an inclusive and equitable model of nation-building.

In Canada, the full formulation is *multiculturalism within a bilingual framework*, but these elements have to a large extent been sheared apart in current political discourse. At least at the federal level, bilingualism has come to almost exclusively signify questions about Quebec nationalism and anxieties about separation. And multiculturalism has become, at least in English-dominant Canada, a discourse about the inclusion and exclusion of racialized Others while it also ingrains the *'essentially* pluralist history' required to maintain the national mythology of a pluralistic society. Even though the limitations on inclusion organized through the contradictory operation of language and culture still continue to function in the present despite their discursive separation, it is vital that the two elements remain discursively interconnected if the white-settler foundations of the nation are to be evident. As Mary Kirtz (1996) states, 'The "bilingual framework" continues to determine the boundaries of the debate over national identity, boundaries beyond which multiculturalism cannot travel and within which ethnic identity must effect its limited transformations' (20). It is bilingualism, as the realization of collective language rights for some, that functions in tandem with multiculturalism as a limiting agent by foreclosing the purported openness of the nation's official linguistic communities.

The ability of language to construct a putatively open community should not be underestimated. As Uli Linke (2003) states in her analysis of linguistic purism and nation-building in Germany: 'This formative power of linguistic systems, which provides centralized regimes with the capacity to absorb and assimilate a diversity of subjects, seems to exhibit a democratic propensity. But such a making of nationals is inherently coercive: through the medium of language, and its strategic deployment in citizenship and immigration politics' (156). Although substantively different from German nationalism, Canadian multicultural nationalism is also based on the purported 'democratic propensity' of language, and the inherent coercion of language as it is deployed through citizenship and immigration in Germany finds its counterpart in Canada as well. Specifically, the emergence of multiculturalism within a bilingual framework in the late 1960s and early 1970s was more than just a new discourse of national mythology; it was also a formulation for national unity that subsequently established a particular system for the racial ordering of 'immigrant' Others. That is, during the course of the B and B Commission, while white-settler national belonging was being rearticulated on the terrain of language and culture, parallel changes were taking place in Canadian immigration policy – which was also moving away from explicitly stated racial preferences. These changes to immigration policy, which began in 1962, meant that by the late 1960s and early 1970s radical changes were occurring in the number and source of immigrants coming to Canada. The result was that, by the time Trudeau responded to the recommendations of *Book IV* in

1971, concerns about the balance between the founding dualities had to be considered, since the increasing number of immigrants was seen as one of the main demographic threats to national unity. In addition, as overt racial preferences for articulating national unity and immigration policy were being jettisoned, the racial composition of the immigrant population began to shift dramatically. Specifically, as source countries for immigration expanded beyond Europe and encompassed more of the global South, more visibly racialized groups were immigrating to Canada, thereby linking these critical changes in immigration policy to the system of racial ordering installed through the policy of multiculturalism in a bilingual framework.

In the present, the normalization of this racial ordering is clear in Kymlicka's (1995) theory of multicultural citizenship. It is instructive to examine this liberal theory of pluralism not only because Kymlicka's framework has become a dominant and ubiquitous model for multicultural citizenship and nation-building, but also because it reveals the durability of the racial ordering that the formulation of multiculturalism within a bilingual framework originally established.

Kymlicka makes a distinction between what he terms 'national minorities' – in Canada, these are the English, French, and a monolithic Aboriginal grouping – who are 'distinct and potentially self-governing societies incorporated into a larger state'; and 'ethnic minorities,' who are 'immigrants who have left their national community to enter another society' (Kymlicka, 1995, 79). The key distinction is that national minorities, at the time of their incorporation, constituted an 'ongoing societal culture and may have or had rights regarding language and land use' (ibid.), whereas ethnic minorities came 'voluntarily,' are not 'nations,' and do not occupy homelands but are scattered throughout the nation-space. These distinctions are based on rationales that closely recall the commission's own reasons for eventually conferring collective language rights on founding groups only, and Kymlicka, like the commission, disavows that these are racial distinctions; instead, he sees them as cultural: 'In talking about national minorities, therefore, I am not talking about racial or descent groups, but about cultural groups' (ibid., 23). For immigrants, their distinctiveness is 'manifested primarily in their family lives and in voluntary associations, and is not inconsistent with institutional integration' since 'they still participate within the dominant institutions of the dominant culture(s) and speak the dominant language(s)' (ibid., 14). In fact, 'immigrants (except the elderly) ... in Canada, must learn either of the two official languages' (ibid., 14–15). As Kymlicka states,

'[T]he commitment to ensuring a common language has been a constant feature of the history of immigration policy' (ibid.). Again, this logic closely recapitulates the narrow reasoning of the integration model that emerged to locate other ethnic groups in relation to the founding dualities in the B and B Commission's *Book IV*.

Kymlicka does admit that there are 'hard cases' which do not fit into either category, with examples being African-Americans, Hutterites, and refugees, among others. However, based on his main group divisions, he has no problem articulating a well-planned hierarchy of 'group-differentiated citizenship' rights. He also gives language as an example of this group-differentiated right, stating that 'the real issue in evaluating language rights is why they are group specific – that is, why francophones should be able to demand court proceedings or education in their mother tongue at public expense when Greek – or Swahili speakers – cannot' (Kymlicka, 1995, 46). For Kymlicka, it is clear that language rights are a major component of the national rights of French Canadians; and furthermore, since immigrant groups are not national minorities, they should not have similar language rights (ibid.). Overall, this hierarchy of rights is presented as a tidy and neat formula. For example, in response to the common charge that at one time even the dominant 'national minorities' were immigrants to the New World, Kymlicka differentiates between English and French colonists and present-day migrants. As he notes, 'there was a fundamentally different set of expectations accompanying colonization and immigration – the former resulted from a deliberate policy aimed at the systematic recreation of an entire society in a new land; the latter resulted from individual and familial choices to leave their society and join another existing society' (ibid., 95). Therefore, the discriminatory project of collective language rights only for some – the national minorities – is premised on a differentiation in migration history, an idea similar to the claims of prior history which were advanced during the commission. Also, the notion of immigration as a choice, which emerged during the commission's public hearings, is a central rationale throughout Kymlicka's theory.

Kymlicka uses the theme of 'choice' as a prime justificatory principle in his gross differentiation of rights between 'national minorities' and 'immigrants': 'After all, most immigrants (as distinct from refugees) choose to leave their own culture' and 'they have uprooted themselves, and they know when they come that their success, and that of their children, depends on integrating into the institutions of English-speaking society' (Kymlicka, 1995, 96). This concept of 'choice' also allows Kymlicka to make statements about the right of immigrants to live and work in their own culture: 'Immigration is one way of waiving one's right' and 'in deciding to uproot themselves, immigrants voluntarily relinquish some of the rights that go along with their original national membership' (ibid.). He is therefore careful to explain that, with respect to the policies designed to accommodate immigrant cultural difference, 'all of these measures take the form of adapting the institutions and practices of the mainstream society so as to accommodate ethnic differences, not of setting up a separate societal culture based on the immigrants' mother tongue' (ibid., 97). In Kymlicka's theory, the foundations of the white-settler *bi-* nation – in his words the 'societal culture' – are a given, and the racial ordering they entrench remains unexamined.

There have been many cogent critiques of Kymlicka's theory that address the depth of historical amnesia upon which his idea of liberal toleration and inclusion is founded. For example, scholars have questioned his idea that immigrants 'choose' to migrate, stating that this ignores the conditions for economic and political survival that imperialism and circuits of global capital have created for many in the global South; as well, they have pointed to the fact that in Kymlicka's model of nation-building, immigrants are forever frozen into the category of 'immigrant' (Padolsky, 2000; Razack, 1998). Other scholars take issue with the form of liberalism he uses, the definition of culture he adopts, and the distinctions he makes between different groups of minorities, in addition to the political and philosophical underpinnings of his work (Parekh, 1997; Young, 1997; Choudhry, 2002). But Kymlicka's theory of multicultural citizenship remains the intellectual basis of the current formulation of multiculturalism within a bilingual framework. It preserves the rationales for the hierarchy of rights that emerged through the B and B Commission, even as it acknowledges group-based claims for Indigenous peoples – albeit only in a limited way that regards these peoples as a homogenized and unspecified grouping without a distinctive history.

The influence of Kymlicka's theory of multicultural nationalism is widespread, and, while it is extensively debated, it is nonetheless used across disciplines to address questions of language, society, and nation-building (see May, 2001). Since language is a key marker of levels of rights and citizenship in his theory, there is also an increasing engagement with Kymlicka's ideas in the area of language rights (see Patten, 2001). Kymlicka acknowledges that 'group-differentiated citizenship rights' are a central element of his theory. In so doing, he makes explicit the contradiction that is lodged at the core of multiculturalism within a bilingual framework; that is, the extension of group rights only to national minorities while ethnic minorities have the standard guarantees of 'freedoms' and choices, or individual rights. Kymlicka's justification is built on historical claims and demographic rationales similar to those used by the B and B Commission, making the link between the two explicit. Based on Kymlicka's rationales, group-differentiated citizenship rights are posited as a rational solution to the dilemma of constructing the unisonant multicultural nation, yet this also elides the disparity in citizenship between the two groupings.

Chantal Mouffe (2001) argues that the liberal logic is a 'logic of the assertion of rights,' and she draws on Arendt's notion of the 'right to have rights' to maintain that it is only 'through being a democratic citizen' that it is possible to have the full exercise of human rights (107). However, the entrenchment of group-differentiated citizenship rights, predicated on a particular reading of national history, makes the assumption of equal citizenship for all members of the polity impossible. Yet this is precisely the formulation that Kymlicka proposes. In the present, his theory of multicultural citizenship, with its mistaken assumption that all members of the polity are equal as citizens, remains enshrined in the Canadian Charter of Rights and Freedoms.

Before the Royal Commission on Bilingualism and Biculturalism, the only provision for language rights in the constitution of Canada lay in section 133, which allowed the use of English and French both in Parliament and the federal court system and required that laws were written in both English and French. In the wake of the royal commission, the expanded set of English and French language rights in the Official Languages Act became part of the Charter of Rights and Freedoms – and was then embedded in the Canadian constitution with its repatriation in 1982 and the subsequent passing of the Constitution Act. Thus, with the Charter as part of the constitution, the collective language rights of the founding groups were entrenched as fundamental rights in Canada; language rights were established in sections 16 to 23 of the Charter, guaranteeing English and French official-language status and ensuring both as the languages of parliament, federal-level public services, and the courts, as well as ensuring official-language minority educational rights across Canada. In addition, section 27 of the Charter was included as the 'multicultural clause' to ensure that the charter was interpreted in a manner consistent with the preservation and enhancement of the multicultural heritage of Canadians.

In an article that analyses Pierre Trudeau's campaign speeches and various government documents from the late 1960s, Robert Charles Vipond (1996) traces the logic of Trudeau's entrenchment of language rights in the Charter as a way of ensuring that citizenship would be seen as a fundamental individual right and as the foundation of a deep sense of belonging (186). According to this reasoning, it was possible to support the constitutional protection of individual rights and the constitutional protection of language rights, for the two were cut from the same cloth; bilingualism was one of the 'fundamental liberties which make us feel proud of being Canadian' (ibid., 183). Language rights could be explained and defended under both rubrics of citizenship – that is, as rights and as belonging – since, as Vipond states, 'Trudeau spoke of minority language rights both as fundamental individual rights and as the foundation for creating a deep sense of belonging, and he moved seamlessly between them as if, by finding an element common to both ideas of citizenship, he could somehow fuse them' (ibid., 186). Vipond draws on Tuohy's (1992) notion of 'institutional ambivalence' (in ibid., 186) to argue that putting language rights first was Trudeau's way of reconciling the tension between these two notions of citizenship as rights and as belonging. And putting them in the Charter in such a way that he could harness other rights – but not language rights – to the override provision of section 33, the 'notwithstanding clause,'[1] was Trudeau's way of institutionalizing this ambivalence (ibid., 186–7).

Terrence Meyerhoff examines the legacy of this 'institutional ambivalence' by considering language rights in the Charter against multicultural rights, as outlined in the Charter's section 27. In his analysis, the collective rights of linguistic dualism, entrenched through the language rights of the Charter, result in a disparity between ethnic minorities and official-language minorities with respect to the rights and status each enjoy (Meyerhoff, 1993–4, 918). Meyerhoff reveals that section 27 has almost never been interpreted to contain any collective rights at all and that 'case law suggests that section 27 is not treated as a substantive provision'; rather, it is at best 'merely an interpretive provision with little impact on other rights' (ibid., 953). In fact, language rights constrain the definition of multiculturalism in the Charter, signalling the genealogical connection of these Charter provisions to the B and B Commission, and in particular to Trudeau's inauguration of a limited and specified definition of multiculturalism through the Multiculturalism Policy of 1971.

Meyerhoff also states that 'the Charter structure reflects the influence linguistic dualism ... has had on shaping multiculturalism and language rights. The upshot of linguistic dualism, as legislation, policy and the Charter exhibit, is a disparity between the rights and status – as to language and culture – afforded official language minorities compared to ethnic minorities' (Meyerhoff, 1993–4, 961). The implications of this relationship of rights are clear; there is an inconsistency in the stated, egalitarian definition of multiculturalism, amounting to an entrenchment of cultural inequality, and these inconsistencies suggest linguistic assimilation and racial ordering, both of which are antithetical to the cultural equality and pluralism that multicultural policy purports to promote (ibid., 967–9).

Meyerhoff begins with the legal inconsistencies that the Charter has promulgated in the present before returning to the contradiction between language and culture that the B and B Commission had set into place for the organization of a hierarchy of belonging – or, in Kymlicka's terms, 'group-differentiated citizenship' rights. In short, the commission's original formulation of multiculturalism within a bilingual framework still speaks to the powerful national mythology it has created, with legal decisions consistently upholding it. As Meyerhoff and Vipond conclude, language rights as envisioned and entrenched by Trudeau, first in the Official Languages Act and then in the Multiculturalism Policy, and eventually as 'institutional ambivalence' in the Charter, did not provide the platform for national unity he had hoped for. Meyerhoff has termed Canada's model of language rights and multiculturalism, premised upon linguistic dualism and a narrow definition of multiculturalism, as 'a weak reed for nation building' and national unity (Meyerhoff, 1993–4, 973). This question of maintaining national unity is the recurrent conundrum that drives the reworking and reiteration of formulations for belonging, with multiculturalism in a bilingual framework as the most durable of all.

We are thus left with the problem of how to promote national unity in a multicultural milieu without establishing a hierarchical relation of rights, without short-circuiting full citizenship rights through a contradiction between language and culture, and without putting into place a racially based social order. This problem has resonance for all states that have to contend with the challenge of addressing minority rights without reverting to an explicitly racial and ethnic form of nationalism.

These are complex issues for which there are no simple formulas or easy models, if exclusions are to be avoided. Perhaps trying to think through the conundrum of national unity and minority rights in a putatively multicultural state requires a questioning of some of the fundamental bases of organizing national inclusion. The preliminary consideration, then, probably has to be about the boundaries that construct any notion of inclusion, whether these are national boundaries or cultural ones (Clifford, 1988). Perhaps Jacques Derrida's radical rethinking of *hospitality* is an entry point into this issue.

Derrida (2000) differentiates between a conditional hospitality and an unconditional hospitality, stating that conditional hospitality is the welcoming of the Other within the limits of the law whereby the host remains the master of the home and retains his authority. Meyda Yegenoglu (2003) draws a parallel between this model of hospitality and multiculturalism, stating: 'The place from which multiculturalist tolerance welcomes the particularity of the other, fortified by codifications such as affirmative action and other legal measures, is what precisely enables the disavowed and inverted self-referentiality of racist hospitality which by emptying the host's position from any positive content asserts its superiority and sovereignty' (10). This is what Yegenoglu calls the inherent paradox of multiculturalism's conditional and lawful welcoming of the Other as guest, best exemplified by immigration laws. The multicultural figure is the 'limit figure' 'which brings into crisis the clear distinction between what is inside and what is outside,' the figure that marks 'cultural and national boundaries' (ibid., 11).

Unconditional hospitality, on the other hand, is the ethics, not law, of hospitality, where hospitality is infinite and cannot be limited – that is, regulated – by a nation's political or juridical practices (Derrida, 2000). Therefore, unconditional hospitality is a reversal, as Yegenoglu states, an 'interruption of a full possession of a place called home,' and 'the question of hospitality cannot be reduced to a multiculturalist tolerance, for there is no longer a question of limiting, restricting, or regulating tolerance of the other' (Yegenoglu, 2003, 20). Between these two limits of hospitality, the conditional and the unconditional, is an *aporia* where the impossibility of hospitality lies. Yet this is a productive impossibility, since the principle of unconditionality is the driving force behind the possibility of a revision of the law of hospitality (ibid., 25): 'As Derrida notes, the law is perfectible and there is progress to be performed on the law that will improve the conditions of hospitality. The condition of laws on immigration has to be improved without claiming that unconditional law should become an official policy. The very desire for unconditional hospitality is what regulated the improvement of the laws of hospitality' (ibid., 22).

The driving force behind the impossibility of unconditional hospitality strains the boundaries of nation and culture, or immigration laws and multicultural tolerance, even though these boundaries can likely never be jettisoned. Unconditional hospitality, as the demand for the immediate transformation of present conditions of hospitality – and as a way to encourage the transformation of the regulations that produce the boundaries of nation and culture – may provide another approach to the conundrum of national unity and multicultural nation-building. Derrida's idea of hospitality, although perhaps not having immediate policy implications, might nevertheless lead to general guiding principles about how we can begin to rethink nation and community. As this book has sought to demonstrate, when questions of 'who we are' reach a crisis point, even symbolic and bureaucratic exercises such as inquiries and commissions may provide a space for counter-discourses and a reimagining of who we are or might become. In the present, the ongoing anxieties and crises about the place of the Other in the nation emerge out of a contradictory set of rights and hierarchical relations, put into place through our current federal formulation of multiculturalism within a bilingual framework, which delineates groupings, their rights, and their mode of national belonging. These crises indicate that our current formulation gives rise to principles for nation-building which cannot accommodate who we are and have become since the B and B Commission was inaugurated.

If we are to seriously reconsider our 'social imaginary' (Castoriadis, 1987) in ways that respond substantively to these crises of national belonging without reproducing a racially based social order, then perhaps the productive impossibility of unconditional hospitality might serve to dislodge the bilingual framework of the anemic state multiculturalism that currently underpins the normalized, white-settler narrative of two founding nations – a narrative that dates back only about forty years to the B and B Commission. Furthermore, this driving force of unconditional hospitality might be harnessed to provide guiding principles for the inquiry into and revision of laws of hospitality governing immigration, citizenship, and refugees, among other areas. Perhaps we can use this principled desire for unconditional hospitality in our next, and overdue, exercise of reimagining nation, community, and belonging.

Appendix: The Terms of Reference

P.C. 1963–1106

Certified to be a true copy of a Minute of a Meeting of the Committee of the Privy Council approved by His Excellency the Governor General on the 19th July, 1963.

The Committee of the Privy Council, on the recommendation of the Right Honourable L.B. Pearson, the Prime Minister, advise that

André Laurendeau,[1] Montreal, P.Q.
Davidson Dunton, Ottawa, Ont.
Rev. Clément Cormier, Moncton, N.B.
Royce Frith, Toronto, Ont.
Jean-Louis Gagnon, Montreal, P.Q.
Mrs. Stanley Laing, Calgary, Alta.
Jean Marchand,[2] Quebec City, P.Q.
Jaroslav Bodhan Rudnyckyj, Winnipeg, Man.
Frank Scott, Montreal, P.Q.
Paul Wyczynski, Ottawa, Ont.

be appointed Commissioners under Part I of the Inquiries Act to inquire into and report upon the existing state of bilingualism and biculturalism in Canada and to recommend what steps should be taken to develop the Canadian Confederation on the basis of an equal partnership between the two founding races, taking into account the contribution made by the other ethnic groups to the cultural enrichment of Canada and the measures that should be taken to safeguard that contribution; and in particular

1. to report upon the situation and practice of bilingualism within all branches and agencies of the federal administration – including Crown corporations – and in their communications with the public and to make recommendations designed to ensure that bilingual and basically bicultural character of the federal administration;

2. to report on the role of public and private organizations including the mass communications media, in promoting bilingualism, better cultural relations and a more widespread appreciation of the basically bicultural character of our country and of the subsequent contribution made by the other cultures; and to recommend what should be done to improve that role; and

3. having regard to the fact that constitutional jurisdiction over education is vested in the provinces, to discuss with the provincial governments the opportunities available to Canadians to learn the English and French languages and to recommend what could be done to enable Canadians to become bilingual.

The Committee further advise:

(a) that the Commissioners be authorized to exercise all the powers conferred upon them by section 11 of the Inquiries Act and be assisted to the fullest extent by Government departments and agencies;

(b) that the Commissioners adopt such procedures and methods as they may from time to time deem expedient for the proper conduct of the inquiry and sit at such times and at such places as they may decide from time to time;

(c) that the Commissioners be authorized to engage the services of such counsel, staff and technical advisers as they may require at rates of remuneration and reimbursement to be approved by the Treasury Board;

(d) that the Commissioners report to the Governor in Council with all reasonable despatch, and file with the Dominion Archivist the papers and records of the Commission as soon as reasonably may be after the conclusion of the inquiry;

(e) that André Laurendeau and Davidson Dunton be co-Chairmen of the Commission and that André Laurendeau be Chief Executive Officer thereof.

R.G. Robertson
Clerk of the Privy Council
(Canada, *Book IV*, 1969, 235–6)

Notes

Introduction

1 'Founding races' is the phrase used by the Royal Commission on Bilingualism and Biculturalism in their terms of reference to refer to the English and French communities of Canada. The use of 'races' to refer to the French and English groups in Canada can be traced back in Canadian history, most notably to Lord Durham's report of 1839.

1. Language, Nation, and Race

1 The individuals most associated with this school are the German Romantics of the eighteenth century (Edwards, 1985, 23), and the leading figure is Johann Gottfried Herder (1744–1803), who is also often credited with being the first to coin the term *nationalism* in a text he wrote in 1774 (Hechter, 2000, 5).

2 Wilhelm von Humbolt (1767–1835), brother of the explorer-scientist Alexander von Humboldt, was a well-known anthropologist and philologist who foreshadowed Sapir-Whorfian relativism, which states that a group which shares a common language also shares a unique way of viewing the world (Edwards, 1985). This is also the theory that thought is inextricably linked to the language in which it is expressed. It is based on the work of the American linguist Edward Sapir (1884–1939) and Benjamin Lee Whorf (1897–1941). Some scholars present Herder, von Humboldt, Fichte, Sapir, and Whorf as part of the same tradition (Crystal, 1987).

3 Fishman's seminal essays on language and nationalism are a bridge between the role of language as a marker of primordialist authenticity and language as a modernist unifying force. Smith describes Fishman's approach as perennialist, in the sense that it is an approach that understands

the power of language and ethnicities – as well as myths of origin and familial metaphors – in rousing popular support for nationalism (Smith, 1998, 224).

4 The Upper Canada Rebellion (1838) and Lower Canada Rebellion (1837) were rebellions by English-Canadian and French-Canadian settlers against the British colonial government of the time.

5 Hage traces a democratization of the aristocratic national identity in Australia – which I feel is also congruent for Canada – from upper-class British to one where 'to be an Australian national aristocrat . . . to feel that one had the right to take a governmental posture towards Australia, one no longer needed to be born to a socioeconomically defined upper-class family, since one's putative Australian Anglo-Celtic Whiteness became in itself the aristocratic national identity' (Hage, 2000, 197–8). I would further argue that anyone who passes for a similar 'Anglo-ness . . . essence' in the Canadian context can also inhabit a sense of governmental belonging as an 'innate right.'

2. Historical Context

1 Until then, Marchand had been a member of the B and B Commission.

2 This was echoed in an *Ottawa Journal* article, which stated: 'The surging millions of Asia and Africa who might want to immigrate lack the skills modern society demands,' and 'the bars against them are therefore as effective as they were in 1947' ('Door to Immigrants,' 1966).

3 Burnet had a significant research role in *Book IV: The Cultural Contributions of Other Ethnic Groups* for the final report from the B and B Commission.

4 The Tory riots, also known as the Montreal riots, were a reaction to the passage of the Rebellion Losses Bill, which was a bill to provide compensation for those in Lower Canada who had suffered losses during the Rebellions of 1837–8 (similar provisions having already been made for those in Upper Canada). Angry Tories in Montreal provoked a riot involving thousands that culminated in the burning of the Montreal Parliament buildings.

5 The conscription crisis of 1917 emerged when Borden attempted to enforce the newly passed Military Services Act, which introduced conscription across the country. Conscription was most vehemently opposed in Quebec and sparked rioting – known as the Easter Riots – in Quebec City between 29 March and 1 April 1918, resulting in the application of the War Measures Act by Ottawa, culminating in the deaths of four civilians, and resulting in hundreds of thousands of dollars in damage. A lesser conscription crisis erupted during Canada's involvement in the Second World War.

6 'Allophone' is a term used ostensibly to denote people in Canada whose mother tongue is neither English nor French.

7 The Rassemblement pour l'indépendance nationale (RIN) was Montreal's first mass-based, separatist political party. The Front de libération du Québec (FLQ) was a 'revolutionary separatist underground of self-styled [f]rancophone urban guerillas' battling against the 'economic colonialism' of Montreal's anglophone establishment (Levine, 1990, 41).

8 See the appendix for the full text of the terms of reference.

9 See the appendix for the full list of commissioners.

3. Preliminary Hearings and Report

1 The commission referred to all non-French, non-English, and non-Indigenous groups as 'other ethnic groups' until the publication of *Book IV*, when they became 'cultural groups.' Indigenous groups were referred to as 'Indians and Eskimos' through most of the commission's work.

2 p.c. = percentage

4. Public Hearings and Research

1 The Mennonite Society for the Promotion of the German Language also submitted a brief calling for the government to take a 'positive attitude to the teaching of secondary languages' and recommending, 'Either French, German, Ukrainian, Jewish or Icelandic – depending on the decision of the respective school district – should be introduced in schools as a second language from grade one' (Mennonite Society, 1963, 2).

2 The profound effects of the war on the Japanese community were underscored in appendix A of the NJCCA's brief, entitled 'A History of the Japanese Canadians in British Columbia, 1877–1958' and written by Ken Adachi. This forty-two-page, extensively researched, and detailed account of the history of Japanese Canadians was in sharp contrast to the short, seven-page, point-form brief to which it was appended, accentuating the significant degree to which community history, in particular internment during the Second World War, informed the positions taken by the NJCCA. The effects of the war on this community were discussed further in a confidential report on a private meeting between three commissioners – Mrs Stanley Laing, Jean-Louis Gagnon, and Paul Wyczynski – and a few members of the Vancouver Japanese community. The meeting took place in the home of Gordon Kadota on 12 May 1965. The report described the war's impact not only on the interned generation but also on the subsequent

Nisei generation: 'To them [Nisei] the war was an important turning point, which as one of them said, forced them out of the ghetto in Steveston into the larger stream of Canadian life. They recognize this was a terrible period for their parents, and say many of them carry scars of bitterness. For themselves it was a good thing, in that they became members of a society at large' (Taylor, 1965, 2).

5. Book I: The Official Language

1 The Study Groups were research groups organized by the commission, each with a specific focus. Study Group D was set up to study matters pertaining to the other ethnic groups.
2 In November 1967 the Confederation of Tomorrow Conference was called by the then-premier of Ontario, John Robarts, to discuss constitutional reform, specifically with regard to Quebec's concerns.
3 In his 1964 report, Rudnyckyj had also included the Dutch language, in addition to this Russian and Ukrainian example, in this category: 'Henry Hudson's third voyage . . . 1609 . . . was made in the service of the Dutch East Indies Co . . . The Netherlands established sovereignty over the area discovered on this voyage, calling it New Netherland' (Rudnyckyj, 1964, 4). However, in his 'Separate Statement' of 1967, the example of the Dutch language was eliminated, possibly to establish a stronger and more focused historical claim for the Ukrainian language.

6. Book IV: The Cultural Contribution of the Other Ethnic Groups

1 N.E. Walmsley, 'Some Aspects of Canada's Immigration Policy.'
2 Foon Sein, 'The Chinese in Canada'; H.H. Potter and D.G. Hill, 'Negro Settlement in Canada, 1628–1965: A Survey'; R.R. Wisse, 'Jewish Participation in Canadian Culture.'
3 The premise that this separation between immigrant and receiving societies was determined by racial and religious 'cultural distance' was reminiscent of an idea expressed in the Introduction to Book I, where the cultural commonality between the English and French groups was deemed to be based on their cultural distance from racialized 'Asian and African cultures' (Canada, Book I, 1967, 9).
4 After the word Eskimos, there was a footnote stating: 'Since the terms of reference contain no mention of Indians and Eskimos, we have not studied the question of Canada's native population' (Canada, Book I, 1969, 4), which echoed the statement made in the blue pages of Book I to justify

the exclusion of Indigenous claims. This evasion allowed the commission to study the history of Canada's people beginning with the colonizing groups – the English and the French – and not have to account for the claims of founding status made by Indigenous peoples. Also, designating the English and French as colonizers – presumably of Indigenous peoples – emphasized their 'founding' difference from Indigenous groups, and the rest of the immigrants could similarly be designated as a group apart under the label of 'immigrants of different ethnic origins,' that is, different from the English and French.

5 One of the examples given was the *padrone* system used in the Italian construction industry.

7. Conclusion

1 The 'notwithstanding clause' is often called an 'override clause'; it allows Parliament or the legislature of a province to declare in an Act of Parliament or of the legislature that the Act or a provision will operate notwithstanding a provision included in section 2 or sections 7 to 15 of the Charter for up to a period of five years.

Appendix

1 On 8 October 1968, following the death of André Laurendeau the preceding June, Jean-Louis Gagnon was appointed co-chairman in his place and André Raynauld was appointed a member of the commission.

2 The resignation of Jean Marchand from the commission was accepted on 21 September 1965. On 22 November of that year, Paul Lacoste, formerly one of the co-secretaries of the commission, was appointed to fill the vacancy created by Marchand's resignation. On 1 May 1966 Professor Gilles Lalande of the Université de Montréal was appointed co-secretary.

References

Abele, F., and D. Stasiulus. 1989. 'Canada as a "White Settler Colony": What about Natives and Immigrants?' In W. Clement and G. Williams, eds., *The New Canadian Political Economy*. Montreal: McGill-Queen's University Press. 240–77.

Adie, R.F., and T. Krukowski. 1966. 'The Other Ethnic Groups and Mass Media: Working Paper Prepared by R.F. Adie.' Ottawa.

'And Those in Between?' 1965. 26 February. Toronto *Telegram*. Library and Archives Canada, RG 33, Series 80, vol. 120, file 606B, 15/3/65.

Andersen, C., and C. Denis. 2003. 'Urban Natives and the Nation: Before and after the Royal Commission on Aboriginal People.' *Canadian Review of Sociology and Anthropology*, 40(4): 373–85.

Anderson, B. 1983. *Imagined Communities*. London: Verso.

Anderson, K. 2000. 'Thinking "Postnationally": Dialogue across Multi-cultural, Indigenous, and Settler Spaces.' *Annals of the Association of American Geographers*, 90(2): 381–91.

Anglican Church of Canada. Council for Social Service. 1965. 'Canada, Unity in Diversity: Report of a Submission to the Royal Commission on Bilingualism and Biculturalism.' Toronto.

Arteaga, A. 1996. *An Other Tongue*. Durham, NC: Duke University Press.

Ashcroft, B. 2001. 'Language and Race.' *Social Identities*, 7(3): 311–21.

Ashforth, A. 1990. 'Reckoning Schemes of Legitimization: On Commissions of Inquiry as Power/Knowledge Forms.' *Journal of Historical Sociology*, 3(1): 1–22.

Bagnato, V.E. 1963. 19 November. Library and Archives Canada, Italian Immigrant Aid Society, RG 33, Series 80, vol. 115, 22, file 101–125.

Balibar, E. 1991. 'The Nation Form: History and Ideology.' In Balibar and I. Wallerstein, eds., *Race, Nation, Class: Ambiguous Identities*. London: Verso. 86–106.

Bannerji, H. 1996. 'On the Dark Side of the Nation: Politics of Multiculturalism and the State of Canada.' *Journal of Canadian Studies*, 31(3): 250–75.

Barnard, F.M. 1965. *Herder's Social and Political Thought: From Enlightenment to Nationalism*. Oxford: Clarendon Press.

Bastarache, M., ed. 2004. Introduction to *Language Rights in Canada*. 2nd ed. Quebec: Yvon Blais. 1–36.

Beaud, J.-P., and J.-G. Prévost. 1996. 'Immigration, Eugenics and Statistics: Measuring Racial Origins in Canada (1921–1941).' *Canadian Ethnic Studies*, 28(2): 1–23.

Bertrand, J., and G. Burgis. 1965. 15 July. 'Our Changing Canadian Community.' Presented at the Lake Couchiching Conference, 30 June–4 July 1965. Library and Archives Canada, RG 33, Series 80, vol. 121, file 677E.

Bhabha, H.K. 1990a. 'DissemiNation: Time, Narrative, and the Margins of the Modern Nation.' In H.K. Bhabha, ed., *Nation and Narration*. London: Routledge. 291–320.

– , ed. 1990b. Introduction to *Nation and Narration*. London: Routledge. 1–7.

Bienkowska, D.I. 1965. 14 April. 'Introduction of the Polish Language.' Toronto: Department of Citizenship and Immigration, Canadian Citizenship Branch. Library and Archives Canada, RG 33, Series 80, vol. 120, file 601–624.

Blodgett, E.D. 1990. 'Ethnic Writing in Canadian Literature as Paratext.' *Signature*, 3: 13–27.

Bourhis, R.Y. 2003. 'Measuring Ethnocultural Diversity Using the Canadian Census.' *Canadian Ethnic Studies*, 35(1): 9–32.

Burnet, J. 1978. 'The Policy of Multiculturalism within a Bilingual Framework: A Stock-Taking.' *Canadian Ethnic Studies*, 10(2): 107–13.

'Cabinet Concerns 30 Years Ago Mirror Today's Problems.' 1996. *Canadian Press Newswire*, 6 February. Retrieved 12 June 2003 from http://cbc1.micromedia.ca/printmaildoc.asp?action=Print&recordnum=30.

Cairns, Alan C. 2000. *Citizens Plus: Aboriginal Peoples and the Canadian State*. Vancouver: UBC Press.

Canada. 1965. 5 March. *Time*, vol. 85, no. 10. Library and Archives Canada, RG 33, Series 80, vol. 120, file 606B, 15/3/65.

Canada Correspondent. (1965, March 6). Our unknown compatriots. *The Economist*. Library and Archives Canada, RG 33, Series 80, Vol. 120, File 606B, 15/3/65.

Canada. Department of Manpower and Immigration. 1966. *Canadian Immigration Policy* (White Paper on Immigration). Ottawa.

Canada Ethnic Press Federation. 1964. 'Brief Presented to the Royal Commission on Bilingualism and Biculturalism.' Toronto.

Canada. *House of Commons Debates*. 1947. 1 May. Vol. 3, 3rd Session, 20th
Parliament. Ottawa: Queen's Printer. 2644–94.
- 1962a. 19 January. Vol. 1, 1st Session, 25th Parliament. Ottawa: Queen's
Printer. 9–27.
- 1962b. 17 December. Vol. 3, 1st Session, 26th Parliament. Ottawa: Queen's
Printer. 2699–755.
- 1963. 16 May. Vol. 1, 1st Session, 26th Parliament. Ottawa: Queen's Printer.
1–8.
- 1966a. 21 April. Vol. 4, 1st Session, 27th Parliament. Hon. Jean Marchand,
Minister of Citizenship and Immigration. Ottawa: Queen's Printer.
4097–150.
- 1966b. 14 October. Vol. 8, 1st Session, 27th Parliament. Ottawa: Queen's
Printer. 8651–713.
- 1967. 5 December. Vol. 5, 2nd Session. 17th Parliament. Ottawa: Queen's
Printer. 4595–5757.
- 1968. 17 October. Vol. 2, 1st Session, 28th Parliament. Ottawa: Queen's
Printer. 1463–1523.
- 1971a. 8 October. Vol. 8, 3rd Session, 28th Parliament. Ottawa: Queen's
Printer. 8545–85.
- 1971b. 8 October. 'Federal Government's Response to Book IV of the Report of
the Royal Commission on Bilingualism and Biculturalism: Document Tabled
in the House of Commons.' Sessional Paper 283–4/101B, Appendix: 8583–4.
'Canada Is Ours.' 1965. June. *Zhinochyi Svit*. Department of Citizenship and
Immigration, Canadian Citizenship Branch, Foreign Language Press
Review Service. Library and Archives Canada, RG 33, Series 80, vol. 121,
file 651–675.
'Canada: Multicultural.' 1970. 7–8 August. Conference held at Hart House,
University of Toronto. Canada: Citizenship Branch, Department of
Provincial Secretary and Citizenship, Government of Ontario.
Canada. Royal Commission on Bilingualism and Biculturalism. 1963.
'Preliminary Hearing.' Transcript. Ottawa.
- 1965a. 'Transcripts of Public Hearings.' Ottawa. Microfilm.
- 1965b. *A Preliminary Report of the Royal Commission on Bilingualism and
Biculturalism*. Ottawa: Queen's Printer.
- 1966. Press Section. 1966. 4 April. 'Working Paper on Definitions of
"Culture" and "Biculturalism."' Library and Archives Canada, RG 33,
Series 80, vol. 124, file 895E.
- 1967. *Book I: The Official Languages*. Ottawa: Queen's Printer.
- 1969. *Book IV: The Cultural Contribution of the Other Ethnic Groups*. Ottawa:
Queen's Printer.

– n.d. 'Quebec Immigration.' Library and Archives Canada, RG 33, Series 80, vol. 128, file 1476–1500.

Canada. *Statement of the Government of Canada on Indian Policy*. 1969. Presented to the First Session of the Twenty-eighth Parliament by the Honourable Jean Chrétien, Minister of Indian Affairs and Northern Development. Ottawa: Department of Indian Affairs and Northern Development. Ottawa: Queen's Printer.

Canadian Citizenship Branch, Department of Citizenship and Immigration. 1964. 22 May. Library and Archives Canada, RG 33, Series 80, vol. 118, file 451–475.

Canadian Council of National Groups. 1964. 'Brief to the Royal Commission on Bilingualism and Biculturalism.' Toronto.

Canadian Cultural Rights Committee. 1968. *Canadian Cultural Rights: Concern: A Conference to Study Canada's Multicultural Patterns in the Sixties*. Ottawa: Canadian Cultural Rights Committee.

Canadian Labour Congress Canada. 1965. 'Submission to the Royal Commission on Bilingualism and Biculturalism.' Ottawa.

Canadian Mennonite Association. 1965. 'Brief to the Royal Commission on Bilingualism and Biculturalism.' Winnipeg.

Cartier, C., and P. Henriquez (Producers), and F. Pelletier (Director/Narrator). 2003. *Public Enemy Number One: The Life and Times of Jacques Parizeau*. Motion picture. Montreal: Macumba International.

Castoriadis. C. 1987. *The Imaginary Institution of Society*. Cambridge, MA: MIT Press.

Caughnawaga Defence Committee. 1965. 'Brief to the Royal Commission on Bilingualism and Biculturalism.' Quebec: Caughnawaga Reserve.

Choudhry, S. 2002. 'National Minorities and Ethnic Immigrants: Liberalism's Political Sociology.' *Journal of Political Philosophy*, 10(1): 54–78.

Chua, B.-H. 1979. 'Describing a National Crisis: An Exploration in Textual Analysis.' *Human Studies*, 2: 47–61.

Clifford, James. 1988. *The Predicament of Culture: Twentieth Century Ethnography, Literature, and Art*. Cambridge, MA: Harvard University Press.

'Confidential – Tentative First Preliminary Draft for Discussion Purposes.' 1964. 25 August. Ottawa. Library and Archives Canada, RG 33, Series 80, vol. 117, file 414E.

Coon, Carleton S. 1962. *The Origins of Races*. New York: Alfred A. Knopf.

Corrigan, P., and D. Sayer. 1985. *The Great Arch: English State Formation as Cultural Revolution*. New York: Blackwell.

Costa, E. 1970. Untitled. Paper presented at Canada: Multicultural Conference. Representing the Federation of Italian Clubs and Associations. Citizenship

Branch, Department of Provincial Secretary and Citizenship, Government of Ontario, 7–8 August, University of Toronto.

Craig, G.M., ed. 1963. *Lord Durham's Report: An Abridgement of Report on the Affairs of British North America*. Toronto: McClelland and Stewart.

Crowley, T. 1996. *Language in History*. London: Routledge.

Crystal, D. 1987. 'Language Planning.' In D. Crystal, ed., *The Cambridge Encyclopedia of Language*. Cambridge: Cambridge University Press. 364–7.

Curtis, B. 2002. *The Politics of Population*. Toronto: University of Toronto Press.

Dean, M. 1994. *Critical and Effective Histories: Foucault's Methods and Historical Sociology*. London: Routledge.

Derrida, J. 2000. *Of Hospitality: Anne Dufourmantelle Invites Jacques Derrida to Respond*. Translated by R. Bowlby. Stanford: Stanford University Press.

Devereux, C. 1999. 'New Woman, New World: Maternal Feminism and the New Imperialism in the White Settler Colonies.' *Women's Studies International Forum*, 22(2): 175–84.

'Door to Immigrants Still Opens Cautiously.' 1966. 17 October. *Ottawa Journal*. Library Archives Canada, RG 33, Series 80, vol. 146, file A-7b.

Edwards, J. 1985. *Language, Society and Identity*. Oxford: Basil Blackwell.

Eggington, W. 1994. 'Language Planning and Policy in Australia.' In W. Grabe, ed., *Annual Review of Applied Linguistics*. Cambridge: Cambridge University Press. 137–55.

'Eskimos Enter Culture Study.' 1964. 12 September. Montreal *Star*. Library and Archives Canada, RG 33, Series 80, vol. 175, file D3, 'Ethnic Minorities 1964–5.'

Farquharson, D. 1966. 14 October. 'Immigration 1963–66.' Ottawa *Citizen*. Library and Archives Canada, RG 33, Series 80, vol. 146, file A-7b, 'Immigration 1963–66.'

Featherstone, M. 2000. 'Archiving Cultures.' *British Journal of Sociology*, 51(1): 161–84.

Ferrabee, J. 1965a. 16 February. 'Highlights.' Montreal *Gazette*. Library and Archives Canada, RG 33, Series 80, vol. 120, file 606B.

– 1965b. 26 February. 'Highlights.' Montreal *Gazette*. Library and Archives Canada, RG 33, Series 80, vol. 120, file 606B.

– 1965c. 27 February. 'Report Comment Varies Widely but Proves Provocative.' Montreal *Gazette*. Library and Archives Canada, RG 33, Series 80, vol. 120, file 606B.

Fichte, J. 1968. *Addresses to the German Nation*. 1922. Reprint, New York: Harper and Row.

Findley, P.C. 1968. 7 May. 'Memorandum.' Library and Archives Canada, RG 33, Series 80, vol. 128, file 1390E.

Fischer, D., and H. Crowe. 1966. 19 October. 'That White Paper Is Anti-Italian.'
    Toronto *Telegram*. Library and Archives Canada, RG 33, Series 80, vol. 146,
    file A-7b, 'Immigration 1963–66.'
Fishman, J.A. 1972. *Language and Nationalism: Two Integrative Essays*. Rowley,
    MA: Newbury House.
Foucault, M. 1977. 'Nietzsche, Genealogy, History.' In D.F. Bouchard, ed.,
    Language, Counter-memory, Practice. Ithaca, NY: Cornell University Press.
    139–64.
– 1982. 'Afterword: The Subject and Power.' In H.L. Dreyfus, P. Rabinow,
    and M. Foucault, eds., *Beyond Structuralism and Hermeneutics*. Chicago:
    University of Chicago Press. 208–28.
Gellner, E. 1983. *Nations and Nationalism: New Perspectives on the Past*. Oxford:
    Basil Blackwell.
Goldberg, D.T. 1993. *Racist Culture*. Oxford: Blackwell.
Grillo, R. 1989. *Dominant Language*. Cambridge: Cambridge University Press.
Hage, G. 2000. *White Nation*. London: Routledge.
Handler, Richard. 1988. Nationalism and the Politics of Culture in Quebec.
    Madison: University of Wisconsin Press.
Harpham, G.G. 2002. *Language Alone*. New York: Routledge.
Haugen, E. 1959. 'Planning for a Standard Language in Modern Norway.'
    Anthropological Linguistics, 1: 8–21.
– 1987. 'Language Planning.' In U. Ammon, N. Dittmar, and K. Mattheier,
    eds., *Sociolinguistics: An International Handbook of the Science of Language and
    Society*. New York: de Gruyter. 626–37.
Hawkins, F. 1988. *Canada and Immigration: Public Policy and Public Concern*.
    2nd ed. Montreal: McGill-Queen's University Press.
Hawthorn, H.B., ed. 1966–7. *A Survey of the Contemporary Indians of Canada:
    Economic, Political, Educational Needs and Policies*. 2 vols. Ottawa: Queen's
    Printer.
Hechter, M. 2000. *Containing Nationalism*. Oxford: Oxford University Press.
Herriman, M., and B. Burnaby, eds. 1996. Introduction to *Language Policies in
    English-Dominant Countries*. Philadelphia: Clevedon Multilingual Matters.
    1–14.
Higonnet, P.L.R. 1980. 'The Politics of Linguistic Terrorism and Grammatical
    Hegemony during the French Revolution.' *Social History*, 5: 41–69.
Horn, K.-T. 1965. 'Brief to the Royal Commission on Bilingualism and
    Biculturalism.'
Imperial Order Daughters of the Empire. 1964. Presentation by the Imperial
    Order Daughters of the Empire (I.O.D.E.) to the Royal Commission on
    Bilingualism and Biculturalism. Toronto.

Indian-Eskimo Association of Canada. 1965. 'A Brief to the Royal Commission on Bilingualism and Biculturalism.' Toronto.

International Institute Canada. 1964. 'Brief to the Royal Commission on Bilingualism and Biculturalism.' Ottawa.

Isajiw, W.W. 1983. 'Multiculturalism and the Integration of the Canadian Community.' *Canadian Ethnic Studies*, 15(2): 107–17.

Jenson, J. 1994. 'Commissioning Ideas: Representation and Royal Commissions.' In Susan D. Phillips, ed., *How Ottawa Spends 1994–95*. Ottawa: Carleton University Press. 39–69.

Johnston, Darlene. 1993. 'First Nations and Canadian Citizenship.' In William Kaplan, ed., *Belonging: The Meaning and Future of Canadian Citizenship*. Montreal: McGill-Queen's University Press. 349–67.

'Kahn-Tineta Horn Critical: Non-Indians in Control.' 1965. 15 August. Regina *Leader-Post*. Library and Archives Canada, RG 33, Series 80, vol. 175, file D3, 'Ethnics Minorities, 1965 II.'

Kallen, E. 1982. 'Multiculturalism: Ideology, Policy and Reality.' *Journal of Canadian Studies*, 17(1): 51–63.

Kirschbaum, J. 1964. 21 November. *The Liberty*. Library and Archives Canada, RG 33, Series 80, vol. 119, file 526–550.

– 1965. 30 January. *The Canadian Slovak*. Library and Archives Canada, RG 33, Series 80, vol. 121, file 651–675.

Knowles V. 1997. *Strangers at Our Gates: Canadian Immigration and Immigration Policy, 1540–1997*. Toronto: Dundurn Press.

Kretzer, D.I., and D. Arel. 2002. 'Censuses, Identity Formation, and the Struggle for Political Power.' In D.I. Kretzer and D. Arel, eds., *Census and Identity: The Politics of Race, Ethnicity and Language in National Censuses*. Cambridge: Cambridge University Press.

Kirtz, M.K. 1996. 'Old World Traditions, New World Inventions: Bilingualism, Multiculturalism, and the Transformation of Ethnicity.' *Canadian Ethnic Studies*, 28(1): 8–21.

Kymlicka, W. 1995. *Multicultural Citizenship*. Oxford: Clarendon Press.

Lam, A. 1965. 22 June. 'Letter from St. John the Baptist Anglican Church to the Commission on Bilingualism and Biculturalism.' Fort Garry, Man. Library and Archives Canada, RG 33, Series 80, vol. 121, file 676–700.

Laurendeau, A. 1962. 'Pour une enquête sur le bilinguisme.' *Le Devoir*, 20 January: 4.

Lee, M.A. 2003. 'Multiculturalism as Nationalism: A Discussion of Nationalism in Pluralistic Nations.' *Canadian Review of Studies in Nationalism*, 30: 103–23.

Levine, M.V. 1990. *The Re-conquest of Montreal: Language Policy and Social Change in a Bilingual City*. Philadelphia: Temple University Press.

Linke, U. 2003. 'There is a Land Where Everything Is Pure: Linguistic Nationalism and Identity Politics in Germany.' In D.S. Moore, J. Kosek, and A. Pandian, eds., *Race, Nature and the Politics of Difference*. Durham, NC: Duke University Press. 149–74.

Lucas, C. 1970. *Lord Durham's Report on the Affairs of British North America*. Edited by C. Lucas. Vol. 2. 1912; reprint, New York: Sentry Press.

Lupul, M.M. 1982. 'The Political Implementation of Multiculturalism.' *Journal of Canadian Studies*, 17(1): 93–102.

Lupul, M.R. 1983. 'Multiculturalism and Canada's White Ethnics.' *Canadian Ethnic Studies*, 15(1): 99–107.

Manitoba Japanese Canadian Citizens Association. 'Statement to the Advisory Committee on Bilingualism and Biculturalism.' Library and Archives Canada, RG 33, Series 80, vol. 115, file 101–125.

Mannil, S.T. 1965. 21 September. 'Immigration.' *Globe and Mail*. Library and Archives Canada, RG 33, Series 80, vol. 146, file A-7b, 'Immigration 1963–66.'

Marais, J.S.B. 1965. July. 'Afrikaans in the Public Service' (1). Translated from Afrikaans by the Foreign Language Division, Translation Bureau, Royal Commission on Bilingualism and Biculturalism. Originally published in *The Public Servant*, May 1959. Library and Archives Canada, RG 33, Series 80, vol. 122, file 743E.

May, S. 2001. *Language and Minority Rights*. London: Longman.

McClintock, A. 1992. 'The Angel of Progress: Pitfalls of the Term: Post-colonialism.' *Social Text*: 1–15.

– 1995. *Imperial Leather*. New York: Routledge.

McGillivray, D. 1966a. 26 May. 'Big Question Mark Hangs over B and B.' *Southam News Services*. Library and Archives Canada, RG 33, Series 80, vol. 124, file 36P.

– 1966b. 26 May. 'Most Controversial Inquiry in History.' *Southam News Services*. Library and Archives Canada, RG 33, Series 80, vol. 124, file 951–975.

McPhedran, A. 1964. 6 November. 'Memorandum to Mrs. Stanley B. Laing – Education of the Native Children in the North West Territories.' Library and Archives Canada, RG 33, Series 80, vol. 118, file 476–500.

McRoberts, Kenneth. 1997. *Misconceiving Canada: The Struggle for National Unity*. Oxford: Oxford University Press.

Mennonite Society. 1963. 16 December. 'Statement of the Mennonite Society for the Promotion of the German Language.' Library and Archives Canada, RG 33, Series 80, vol. 115, file 101–125.

Meyerhoff, T. 1993–4. 'Multiculturalism and Language Rights in Canada: Problems and Prospects for Equality and Unity.' *American University Journal of International Law and Policy*, 9: 913–1013.

Momryk, M. 1988. 'J.B. Rudnyckyj and the Bilingualism and Biculturalism Commission.' *The Archivist* 15(3): 18–19.

Montreal Star. 1965. 27 April. 'Submission to the Royal Commission on Bilingualism and Biculturalism.' Montreal.

Morrison, N. 1966. 1 March. 'Memorandum.' Library and Archives Canada, RG 33, Series 80, vol. 123, file 836E.

– 1989. *'Bilingualism and Biculturalism': Language and Society: Special Report: On the 25th Anniversary of the B and B Commission and the 20th Anniversary of the Official Languages Act – English and French in Canada.* Ottawa: Commission of Official Languages / Ministry of Supply and Services.

Mouffe, C. 2001. 'Every Form of Art Has a Political Dimension.' Interview by R. Deutsche, B.W. Joseph, and T. Keenan. *Grey Room,* 2: 98–125.

Multiculturalism for Canada Conference. 1970. *Report of the Conference.* 28–9 August, University of Alberta.

Mutual Co-Operation League of Canada. 1964. 'Brief to the Royal Commission on Bilingualism and Biculturalism.' Toronto.

National Japanese Canadian Citizens Association. 1965. 'Brief to the Royal Commission on Bilingualism and Biculturalism.' Toronto.

Ng, R. 1995. 'Multiculturalism as Ideology: A Textual Analysis.' In M. Campbell and A. Manicom, eds., *Knowledge, Experience and Ruling Relations.* Toronto: University of Toronto Press. 35–48.

Oliver, M. 1963. October. 'Memorandum to the Royal Commission on Bilingualism and Biculturalism.' Library and Archives Canada, RG 33, Series 80, vol. 115, file 47E.

'Once Again: Two Languages – Yes! Only Two Cultures.' 1964. 12 September. Montreal *News.* Department of Citizenship and Immigration, Canadian Citizenship Branch, Foreign Language Press Review Service. Library and Archives Canada, RG 33, Series 80, vol. 118, file 476–500.

O'Neil, M. 2001. 'Why We Need More Royal Commissions,' *Herizons,* 15(2): 14–16.

Padolsky, E. 2000. 'Multiculturalism at the Millennium.' *Journal of Canadian Studies,* 35(1): 138–60.

Parai, L. 1974. 'Canada's Immigration Policy: 1962–73.' London, ON: University of Western Ontario, Department of Economics.

Parekh, B. 1997. 'Dilemmas of Multicultural Theory of Citizenship.' *Constellations,* 4(1): 54–62.

Patten, A. 2001. 'Political Theory and Language Policy.' *Political Theory,* 29(5): 691–715.

Pelletier, G. 1989. *Language and Society: Special Report: On the 25th Anniversary of the B and B Commission and the 20th Anniversary of the Official Languages*

Act – English and French in Canada – 'The Kick-Off.' Ottawa: Commission of
Official Languages / Ministry of Supply and Services Canada.

Porter, J. 1969. 'Bilingualism and the Myths of Culture.' *Review of Canadian
Sociology and Anthropology*, 6(2): 111–19.

Potter, Harold, H., and Hill, Daniel G. 1966. *Negro Settlement in Canada,
1628–1965: A Survey.* Ottawa: s.n. Series: Canada. Royal Commission on
Bilingualism and Biculturalism Research Studies Div. VIII-B, no. 14.

Rabinow, P., and N. Rose. 2003. *The Essential Foucault.* London: The New Press.

Rassool, N. 1998. 'Postmodernity, Cultural Pluralism and the Nation-state:
Problems of Language Rights, Human Rights, Identity and Power.' *Language Sciences*, 20(1): 89–99.

Razack, S. 1998. *Looking White People in the Eye.* Toronto: University of Toronto
Press.

– 1999. 'Making Canada White: Law and the Policing of Bodies of Colour in
the 1990s.' *Canadian Journal of Law and Society*, 14(1): 159–84.

'Report on Canada Intended to Shock.' 1965. 4 March. Manchester *Guardian*,
vol. 92, no. 9. Library and Archives Canada, RG 33, Series 80, vol. 120, file
606B.

Rose, N., and P. Miller. 1992. 'Political Power beyond the State: Problematics
of Government.' *British Journal of Sociology*, 43(2): 173–205.

Rudnyckyj, J.B. 1963. 14 September. 'Bilingualism and Biculturalism in
Canada: Preliminary Review of Concepts and Definitions. Research Report
Presented in Winnipeg.' Library and Archives Canada, RG 33, Series 80,
vol. 115, file 15aE.

– 1964. 30 January. 'Ethno-lingual Groups in Canada.' Library and Archives
Canada, RG 33, Series 80, vol. 115, file 145E.

– 1965. 23 December. 'Formulas in Bilingualism and Biculturalism' (excerpts
from an address). Library and Archives Canada, RG 33, Series 80, vol. 122,
file 771E.

– N.d.a. 'Biography.' Archives of Manitoba, MG 14, C98, box 1.

– N.d.b 'Unilingualism versus Bi and Multilingualism in Manitoba.' Archives
of Manitoba, MG 14, C98, box 1.

Ryder, N.B. 1955. 'The Interpretation of Origin Statistics.' *Canadian Journal of
Economics and Political Science*, 21(4): 466–79.

Said, E. 1979. *Orientalism.* New York: Vintage Books.

Satzewich, V. 1989. 'Racism and Canadian Immigration Policy: The Government's
View of Caribbean Migration, 1962–1966.' *Canadian Ethnic Studies*, 21(1): 77–97.

Schmidt, W.H.O. 1965. 23 September. 'Report to Professor MacRae, Royal
Commission on Bilingualism and Biculturalism.' Library and Archives
Canada, RG 33, Series 80, vol. 121, file 701–25.

Shepherd, H. 1965. 12 February. 'Indian Cheated by White Man, Says
Mohawk Model.' *The Varsity*, 1, 3. Library and Archives Canada, RG 33,
Series 80, vol. 175, file D3, 'Ethnic Minorities 1964–5 I.'

Sien, Foon. 1967. 'The Chinese in Canada.' Essay Submitted to the Royal
Commission on Bilingualism and Biculturalism. Ottawa: s.n. Series:
Canada. Royal Commission on Bilingualism and Biculturalism Research
Studies Div. VIII-B, no. 10.

Sloan, T. 1989. 'Opinion Takers, Opinion Makers.' *Language and Society:
Special Report: On the 25th Anniversary of the B and B Commission and the
20th Anniversary of the Official Languages Act – English and French in Canada.*
Ottawa: Commission of Official Languages / Ministry of Supply and
Services.

Smart, P. 1991. *The Diary of André Laurendeau.* Translated by P. Smart and
D. Howard. Toronto: James Lorimer.

Smith, A.D. 1998. *Nationalism and Modernism.* London: Routledge.

Smith, D. 1999. *Writing the Social.* Toronto: University of Toronto Press.

Social Study Club of Edmonton. 1964. 'Brief to the Royal Commission on
Bilingualism and Biculturalism.' Edmonton.

Stasiulus, D., and N. Yuval-Davis. 1995. 'Introduction: Beyond Dichotomies –
Gender, Race, Ethnicity and Class in Settler Societies.' In Stasiulus and
Yuval-Davis, eds., *Unsettling Settler Societies: Articulations of Gender, Race,
Ethnicity and Class.* London: Sage Publications. 1–38.

Stinson, A. 1966. 19 January. 'Confidential: Private Meeting, Department of
Citizenship and Immigration, October 11, 1965.' Library and Archives
Canada, RG 33, Series 80, vol. 122, file 785E.

Study Group C. 1966. 7 July. Minutes. 8th Meeting, Ottawa. Library and
Archives Canada, RG 33, Series 80, vol. 125, file 1007E.

Study Group D. 1963. December. 'Working Paper.' Library and Archives
Canada, RG 33, Series 80, vol. 123, file 801–825.

Tamboukou, M. 1999. 'Writing Genealogies: An Exploration of Foucault's
Strategies for Doing Research.' *Discourse: Studies in the Cultural Politics of
Education*, 20(2): 201–17.

Taylor, J. 1965. 3 June. 'Confidential Report: Private Meeting with Japanese-
Canadians, Vancouver.' Library and Archives Canada, RG 33, Series 80,
vol. 120, file 631E.

Taylor, K.W. 1991. 'Racism in Canadian Immigration Policy.' *Canadian Ethnic
Studies*, 23(1): 1–20.

'The Shame of Our "Mississippi" Indians.' 1965. 22 November. Toronto
Daily Star. Library and Archives Canada, RG 33, Series 80, vol. 175, file D3,
'Ethnic Minorities 1965 II.'

Todorov, T. 1993. *On Human Diversity: Nationalism, Racism, and Exoticism in French Thought*. Translated by C. Porter. Cambridge, MA: Harvard University Press.

Touhy, Caroline J. 1992. *Policy and Politics in Canada: Institutionalized Ambivalence*. Philadelphia: Temple University Press.

Troper, H. 1993. 'Canada's Immigration Policy since 1945.' *International Journal*, 48: 255–334.

'Two Soliloquies.' 1965. 26 February. Ottawa *Citizen*. Library and Archives Canada, RG 33, Series 80, vol. 120, file 606B.

– 1965. 15 March. Ottawa *Citizen*. Library and Archives Canada, RG 33, Series 80, vol. 120, file 606B.

Ukrainian Canadian Committee. 1971. 14 July. Letter to Trudeau. Archives of Manitoba, MG 14, C98, box 1.

Ukrainian Canadian Council of Learned Societies. 1968. 22 January. 'Blueprint for the B.N.A. Act, Section 133: A Simplified Version of Bilingualism and Biculturalism, Rudnyckyj's Formula.' Library and Archives Canada, RG 33, Series 80, vol. 128, file 1476–1500.

Ukrainian Self-Reliance League of Canada. 1965. 'Brief submitted to the Royal Commission on Bilingualism and Biculturalism.' Presented by the Dominion Executive of the Ukrainian Self-Reliance League of Canada. Toronto.

Ukrainian Voice. 1964. April. 'Senator Yuzyk's Maiden Speech.' English series, pamphlet no. 5. Winnipeg: Ukrainian Voice.

United Church of Canada. 1964. June. 'Brief Presented to the Royal Commission on Bilingualism and Biculturalism.' Toronto: United Church House.

Vallee, F.G. 1966. 'Indians and Eskimos of Canada: An Overview of Studies of Relevance to the Royal Commission on Bilingualism and Biculturalism. s.l.: s.n. Amicus number 12033571.

Varjassy, I.M. 1964a. 'The Canadian Eskimos.' Library and Archives Canada, RG 33, Series 80, vol. 117, file 408E.

– 1964b. 20–22 November. 'Confidential Distribution: The Ontario Conference of the Indian Eskimo Association,' London, Ont. Library and Archives Canada, RG 33, Series 80, vol. 119, file 537E.

– 1964c. 26 November. 'Report on Private Meetings.' Library and Archives Canada, RG 33, Series 80, vol. 119, file 538E.

– 1966a. 7 June. 'Cultural Contribution.' Library and Archives Canada, RG 33, Series 80, vol. 124, file 951–975.

– 1966b. 8 July. 'Cultural Contribution.' Library and Archives Canada, RG 33, Series 80, vol. 124, file 973E.

Vipond, R.C. 1996. 'Citizenship and the Charter of Rights: The Two Sides of Pierre Trudeau.' *International Journal of Canadian Studies*, 14: 179–92.

Voice of Canada League. 1964. 'Brief to the Royal Commission on Bilingualism and Biculturalism.' Ottawa.

Walmsley, N.E. 1965. *Some Aspects of Canada's Immigration Policy*. Report for the Royal Commission on Bilingualism and Biculturalism, Canada. Amicus number: 23342539.

Wardaugh, R. 1983. *Language and Nationhood: The Canadian Experience*. Vancouver: New Star Books.

Watts, R.L. 1970. *Multicultural Societies and Federalism*. Studies of the Royal Commission on Bilingualism and Biculturalism. Ottawa: Information Canada.

Wayland, S.V. 1997. 'Immigration, Multiculturalism and National Identity in Canada.' *International Journal on Group Rights*, 5: 33–58.

Weitzer, R. 1990. *Transforming Settler States*. Berkeley: University of California Press.

'West Seen Rejecting Biculturalism Issue.' 1965. 26 February. Winnipeg *Free Press*. Library and Archives Canada, RG 33, Series 80, vol. 120, file 606B.

'Why Is the Voice of the German-Canadian So Weak?' 1965. 25 May. *Der Nordwesten*. Canadian Citizenship Branch, Foreign Language Press Review Service. Ottawa. Library and Archives Canada, RG 33, Series 80, vols. 120, file 626–650.

Willinsky, J. 1998. *Learning to Divide the World*. Minneapolis: University of Minnesota Press.

Wilson, W.A. 1966. 15 October. 'Immigration 1963–66.' *Montreal Star*. Library and Archives Canada, RG 33, Series 80, vol. 146, file A-7b, 'Immigration 1963–66.'

Wisse, Ruth R. 1965. *Jewish Participation in Canadian Culture*. Ottawa: s.n. Series: Canada. Royal Comission on Bilingualism and Biculturalism Research Studies Div. VIII-B, no. 6.

Woodbridge, A., L. Morrow, and E. Hepner. 1965. 12 January. 'Royal Commission on Bilingualism and Biculturalism Press Survey.' Library and Archives Canada, RG 33, Series 80, vol. 122, file 761B.

Woodsworth, J.A. 1964. 'On Bilingualism as Applied to Canada: A Report by John A. Woodsworth to the Royal Commission on Bilingualism and Biculturalism, Submitted November 30, 1963.' Vancouver.

Wright, S. 2000. *Community and Communication*. Buffalo, NY: Clevedon Multilingual Matters.

Wyczynski, P. 1966. 28 May. 'Les autres groupes ethniques – Rapport Préliminaire.' Library and Archives Canada, RG 33, Series 80, vol. 124, file 966E.

Yegenoglu, M. 1998. *Colonial Fantasies*. Cambridge: Cambridge University Press.

– 2003. 'Liberal Multiculturalism and the Ethics of Hospitality in the Age of
  Globalization.' *Postmodern Culture*. Retrieved 13 January 2005 from http://
  www.iath.virginia.edu/pmc/text-only/issue.103/13.2yegenoglu.txt.
Young, I.M. 1997. 'A Multicultural Continuum: A Critique of Will Kymlicka's
  Ethnic-nation Dichotomy.' *Constellations*, 4(1): 49–53.
Yuzyk, P. 1968. 1 May. 'Thinker's Conference on Minority Rights Planned.'
  Library and Archives Canada, RG 33, Series 80, vol. 128, file 140–3.
Zink, L.J. 1966a. 19 October. 'The True North White and Free?' Toronto
  Telegram. Library and Archives Canada, RG 33, Series 80, vol. 146, file A-7b.
  'Immigration 1963–66.'
– 1966b. 20 October. 'A Hollow Equality.' Toronto *Telegram*. Library and
  Archives Canada, RG 33, Series 80, vol. 146, file A-7b, 'Immigration
  1963–66.'

Index

219, 222, 226, 229, 230; rejection
of by Japanese community, 105;
rejection of by Voice of Canada
League, 111–12; in Rudnyckyj's
statement, 178; as stepping
stone to multiculturalism,
99–100; United Church support
for, 114; as vestige of past, 105
bi-culture: contestation of, 122;
white-settler, 14, 43
bilingualism: in blue pages, 152–6;
in *Book I* of final report, 164–5,
169, 170–1; Canada Ethnic
Press Federation and, 101–2; as
central term of reference, 57, 58;
challenges of, 131; challenges
to by Ukrainian community,
108; in civil service, 44; CLC
support for, 113; and collective
language rights, 243; comparison of Canada and South Africa,
131, 170–1; dangers of, 99;
definitions of, 152–3; disenfranchisement and, 154; dismissal
of, 97; as distinction between
Canada and U.S., 112–13;
and distinctiveness of English
and French communities, 164,
169; as entrenched feature of
Canadian identity, 104–5; of
ethnic groups, 153, 154; evolution of term in Manitoba, 64–7;
extensive, 153; extent of in
federal bureaucracy, 5; factual,
102, 123; hegemony of En-
glish and French, 67, 197, 199,
206–8, 223–4, 235; Indigenous
groups' views on, 120–3; individual, 153–4, 156; individual
rights and freedoms vs., 225;

institutional, 153–4, 156, 158, 163;
IODE support for, 112–13; Italian community support for, 106;
lack of correlation with biculturalism, 133–4; Laurier-Greenway
agreement on, 65–6; linguistic
expertise in, 133–4; majority
status of English and French
and, 169; modification of, 230;
multiple, 57, 153, 177, 180;
national, 153; official, 152, 177,
180; opportunities provided to
ethnic groups by, 174; personality principle of, 169–71; persua-
sion of non-English/non-French
to accept, 226; prior history
claims and, 169; and Quebec
nationalism, 242; redefinition
of, 65; regional, 180; rejection of by Manitoba Japanese
community, 105; rejection of
by Ukrainian community, 109;
rejection of by Voice of Canada
League, 111–12; repudiation of,
229; repudiation of by Iroquois,
121; in Rudnyckyj's statement,
178, 180; spending on, 227; as
stepping stone to multiculturalism, 102; as stepping stone to
multilingualism, 99–100; and
support for multiculturalism,
234; territorial, 170–1; types
of in Canada, 177; United
Church support for, 114;
unofficial/'inofficial,' 102, 152–3,
156, 177; in Upper and Lower
Canada, 43; as vestige of past,
105; Western definition of, 65
Bill C-120, 140, 172. *See also* Official
Languages Act